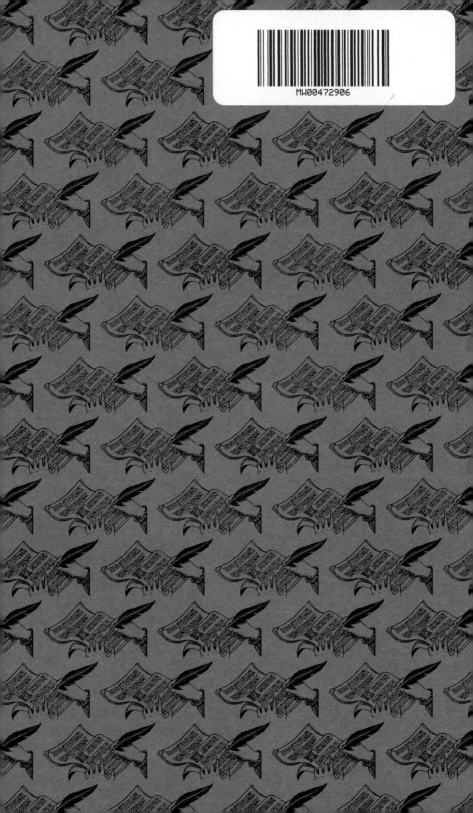

A LITTLE HISTORY OF MUSIC

ROBERT PHILIP

A LITTLE HISTORY

HISTORY

of

MUSIC

YALE UNIVERSITY PRESS
NEW HAVEN AND LONDON

Illustrations by Emily Louise Howard ('The Diggingest Girl').

For information about this and other Yale University Press publications, please contact:
U.S. Office: sales.press@yale.edu   yalebooks.com
Europe Office: sales@yaleup.co.uk   yalebooks.co.uk

Set in Minion Pro by IDSUK (DataConnection) Ltd
Printed in Great Britain by TJ Books, Padstow, Cornwall

Library of Congress Control Number: 2022948962

ISBN 978-0-300-25774-8

A catalogue record for this book is available from the British Library.

10 9 8 7 6 5 4 3 2 1

Contents

CHAPTER 1

The What and Why of Music

What is music? A simple enough question, you might think, but it is not as simple as it looks. You could say that music is pleasing sound, produced by someone singing, or playing an instrument. But what is this 'pleasing sound', and what are we doing when we sing or play? You might say that people make tunes, chords, harmony, rhythm, beat. These are certainly ingredients of music. But they don't explain what music *is*, fundamentally.

We are first exposed to elements of music in the womb. As unborn babies we begin to hear at about fifteen weeks. The sound that dominates our life is the beat of our mother's heart. The heartbeat is always there, in partnership with our mother's breathing. So even before we are born, we are aware of these two rhythms that carry on all the time, each of them speeding up and slowing down with our mother's level of activity. No wonder, therefore, that most people are born with some sort of sense of rhythm.

After we are born, before we are one year old we respond to a basic sort of 'meaning', perhaps even 'music'. You know what 'baby talk' sounds like. It involves making the voice go up and down in an exaggerated way, to emphasise the mood of what is meant: '*There's a good girl!*', 'Oh *dear!*', 'Oops! *Silly* me!' This exaggerated speech, almost like a song, is used in very different cultures across the world. The baby responds by smiling, laughing, becoming serious, finding the words and the tone in some way 'meaningful', even without understanding the words. And people have argued that this is perhaps one of the origins of human music.

I say 'human' music. Here's another question: is music just a human activity, or do other animals have it?

We are a species of ape, and all apes and monkeys have a wide range of sounds – whoops, shrieks, whistles, calls, growls – to express emotions and specific meanings: delight, fear, agitation, danger. Like baby talk, the calls of apes can seem quite 'musical'. Other animals have calls which sound so musical that we refer to them as 'song'. Humpback whales sing a huge variety of sounds, from high chirrups to deep moans and groans, organised into 'themes', and a song can go on for twenty minutes or more. We describe birds as 'singing'. There are features of the most complicated birdsong that are like human music, but sung so fast that we don't hear the details. If you slow the song down, you can hear that, like whales, birds arrange the notes of their song in ways that seem organised, not just random.

Are apes, whales or birds singing 'music'? Well, it depends how you choose to define 'music', so maybe it's not even a useful question. Do the complex sounds of whales and birds even amount to some sort of 'language'? Again, it depends how you choose to define 'language'. We don't yet have answers to these questions. What we do know is that human brains and throats have evolved so that we speak human languages, and that this has gone hand in hand with the development of music. Indeed, it is because we have both language and music that there is a 'history of music' to write about.

Rhythm is one of the basic ingredients, not only of music but of life. From before we are born until we die, we are surrounded by rhythm. Our own heart beats. When we walk, our feet move in a regular rhythm which is different from the rhythm of an animal with four feet. Limping, skipping and running have different rhythms, and so do the hooves of a horse when it walks, trots, canters or gallops.

Many age-old tasks have inspired music because of their characteristic rhythms: digging, rowing, pulling on ropes, breaking rocks. The Industrial Revolution introduced many mechanical rhythms to add to natural rhythms. When a rhythm is interrupted or changes – when a galloping horse jumps a fence, when someone breaks into a run, or pauses – we experience a moment of suspense, expectation, surprise. From all these rhythms have arisen the rhythms of music and dance.

Some natural rhythmic patterns are changing all the time: the way the air moves, the way branches sway in the wind, waves breaking on the shore. There are silent rhythms: the days have their repeating rhythm, with the sun rising at dawn, travelling across the sky (as it seems to us), and setting at dusk. The days gradually lengthen and then shorten, creating the rhythm of the year. There is also the rhythm of life itself, from birth through growth and decline to death. Within that life, we experience many rhythmic patterns, physical and psychological: striving to achieve something (mental or physical) and then relaxing; falling ill and recovering; being pregnant and giving birth.

So our lives supply us with plenty of sources of rhythm to inspire our music. There are cultures in different parts of the world where rhythm is the dominant element in music. But usually there is also melody – singing or playing a tune – and harmony. Of these two, the melody is most obvious, but harmony is fundamental. Even when someone is singing on their own, unaccompanied, there is harmony in their choice of notes.

That may sound puzzling, so let me explain what I mean. Everyone understands the meaning of 'harmony' at some level: we talk about a family 'living in harmony'. That is just a metaphor, but it is derived from a natural phenomenon that creates the possibility of musical harmony.

If you have ever played a wind instrument, you'll know that you can change the note just by how you blow. Depending on the instrument, if you blow harder, or squeeze the reed tighter, or adjust the shape of your lips, you will get a higher note, and if you do this even more, you'll get an even higher note. This is because the tube of air inside the instrument can vibrate in several ways – altogether, divided into two half-lengths, divided into three, divided into four, and so on. The more energy you put into the tube, the more parts the air will divide into as it vibrates. When it divides in two it vibrates twice as fast, when it divides in three it vibrates three times as fast, and so on, producing a higher and higher note. You can do the same with the strings of a violin, guitar or harp. Touch the string halfway along, or a third along, or a quarter, and the vibrations divide into shorter sections and you get a series of higher and higher notes, called 'harmonics' or 'overtones'.

This series of notes is called the 'harmonic series'. It exists not just as a series of individual notes; it also combines to create tone-quality. If you play or sing a single note, the string or air will simultaneously be vibrating in its various possible divisions – halves, thirds, quarters, and so on – to produce the various harmonics *above* the basic note. It is this mixture of different pitches that gives the note its characteristic tone-quality. We use this phenomenon every day in our voices. The difference between different vowels – a, e, i, o, u – is the difference between mixtures of harmonics, which we adjust from one vowel to another by changing the shape of our mouths.

Our ears are designed to hear all these subtleties. The harmonic series sets our ears vibrating with all these different combinations, and we sense the 'harmonious' relations between its notes.

If this all sounds rather theoretical, here's a practical illustration of how we instinctively understand the 'harmony' of the harmonic series. The first interval of the harmonic series – the jump from the first note to the second – is known as an 'octave'. You may not think you know what an octave is, but you do.

Imagine yourself in a group of people singing 'Happy Birthday'. Men, who have deeper voices, will sing at the pitch that suits them, while women and children, who generally have higher voices, will sing at the pitch that suits their voices, an octave higher than the men. We do this instinctively. The relationship between notes an octave apart is so close that we don't really think that the men and women are singing different notes: it is more that they are singing the same note, one above the other. This is because the two notes are in the simplest possible relationship: they are the first and second notes of the harmonic series, with the second note vibrating at twice the frequency of the first. If you go up one more note in the harmonic series, you get a note with three times the frequency of the bottom note. This gives you the interval of a 'fifth' between the second and third notes. This is, apart from the octave, the most common interval to be found in almost all musical cultures across the world. Again, this is because we hear the simple relationship between the second and third note (a ratio of 3 to 2).

The harmonic series provides the basis of harmony. It is the natural phenomenon which leads to the possibility of making choices: the choice of notes in a melody, or the choice of combinations of notes. Some notes sound more 'harmonious' in relation to others, because the relationships are simple. Some sound 'clashing' or dissonant because the relationships are less simple. It is a matter of taste and culture how much dissonance we want, but that taste is based on the sensitivity of our ears and brains to the harmonic series.

So nature has supplied us with the basic ingredients for music, just as the earth has given us the materials for other arts: colours, clay, wood and stone. Paintings, sculptures and buildings can last for thousands of years. But music vanishes once the musicians stop. So why do we value it? What is music *for*?

Your answer to this question will depend on whether you play or sing music yourself, go to concerts, attend places of worship where there is singing, or simply listen to music at home or as you travel around. Of course, the music you listen to would not exist without someone having created it. If you yourself make music, you'll know that there is a particular range of feelings evoked by singing or playing which is different from the effect of just listening. People who sing in choirs often say that, however tired they were when they arrived at the session, they leave at the end feeling refreshed. This is partly because the physical act of singing affects our bodies and brains, but also because it is a communal act that connects us to other people with a common purpose.

One of the most widespread communal acts of music through the ages has been as part of religious ritual. Many ancient cultures – in India, Mesopotamia, China, Egypt, Greece – believed that the vibrations of sound are everywhere in the universe, providing energy and, ultimately, music, and giving rise to harmony. In the early centuries of Christianity, these concepts were taken up as part of the attempt to explain the order of God's universe, and music as an expression of that order.

Similarly, many cultures that preserve ancient traditions see music as a vital part of the story of creation. From here it is a short step to the idea of music as a way of establishing the relationship between humans and the natural world, and a way of communicating with animals and the spirits of ancestors. Music is seen to have power, for good or ill. Sometimes it is believed to heal the sick, but music has also often been thought dangerous, or potentially immoral.

Music can have so many uses and effects that it is not always useful to think of 'music' as if it were just one thing. Some languages do not even have a word for 'music', in the general sense that we give it in English, but distinguish instead between singing poetry, chanting religious texts, playing instruments, drumming, and so on. Often, religious music is specifically not considered as 'music', but simply as an act of worship (in Islam, for example). But singing the words is seen to raise them to a higher level, to make them more worthy of being offered to God.

It is not far from here to the thought that singing any words raises them, or at least transforms them. It is not just a question of making the words clearer. Often the words are less clear when they are sung, but if you know what the words are, you can appreciate that their message has somehow been intensified by music.

You could say something similar about dance: dance is a musical way of intensifying the experience of rhythm through the body. And this can extend from wild, ecstatic energy through to the solemn procession of ceremonies and ritual.

In some societies, religion, dance and music are primarily expressions of community. But in many societies, and particularly today, there is a strong emphasis on performing music to an audience, and on the qualities of individual musicians. To be a musician is a specialist skill, often with status or prestige attached to it. Individual musicians become famous, particularly in the modern, super-connected world.

Instruments have existed for thousands of years. Why do we need instruments when we all have voices? The basic answer is that instruments enable us to make a greater range of sounds. We can play higher, lower, louder, and produce patterns of notes more elaborate than anything we can achieve with our voices. The rhythms of percussion instruments have an impact that enhances the rhythms of dance or heightens the solemnity of ritual. Instruments sometimes acquire such importance that they come to be considered as precious objects in themselves, dedicated to rulers or gods, or representing the voices of ancestors.

All these musical activities share an obvious background: music, like everything else, is partly a reflection of society. Music is *for* whatever society needs it to be for. It also, as researchers are increasingly finding, stimulates chemicals in the brain that give us a sense of deep pleasure and satisfaction. And I don't need to tell you that sharing deep pleasure with others is one of the things that not only enhances our individual lives but helps to bind us all together. We'll see how varied the results of music's power can be as we begin our journey through the centuries and across the globe.

CHAPTER 2

Shadows of an Ancient Dance

As with any journey, it would be good to start at the beginning. But what is the beginning? There are rarely simple starting points in history: if something happens, it is usually because something led up to it, and you end up tracing the origins further and further back. It is the same with music.

It was in eastern Africa that the earliest forms of the ape that we call 'human' evolved about four million years ago, and by about three million years ago they were making stone tools. It is difficult to think of these staggeringly old artefacts without imagining early humans developing more sophisticated versions of what other apes do: singing, clapping, dancing, hitting. Human evolution made these activities possible in various ways. Standing upright was a crucial factor, one of the most important features of these early humans. Anthropologists continue to argue about why we did this, but one thing they agree is that it had the effect of freeing our hands. Over time, we developed many different ways of using our hands, including potentially musical ones. But standing upright also had an important effect on our heads and throats. As our head was raised above our spine, our larynx – the voice box with which we produce speech and other sounds – fell to a lower position in our throat and became longer. This made it possible for humans to produce a greater range of sounds than other apes. Changes in the shape of the tongue, and the ongoing development of the human brain, added to this potential. This ultimately made it possible for humans to develop both music and language.

How the development of music and language related to each other is the subject of ongoing debate, and nobody has clear-cut answers. But this was obviously a very slow process, taking place over millions of years. Some anthropologists suggest that the earliest human languages might have developed in Africa as long as 350,000 years ago. If so, it is difficult to imagine the lives of those people without some sort of music. Again, anthropologists continue to debate the role of music for early humans. Theories range from emotional expression as a way of strengthening the bonds of the group (an extension of the role of ape calls), to singing together to ward off predators.

Of course, this is conjecture, based on the development of human anatomy and our knowledge of later human and animal behaviour. There is no surviving evidence of this earliest music. The oldest physical evidence that might suggest music is the evidence for ritual, particularly the formal arrangements for burying the dead.

A burial site discovered in southern France in the 1970s included the body of a two-year-old child, dated to around 40,000 years ago. There were no surviving possessions with the body, but it had been carefully arranged as if lying at rest. Music has, throughout later centuries, been closely associated with ceremonies relating to burial and ancestors, so it is easy to imagine that some kind of music might have accompanied the burial – singing or chanting, dancing or procession.

It is from the same period that we find the earliest surviving musical instruments. In a cave in southern Germany, excavators in the 1990s found flutes made from the ivory of mammoth tusks dating from about 40,000 years ago. Ten years later another flute made from a wing-bone of a vulture was found in a nearby cave. None of these flutes are complete enough to be playable, but attempts at reconstruction give some idea of what they might have sounded like.

One thing that is clear is that whoever made these flutes had not spontaneously 'invented' them. They are highly sophisticated instruments. They have been carefully shaped and refined, the finger-holes placed not just randomly, but with the purpose of producing particular notes. They were blown from one end, and some show evidence of having had a hole near the end shaped to produce a whistle, rather as on a recorder. These instruments are clearly the product of a tradition of craftsmanship. Certainly they must also have been made in all kinds of other materials, most commonly natural tubes such as bamboo and reeds, but these would have rotted and disappeared over the years. One of the German caves where the bone flutes were found is also the source of the earliest known 'Venus' figure, the 'Venus of Willendorf', a small figure of a large-breasted naked woman. Such figures, found in many sites across Europe and Asia, are thought to have had ritual significance, to do with fertility or worship of goddesses. Ritual will be associated with music in many societies over the next many thousands of years, so it is plausible to think that these elaborately carved flutes might have had some part in the rituals of these ancient cave-dwellers.

The earliest flutes that are still playable come from China. In the 1980s, twenty complete flutes were found in a series of graves at Jiahu, near the Yellow River. They are between 9,000 and 8,000 years old and, like the earlier fragments of German flutes, were made from the wing-bones of large birds. As these flutes were buried in graves, alongside pottery and other objects, they must have had great importance. But for us they are particularly fascinating because they can be played, and we get a very early indication of the range of notes that the ancient Chinese wanted to achieve from their flutes. The player blew across the open end of the tube to produce the note. The earliest examples have five finger-holes, the later ones seven, making it possible to play a selection of notes –

what we now call scales – similar to those that were to be common across Asia thousands of years later.

Apart from instruments, evidence for musical activity also survives in prehistoric paintings and carvings. Many of these show images of dancers. One of the earliest painted examples, perhaps as much as 20,000 years old, is in Borneo, and shows pairs of stick figures holding hands and dancing, or at least leaping. The Bhimbetka Rock Shelters in India have rock paintings about 10,000 years old. Alongside paintings of animals and hunting, these include stick figures of people dancing in rows, possibly also holding hands. Some rows face each other, one dancer holds something circular, perhaps a tambourine or small drum. In the Sahara Desert, there are caves with thousands of paintings dating from around 6,000–8,000 years ago, before the Sahara became a desert. Amid scenes of cattle-herding and hunting there are paintings of people dancing, in pairs with co-ordinated arm movements, and in larger groups, as if in ritual procession. A painting from nearby shows women clapping, singing and dancing, while one plays a drum. On rockfaces in Chad, a line of four women dance, again with one holding what might be a drum.

The evidence for music-making increases dramatically with the growth of larger settlements and cities from around 6,000 years ago. Soon there were major centres in Mesopotamia (the area centred on present-day Iraq), Persia (Iran), Egypt, the Indus Valley (present-day Pakistan) and China. These were to be important areas for the development of music over the next thousands of years, and they communicated ideas and instruments with each other from astonishingly early on.

In Egypt, illustrations from 5,000 years ago – on tomb walls, pottery, the handles of daggers – show dancers, often women holding hands. There are clay seals and pottery from Persia that show dancers in groups, together with one of the very earliest surviving statuettes of a solo dancer. These different forms of dance must be much more ancient than the surviving evidence, and similar groupings and shapes are still common in folk dances to this day. There is clearly something absolutely fundamental to human nature about the dance, both as individual expression and as a bonding ritual with fellow human beings.

Around the same time, there is the earliest evidence for various kinds of trumpet. You make the note on a trumpet by pursing your lips against the mouthpiece and blowing a 'raspberry'. This principle had been used to blow conch shells (large seashells) as early as 17,000 years ago, and animal horns must have been blown in a similar way across the world. It is in Jewish literature that we read about the ritual use of trumpets. The ceremonial ram's horn, the *shofar*, was blown in Solomon's Temple in Jerusalem, around 5,000 years ago, and after the ritual sacrificing of animals, silver trumpets were sounded. Silver trumpets were also found in the tomb of the young Egyptian Pharaoh, Tutankhamun, who reigned 3,500 years ago. These early trumpets were not designed to produce a wide range of notes. They would have been used to blast out one or two notes as a signal, or a moment of ritual; they were ceremonial instruments, rather than instruments to make 'music'.

Stringed instruments, on the other hand, were used to make real music from very early times. Hunting bows for shooting arrows have existed for many thousands of years, and you can produce a note by stretching the string and twanging it or scraping a stick across it (such instruments are still used in parts of Africa). It was in ancient Mesopotamia and Egypt that the earliest sophisticated musical instruments were based on this principle. Excavations at Ur, at the southern end of Mesopotamia, revealed from 5,000 years ago large numbers of illustrations of musical instruments, together with singers, dancers, acrobats and religious rituals which give us some background to the music. There are even a few surviving harps and lyres (like small harps), the wood long decayed, but the remains held in place by the lavish coverings of precious metals. The most common form of lyre in Mesopotamia at this period had strings running vertically, mounted on a soundboard in the shape of a bull, with its head elaborately carved. The bull was the symbol of the god of rain and thunder, so the lyre was clearly more than just an instrument for entertainment. The lyres found at Ur each had from eight to ten strings. We don't know how they were tuned, but clay tablets from about a thousand years later show that by that date Mesopotamians had an understanding of the maths of the harmonic series. With this knowledge they were able to tune several strings on an instrument by using a succession of fifths (the interval between notes 2 and 3 of the harmonic series). This tuning principle, and the scales that Mesopotamians used, were to prove influential across Asia and across the centuries – the modern Western major and minor scales, and the methods used to tune Western instruments, owe their existence to the theories developed in Mesopotamia at least 4,000 years ago.

This was not just a matter of musical theory. In ancient Mesopotamia, music was closely linked to the understanding of the cosmos and its mathematical relationships, from which harmony derived. These ideas were to spread as far east as China, and as far south as Egypt. From there they reached Greece, where the concepts of the 'harmony of the universe' and the 'music of the spheres' took root. In the early centuries of Christianity, these concepts were taken up as part of the attempt to explain the order of God's universe, and music as an expression of that order.

Mesopotamian-style instruments were also found in ancient Egypt. The lyre and the harp frequently appear in Egyptian paintings. The lute (played like a guitar) is another instrument shared between Mesopotamia and Egypt. This was an instrument with a small body and a long neck. There's a Mesopotamian illustration of a musician playing one from about 5,000 years ago, looking uncannily like a modern player of a guitar, with one hand plucking the strings, the other curled round the neck and pressing the string on the fingerboard. Egyptian illustrations clearly show that these lutes had frets: ridges to mark the position of each note on the fingerboard (again, as on the guitar). There is a famous set of paintings from the tomb of an Egyptian civil servant, dating from about 3,500 years ago, in one of which women play lutes with two strings. In the same tomb, another scene shows two naked women dancing, with elegantly curved gestures. Other women sit clapping, and a musician plays a wind instrument consisting of two long pipes, both blown at the same time. This is a double *aulos*. The *aulos* was an instrument with a small double reed, as in the modern oboe, and that too (played singly and in pairs) had come from Mesopotamia to Egypt. This painting seems to show a scene of domestic entertainment. But music was also an important part of religious ritual and royal ceremony. There were professional musicians, men and women, at every level. The highest rank was that of temple musicians, who were dedicated to the worship of the god of that temple, and some had the status of priest- and priestess-musicians. There were many gods, some of whom were particularly associated with music and dancing.

CHAPTER 3

The Poet Sings

'Classical Greece' is the imposing title that is given to the civilisation that reached its climax in Greece in the fifth century BCE. The word 'classical' is used because the ideas and achievements of the ancient Greeks came to be seen as the most important inspiration for later developments in Europe. It is only in recent decades that scholars have made us aware that the achievements of Greek civilisation owed a great deal to other, older cultures, particularly from Mesopotamia in the east and Egypt in the south.

As we have seen, Mesopotamia and Egypt shared many ideas and instruments in common, long before Greece rose to cultural prominence. I've already mentioned that the Mesopotamians understood the maths of the harmonic series and developed ways of tuning stringed instruments. How do we know this? Because the Mesopotamians were the earliest civilisation to leave us written documents, in a language that scholars have been able to decipher. Their writing was stamped in a wedge-shaped script ('cuneiform') into clay. They not only wrote about music, but even developed a way of writing down musical notes. This was nothing like modern notation, but, again, scholars have been able to make some attempt to work out what it means. The oldest example to survive is on a clay tablet from Ugarit (a city to the north of Mesopotamia), dating from about 3,400 years ago. It is a song to a goddess, with the notes and the text, and indications of how it is to be sung. Though there are many things about this ancient music that remain obscure, it seems clear that the Mesopotamians and their neighbours formed their melodies in a selection of modes (akin to our modern scales), which were linked to their mathematical understanding of tuning. It was this knowledge that was passed on to the Greeks.

Music was very important to the Greeks and was intimately tied to poetry. The early epics, the *Iliad* and the *Odyssey*, date from the seventh century BCE. Although they carry the name of an author, Homer, they probably derive from a long tradition of epic poems that were memorised and passed from one generation to another by ear. They reached a fixed version only when they were eventually written down. Poems of this ancient vintage often refer to 'singing' rather than 'telling' the story, and the poet, or 'bard', would probably have sung these epics. Homer in the *Odyssey* describes a bard singing while accompanying himself on the lyre, and this would have been a familiar picture. Seven-string lyres, similar to those of Mesopotamia and Egypt, were in use in the Greek world in Homer's time. This tradition of memorised poetry, semi-improvised with accompaniment, is a model that runs through many centuries, as we shall see.

The climax of ancient Greek civilisation came two centuries after Homer, in the fifth century BCE, centred on Athens. It was then that the Greeks achieved all the things that have inspired later generations, in the fields of literature, drama, sport, art, sculpture, architecture, philosophy and politics. The main focus of Greek arts were the festivals held across the country, some small and local, others involving people from all over Greece. These were held in honour of the gods – Greece, like Egypt and Mesopotamia, was a culture of many gods and goddesses. The festivals involved religious processions, animal sacrifices, sporting competitions, music and drama.

The most important festival for drama was the Dionysia, held in spring in Athens, in honour of Dionysus, the god of wine. The central event was a competition for new plays, tragedies and comedies, and the list of winners included the four great dramatists whose names are still famous today: Euripides, Aeschylus and Sophocles for tragedy, and Aristophanes for comedy.

Music was a vital part of the performances. The plays are structured into sections for the principal actors interspersed with passages for chorus (all the performers were men, playing both male and female roles). The principal actors are the main drivers of the story, which often involves tragic situations and the moral problems that they raise. The chorus of a dozen or so comment on the action, expressing dread at what is to happen, pity for the fate of the main characters, warning them of the consequences of their actions, and so on. The chorus's lines are written in poetry intended to be sung rather than spoken, and the chorus also danced as they sang, accompanied by lyre or *aulos* players. They danced and sang in a space in front of the stage called the 'orchestra', which literally means 'dancing place' (it was much later that this word came to mean a group of instruments in that place).

Music was important across a wide range of contexts. The processions and sacrifices at the major festivals were just the largest-scale versions of religious rituals carried out at local shrines and temples across Greece. Each god and goddess had their own cult and sites of worship, accompanied by the chanting of hymns and ritual dancing. The Greeks thought of dance as a gift from the gods, and dancing was part of religious ceremonies. These ranged from public festivals to secret cults, and from solemn procession to wild and ecstatic dance. The character of the music that accompanied the dance would have had a similar variety. Illustrations of dance are found on many Greek vases, showing people dancing in religious ceremonies, at banquets, groups of women and groups of men (but not together, except for children), and ranging from formal and dignified to wild and drunken.

But wild dancing was not just self-indulgent, though no doubt it sometimes was. In the cult of Dionysus, worshippers would take part in *orgia*, from which our word 'orgy' comes. Men and women (separately) attained a state of drunken ecstasy, as a way of feeling in touch with the god. The instruments associated with this dancing were, of course, loud. The *aulos* – the penetrating reed instrument inherited from Mesopotamia and Egypt – is often shown on pottery accompanying wild dancing, and the player sometimes seems to be joining in the dance, provoking the dancers to greater excitement. One of the most popular of these wild dances originated from Persia, and was brought to Athens after wars between Greece and Persia – war often brought the music and arts of different cultures in contact with each other.

By contrast with the *aulos*, the lyre was for quieter music, and was used to accompany sung poetry as in Homer's day. Like the Mesopotamians, the Greeks had a way of being able to write music down, and there are some surviving texts of hymns with an indication of the music. They need some imagination to interpret, because this was nothing like our modern notation, but what is clear is that the Greeks worked with a musical system that they had inherited from the Mesopotamians. From the harmonic series and the maths associated with it, they derived a set of modes (roughly the equivalent of what we call scales), and a method for tuning instruments to produce them. This involved the use of the lowest interval in the harmonic series (the octave) and the second interval (the fifth). It was the philosopher-mathematician Pythagoras who is most associated with the refinement of this method, and to this day we speak of tunings based on pure fifths as 'Pythagorean'.

By the third century BCE a Greek engineer had invented an instrument called the *hydraulis*, a sort of prototype of the organ. Air was pumped by hand into a row of pipes, via a chamber that was kept under pressure by a tank of water. This kept the flow of air constant (the same effect achieved by the bag of the bagpipes). The player opened each pipe by pressing a key. This was an impressively loud instrument that was played during outdoor ceremonies.

The most important aspect of ancient Greek music was its close association with words, as in the plays performed at festivals. Not only was poetry sung, but the rhythm of the music was determined by the rhythm of the spoken words. The rhythms of Greek poetry were not just a question of emphasis, strong and weak beats, such as we are used to in English poetry. The lines had traditionally been formed from different *lengths* of syllable, in alternating patterns of long and short, or long followed by two short syllables. The poems were therefore already highly rhythmic, in an almost musical way. So naturally a singer-poet would sing in the rhythm of the poetry, with longer and shorter notes in the appropriate pattern. The art of the singer was to enhance the natural rhythm by sometimes drawing out important syllables, and by the way the melody went up and down. One of the modes would be chosen for the melody depending on the mood and purpose of the song, rather as later European musicians might choose a major or a minor key. But singers would also add expressive touches to the melody by 'bending' notes away from the note of the mode – perhaps we can imagine this as being like the 'blue' notes of jazz musicians. This repertoire of modes, their identification with particular moods, and the flexibility with which they were interpreted, was, in later centuries, shared across a wide range of western and central Asia, as far as India.

Greek thinkers were well aware of the power of music. The philosopher Plato described music as having moral power, gripping the soul of the listener. It was good for purification, or for relaxation, but also potentially harmful. For this reason it needed careful training, and an avoidance of excessive emotion (as in the 'orgies' of Dionysus). Different modes were suitable to strengthen the courage of a warrior, or to express peace, but some were too mournful to be suitable for general use.

Underlying all Greek musical activity and thinking was the belief that music was fundamental to the understanding of the world and its place in the universe. The mathematical relationships of musical notes, their 'harmony', was an expression of the relationship and harmony of the universe and the bodies within it, the 'harmony of the spheres'. This concept was to last for many centuries.

CHAPTER 4

Improvising to the Lute

In the previous two chapters, my focus has been on the distant past. Now I'm going to devote several chapters to some of the world's major surviving musical traditions, covering a wide spread of countries across the globe. One important factor that links many of these traditions is that they really were, and still are, traditions, in the sense that they have continued largely unbroken over the centuries. This is not to say that traditions do not change: nothing remains static for long, and musical traditions are always in a state of evolution. But their continuity over long time spans means that we can link the music of the past with the music of the same tradition today, so as to get a handle on what has gone on over the centuries. The past is, you might say, still active in the music of the present. This is a characteristic that distinguishes most of the world's music cultures from the music of the West, with its history of sudden and radical change. I hope, by the time we come to consider the music of the West, this tour of the world's other cultures will not only have been valuable in itself, but will also have given us some useful perspective.

I've already talked about the spread of ideas, including musical ideas, in the ancient world. It's worth pausing to think about the implications of this. We are so used to the instant communications of today through the Internet that it is easy to assume we are more connected with the rest of the world than any previous generation. In a narrow sense, that is true. But when it comes to deeper communication and the understanding of different cultures, it is worth thinking about how things were before computers, telephones, radios and even books existed. Although there was some writing in the ancient world, on stone, clay, and, in some countries, parchment, few people had access to it or could read, and almost all communication was from person to person, speaking and listening. To reach someone at a distance, you travelled to find them, or sent someone.

It is astonishing to realise what a wealth of communication between distant people went on. Much of this was associated with trade. Across Asia, from Turkey in the west to China in the east, a distance of 5,000 miles, there was for thousands of years a network of regular trade routes. Around the second century BCE these coalesced into what became known as the Silk Road, named after one of the major goods that travelled along it. This network of routes was so much used that, over the years, communication between different cultures led to the development of new languages, new ways of thinking, new scientific knowledge, new religious ideas, new ways of making music. A merchant travelling by camel or mule could be away from home for years, staying in places on the route for long periods of time. This meant that there was an opportunity for new ideas and customs to be absorbed in depth.

Another way that cultural exchange took place was through invasions, war and the resulting migration. These too were very different from modern notions of such things. Instead of the massive, instant destruction of modern explosives, we have to imagine a much more laborious process, with armies of soldiers equipped with swords, shields, battering rams, and the like. War was quite destructive enough, but it tended to leave places more or less intact, unless there was a particular reason for wanting to destroy them, stone by stone. War was also less remote. It most often took place between neighbours who were familiar with each other's culture through trade and other exchanges. An invader would generally want to preserve as much of the structure and working population of the country as possible: a functioning society was far more useful to an invader than a wasteland. Among the people whom invaders would often want to preserve were artists and musicians. Indeed, they were likely to be well known across a wide area, and incoming rulers often took on the local top artists and musicians as their courts replaced those of the defeated rulers.

The consequence was that, across a huge swathe of Asia, for many centuries different cultures and religions mixed – Arabs, Persians, Turks, Jews, Christians and Muslims – learning from each other and, in many areas, living side by side in reasonably peaceful coexistence, sharing ideas, including music. I have already talked about Mesopotamia as an important source of these ideas. Another powerful influence was Persia, whose empire at its height, nearly 3,000 years ago, extended all the way from Greece and Libya in the west to India in the east. Wars between Persia and Greece two hundred years later reinforced the links between Greek and Persian culture.

Many elements of Persian music, including instruments, had, as with the Greeks, come from Mesopotamia. One instrument that was to become very important was the *oud*, a short-necked lute which the Persians developed into a refined instrument for accompanying a singer. And it was the poet-singers who were most valued among musicians at Persian courts. Singing to the *oud* was to become one of the most important musical arts across a wide area in the following centuries, with Persian musicians admired over the Arab world, and spreading their influence from Turkey to India. From the seventh century CE, Arab armies swept across Asia, bringing the new religion of Islam and the teachings of the Prophet Mohammed. Ancient learning and music were highly respected in the Arab-Islamic world, and the Persian style of singing to the *oud* was treasured. To this day, the accompanied singing of much of Asia owes its origins to Persian musicians of 2,000 years ago.

In the Islamic world over many centuries, a style and tradition of singing was established that, though it varied from region to region, had its roots in a common approach to music-making. The system of modes, which the Persians had inherited from the Mesopotamians, became the basis of sophisticated music across a wide area. The Persian court was already a great centre for music, reaching a climax under King Khosrow II around 600 CE. He employed a number of famous musicians, chief among them Barbad, who was widely credited with having organised the Persian system of modes and melody-building principles that influenced musicians well beyond Persia. Several hundred melodies composed over the centuries were brought together in a collection called the *radif*. To this day, Iranian/Persian musicians memorise the *radif*, and use it as a basis for learning to improvise.

The spread of Islam over the next centuries, with courts established in Damascus, Baghdad, Córdoba and other cities, meant that a Persian-Arab style became the norm across thousands of miles. The Persian *oud* was widely adopted. Its tuning was based on the principles handed down from the Mesopotamians and already adopted by the Greeks, in which the tuning of strings was derived using the fifths of the harmonic series. However, you may remember that the Greeks liked to 'bend' notes for expressive effect. Persian and Arab musicians went further, developing subtle tunings within the scales themselves.

In the modern West, we are used to tuning keyboards with a system in which the smallest interval, the semitone, is always the same, and a tone is two semitones wide (singers and players of string and wind instruments vary this a bit, but the basic principle remains). We are used to thinking of the resulting scales that we use for our melodies as sounding 'natural'. But Persian and Arab scales are very different. They have not only semitones and tones, but also an interval between a semitone and a tone, and another slightly bigger than a tone. In the West we have the major third and the minor third. But in Arab and Persian tuning, there is a third which is between our major and minor third.

Baghdad (the capital of present-day Iraq) was a major centre of Islamic culture in the ninth and tenth centuries, with an institution known as the 'House of Wisdom' attracting scholars dedicated to the study of philosophy, astronomy, mathematics, music and other subjects. A major project was the translating of classical Greek texts. Prominent among these translators was Al-Farabi, who wrote a famous book on music bringing together Greek and earlier Arab theory.

It was a musician from the court of Baghdad, Ziryab, who travelled to accept an appointment at the court in Córdoba in the ninth century, taking with him the latest ideas. Córdoba was the principal musical centre of southern Spain, which Islamic armies from North Africa had conquered in the previous century. Al-Andalus, as the conquerors called the country, was a great centre of the arts, a multi-cultural civilisation that, although ruled by Muslims, allowed the peaceful coexistence of communities of Jews and Christians. Among the results of this multi-culturalism was the development of a highly successful style of music, which came to be known as Andalusian. Ziryab, a man of very wide knowledge and education, was highly influential at the court in Córdoba, and founded an important music school at which both men and women were trained. This was while the great mosque of Córdoba was under construction, which remains one of the great buildings of the world. You only have to wander among its endless forest of elegant columns and arches to get a sense of Córdoba as a centre of extraordinarily rich culture in those times.

The tradition of high musical accomplishment that Ziryab established fed into an important development in music that was to take the Arab musical world by storm. There was a tradition, as in many other cultures, of long poems being sung. In Al-Andalus, where Muslims, Christians and Jews influenced each other, there emerged a new style of Arabic poetry, with a formal arrangement of groups of lines into verses, with various rhyming schemes. This was new in

Arabic poetry, and its elegance gave it an immediate appeal. The verses with their repeating rhyming schemes made them much easier to memorise than the traditional, more loosely constructed poems of earlier Arab literature, particularly when sung to melodies that also repeated in a pattern. This new 'Andalusian' style of sung poetry gradually spread across the Arab world.

Andalusian poetry often evokes romantic images: the intoxication of love and wine, a glimpse of the beloved in a garden. These are themes common to many cultures, from Mesopotamian via Egyptian and Greek to Jewish and Christian (examples in the Jewish and Christian Bibles include the Garden of Eden and the Song of Solomon). In Al-Andalus, the poetry and music reached a high level of refinement, particularly at the court of the emir (ruler) at Córdoba. Here there were many singers, some of them highly trained female slaves who entertained guests by singing and playing behind a curtain, improvising for hours at a time.

One important aspect of Islamic music arose from its style of worship. Three religions – Judaism, Christianity and Islam – share a belief in the one God with whom each person can have a relationship, a belief that all three trace back to the ancient religious leader, Abraham. Jewish worship was the earliest to develop, followed by Christianity and then Islam. Unsurprisingly, both Christians and Muslims owed much to Jewish traditions. I'll come to Jews and Christians in Chapter 10. In Islamic worship, the sacred texts from the Qur'an are chanted, and the faithful are summoned with the 'call to prayer'. One important aspect of these chants is that they do not have fixed melodies (this is also true of the more ancient Jewish chant). The singer (the muezzin, the equivalent of the Jewish cantor) responds to the rhythm of the words, and sings appropriate shapes of melody, based on long training in the traditional modes and their different characters.

The chanting is, therefore, to some extent 'improvised', and this is also true of the music sung and played across the Arab-Islamic world, as it must have been ever since the earliest days of singer-poets. There developed a highly sophisticated tradition of semi-improvised music-making which came to be known in the Arab world as *maqam*. It has retained its religious basis, but has also embraced themes of love and earthly delights (as in the Andalusian tradition). Singers have been accompanied just by an *oud*, or by larger ensembles, and in all cases the instrumentalists shadow the singer with variations of the melody. *Maqam* can also be played by instrumentalists without a singer, the *oud* being a particularly favoured instrument through the centuries.

Maqam has had many varieties of style in different cultures and countries, from Tajikistan, which borders China in the east, to Turkey in the west, and south to Egypt and Sudan. It was widespread practice to perform 'suites' of several movements, in which each suite would be based on a different melody. From the seventeenth century, musicians took to moving between different modes as the melody changed. This is akin to the changes of key we are used to in Western music, 'modulation'.

CHAPTER 5

Music as Meditation

Amid all the rich and ancient musical cultures of Asia, India occupies a special place. Indian musicians today, despite centuries of invasion, colonisation and modernisation, retain a strong sense that their art is rooted in philosophies and beliefs thousands of years old. Their earliest works of literature, the *Vedas*, date from more than 3,000 years ago. Over the succeeding centuries these formed the basis of complex spiritual interpretations of the origins and nature of the cosmos, the Supreme Being who created everything, the many gods responsible for aspects of nature, and the relationship between humans and the divine. They also contain hymns, both words and a form of musical notation, which laid the basis for future developments. Unsurprisingly, there are echoes of ideas going back to the even earlier beliefs of Mesopotamia and Egypt. This religion, Hinduism, gave rise to a strong tradition of mysticism, in which the aim was to arrive at a sense of identity with the Supreme Being by achieving complete stillness of the mind. There was also a belief in the reincarnation of the soul, and of the transience and 'unreal' nature of our brief life as a human being. This was most powerfully expressed in Buddhism, which grew out of Hinduism around 500 BCE. Its founder, Buddha, taught that, through meditation, right behaviour and thinking ('mindfulness'), it was possible to escape the endless cycle of reincarnation, and achieve the ultimate 'enlightenment'.

These ideas are helpful in finding our way into Indian music. As in many other ancient cultures, music and religion are closely linked, and in India music as meditation lies at the heart of it. This is partly expressed by the use of drone instruments, which give the music a sense of having no beginning and no end.

India, with its vast area and population, has developed different musical traditions in different places over time. In particular, there grew up a strong difference between the music of the south and the music of the north (including Pakistan, which was part of northern India until it was separated from southern India by the British in 1947). The north was, from ancient times, more open to incursions from the west. Successive invasions brought the influences of Greek and Persian culture, Buddhism and Islam, resulting in a rich cultural and religious mix.

Local courts of rulers encouraged local styles, though the under-lying philosophies that stemmed back to the *Vedas* were never far away. It was with the establishment of the Mughal Empire in the fifteenth century that there began to be a sense of a wider northern Indian style of music. The Mughal conquerors, from central Asia, combined the Islamic faith with a strong Persian influence and a tolerance of other cultures, and a desire to embrace the best of them. (This was at the time when a more austere view of music had taken over in Persia, with the rise of Shi'ism.) Akbar, the Mughal emperor around 1600, had a particularly splendid and multi-cultural court at Agra. He had brought into India players of the long-necked lutes that we first encountered in ancient Mesopotamia and Egypt, and these became popular in India. But he also embraced the local Hindu singers, who were already famous for their sophis-ticated and refined art. They sang songs in a style that already had the main features of what we know as the classical north Indian ('Hindustani') way of performing a *raga*.

This style was developed from principles that had been described as early as about 800 CE, and now reached a new level of refinement. To understand it, and the whole course of Indian music, I need to explain two Indian terms: '*raga*', which is to do with melody, and '*tala*', which is to do with rhythm. Indian music, like Arab and Persian music, forms melodies from a choice of notes, a mode or scale, that remains stable, and gives a sense of continuity in performance. But the Indian *raga* is far more than what we understand in the West as a scale. Already in Mesopotamian, Greek and Arab music, we have seen individual modes being associated with different qualities and moods. Indian music has a similar approach. Within the chosen scale, each *raga* has characteristic ways of shaping phrases of the melody, a way of going up, a way of coming down, a way of turning corners. Particular *ragas* have associations with times of day, aspects of nature, seasons, and so on.

The *tala* is the rhythmic cycle that creates a structure in which to place the melody. This is a repeating metre, which is chosen from many different possibilities with different numbers of beats and complex patterns within them. The ancient *Vedas* already gave a method of learning these patterns through hand and finger shapes, at a time when these traditions were passed down the generations by ear, and had to be memorised without the help of written texts. All of this was, and to a large extent still is, learned by long study with a master (increasingly either a man or woman), whose knowledge and understanding are passed on orally from one generation to the next. Although some form of notation has existed since ancient times, it has never been widely used in teaching or performing, but only for reference. This is partly because of the tradition of learning by ear, but also because the basic musical material – the *raga*, the mode, the composition – is no more than a framework on which to build through elaboration and improvisation. In the past, performances used to last for hours, and even today a single *raga* can easily last half an hour or more.

A *raga* can be sung, or played by one or more instruments – the complex, long-necked lute called the *sitar* is the most common solo instrument. Singers are usually accompanied by a small group of instruments. Often, a melody instrument (these days usually a small harmonium) tails the singer, echoing what he or she does with overlapping phrases, or different elaborations. Underneath is one or more drone instruments, usually one of the long-necked lutes, that plays a bass note, constant but gently pulsating. Then there are the drums. These vary, but most often in northern India they consist of the *tabla*, a pair of small drums. They are played with the hands and fingers to produce a wide range of percussive and 'speaking' effects. The *tabla* player elaborates the *tala* in a manner that underpins and ornaments the performance of the singer or principal player.

The most common way to perform a *raga*, in the tradition established around 1600 and still current today, is to begin with a free, slow introduction, without any beat, in which the singer (or player) explores the melodic shapes that are characteristic of that particular *raga*. Then the *tabla* player enters, and the regular rhythmic cycle, the *tala*, begins. What follows is, to use a Western analogy, like a set of variations. Parts of the performance will take a pre-existing composition, and elaborate it through all manner of rising and falling shapes and ornaments, all within the character of the predominant *raga*. There may be two or three compositions within the performance, interspersed with passages of free improvisation. Sometimes the singer will take a rest, and let the harmonium player or other instrumentalist improvise a passage. Generally speaking, the performance will begin slowly, settle into a moderate tempo, and end by accelerating to an energetic conclusion. Throughout, the drone instruments keep the music anchored to the same, unchanging bass note, unlike in Arab *maqam*, in which the musicians will sometimes shift from one mode to another.

The music of southern India has similar roots to that of the north, in the ancient literature of the *Vedas* and Hinduism. But north and south diverged in style as the Islamic courts of the Mughals came to dominate the north, bringing in other influences. In the south, the old traditions remained more intact, and, because there was less influence of Islam, the links between music and the ancient religions, predominantly Hinduism, were even stronger than in the north. The classical music style of southern India is known as Karnatak (or Carnatic; Karnataka is the largest state in southern India), and it draws on traditions deriving from the languages and literature of the south. Many of the prominent musicians over the centuries have been poets, a traditional link that goes back as far as the thirteenth century. This tradition reached a golden age in the eighteenth century, when three great musician-poets were at the royal court in Tanjore. Chief among them was Tyagaraja, revered not only as a poet and musician, but also as a spiritual leader, a devotee of Rama, one of the principal Hindu gods. There was a strong tradition of temple music in south India, and Tyagaraja brought hymns into the repertoire of Karnatak music. It is from this generation that a repertoire of compositions comes, passed down and augmented from master to pupil, and these compositions form the core of Karnatak music to this day.

As in the north, however, the pre-existing compositions are only the starting point for a performance. There is the same emphasis on the *raga*, each with its characteristic melodic shapes and conventions. The way that the melody is shaped and ornamented is even more elaborate in the south than in the north, and there is a different range of *tala* (rhythmic cycles) to go with them. The traditional instruments are slightly different to those of the north, with larger drums and, since the early nineteenth century, a preference for the violin to shadow the voice or principal instrument. But the basic principles of *raga*, *tala* and improvisation are quite close to those of the north.

The northern and southern versions of *raga* performance have come to be seen as the great 'classical' traditions of Indian music. With their long history, their origins in ancient religious teaching and ritual, their modes, compositions and improvisation, they have much in common with the Arab and Persian traditions. They have the status of classical because they are the most enduring of many forms of music across India over the centuries. There are also many kinds of folk music and temple music, each with their regional variations. And India has a long history of theatre at all levels of society. Dance is an important element of all these genres.

Two classic types of dance are *Bharatanatyam* in the south and *Kathak* in the north. Both express stories of gods and goddesses from the ancient epics, through highly elaborate movements and gestures, of hands, feet, face and eyes. The tradition began more than 2,000 years ago as dance-drama danced by women in the temple courtyards. Later, during the rule of the Mughals, *Kathak* moved to the courts, and became an entertainment for aristocrats which even royal children were encouraged to learn. There are other, equally ancient story-telling dance traditions in different parts of India. Some of these are danced by women, others by men, and they have a long history of connection with the temples and courts. They vary according to local religion and history, but share the basic characteristics of complex rhythm and expressive gesture to create a narrative.

CHAPTER 6

The Eternal Sound of Gongs

I have already mentioned flutes found in China that date from 9,000 years ago. China's civilisation stretches back to the distant past, and, like India's, it was closely linked to religion and philosophy. The ancient religion centred on the relationship of the living with their ancestral spirits. Around 2,000 years ago this religion was joined by two new philosophies. Daoism focused on achieving harmony with the universe (a link to Mesopotamian thought). Around the same time, the philosopher Confucius developed the idea that the health of society depended on individual order and discipline. When monks first brought Buddhism from India to China, it chimed with both of these philosophies, developing by around 600 CE into Zen Buddhism.

Zen Buddhism aims, through meditation, to abandon the sense of past, future or self, and to lose oneself in the immediate reality of breath, nature and the cosmos. This philosophy had a profound effect on music and the other arts. The artist receives inspiration, 'heavenly music', and should simply express it without personal intervention. Religious chanting is not a personal address to a god, but an expression of the eternity of which we are an insignificant part. This sort of philosophy permeates the history of China in all areas of life and across the centuries. And Chinese music and instruments have always been intimately bound up with this cultural and religious history.

An important element in the development of Chinese instruments was the production of bronze, a metal created by combining copper with other metals to harden it. Royal tombs from around 3,000 years ago have yielded many magnificent bronze vessels, which were used for sacrifices to the spirits of ancestors. Some tombs also contained sets of bronze bells, known as *bianzhong*, whose main purpose was to please those ancestors so as to receive their blessing. The most spectacular set of bells, from the tomb of the Marquis Yi of Zeng, dates from 433 BCE – this date is inscribed on one of the bells with a dedication from the king. It consists of a unique assembly of sixty-five bells of different sizes and pitches, ranging over five octaves and suspended from frames. The bells would have been struck with mallets, and each bell produces two notes, depending on where you hit it. In later centuries, sets of sixteen bells became standard for use in court ritual.

At the opposite extreme from these ceremonial instruments there were also instruments for private use. Chief among these was a kind of zither called the *qin*. It is mentioned in Chinese poetry from 2,500 years ago, and Confucius himself played it. Traditionally the *qin* was associated with intellectuals as an aid to meditation and wisdom, evoking nature and the cosmos, and it retained this association for many centuries.

The *qin* has seven strings tuned to a five-note (pentatonic) scale, such as you find by playing all the black notes on a keyboard. Since ancient times, it has been tuned by the method developed by the Mesopotamians, using a succession of fifths (the second interval of the harmonic series). This basic method would also have been applied to the tuning and scales of the bells of the *bianzhong*. But large sets of bells had extra notes apart from those of the pentatonic scale, and the tuning of surviving bells often deviates from any 'correct' tuning system. Traditional *qin* playing also involves the 'bending' of notes. So playing the instruments of ancient China clearly involved complexities and subtleties, which are not fully understood.

During the Tang Dynasty (seventh–tenth century CE), the music of the emperor's court entered a golden age of Chinese arts. In the courtyard, a large group of musicians and dancers offered praise to heaven. Inside, smaller groups praised the emperor and his ancestors. Many of the musicians had been brought from abroad, together with their instruments including Persian lutes. They performed music for banquets, which, known as *Gagaku*, were imitated in Japan, where the tradition survives to this day.

For many centuries, there were dramatic presentations at temples and in rural communities across China. In the fourteenth century these came together into a more refined art form, encouraged by the intellectual community at court. This became 'Chinese Opera' (or specifically 'Peking Opera'), which was developed right through to modern times. Because of its traditional origins, much of the music was based on existing 'folk' tunes, but these were increasingly elaborated, with a highly sophisticated and complex style of singing.

In the sixth century, diplomats were sent from the Japanese court to China, to learn about Chinese culture so that the Japanese court could emulate it. Buddhism and Confucianism were introduced into Japan, where they merged with traditional beliefs in divine spirits of nature. The Japanese delegates also brought back Chinese banquet music, *Gagaku*, and the instruments to play it, including a kind of large zither which they called the *koto*, and the long-necked lute which they called the *shamisen*. In *Gagaku* every instrument plays simultaneous variations of the same melody. The tempo is immensely slow, with pauses. This illustrates an important concept in Japanese music, *ma*, translated as 'silence' or the 'space' between notes, which is as important as the notes themselves. This idea is closely linked to Buddhist meditation.

The *koto*, like the Chinese *qin*, came to be particularly associated with private music-making. It features in *The Tale of Genji*, written around 1000 CE by a lady-in-waiting at the Japanese court, Murasaki Shikibu. She describes it as an instrument of nature and love. The hero, Prince Genji, is a master of the *koto*, and encourages young ladies to learn it, both as a musical accomplishment and so that they will be seen at their most graceful. Genji and a young lady often play music together by moonlight.

In many cultures, the use of instruments changes over the centuries. By the seventeenth century, the *koto* had been taken up by musicians from a lower social class, and it gradually became an instrument available to anyone. A parallel development occurred with the *shakuhachi*, an end-blown flute. Like the *koto*, it was a member of the court ensemble. But by the thirteenth century it was particularly associated with blind Buddhist monks, who travelled the country earning a living as musicians. By the nineteenth century it had become a popular instrument for playing chamber music, together with the *koto* and the *shamisen*. The *shakuhachi* has become an internationally known instrument in recent years, valued for its evocative range of expression.

There are two great theatrical traditions of Japan, *Noh* and *Kabuki*. *Noh* is the older of the two, with its origins in religious folk theatre. From the fourteenth century, groups were invited to perform *Noh* for the upper classes, and soon it was established as an art enjoyed by both the ordinary people and the military elite, the *Samurai* with their ruler the *Shogun*. Once it became a respected art form, *Noh* took on an intensely serious character, which it has preserved to this day. The pace is generally very slow, the singing somewhat like Buddhist chanting, and the style of acting is similarly austere. The performance takes place on a bare stage, and the singers are accompanied by a flute and drums. The overall character is highly disciplined and ritualistic. The performers have until recently all been male, with principal characters and a unison chorus, and they all wear masks.

When the cities of Japan were developing in the seventeenth century, the new middle class of professionals and merchants needed something more in tune with their style of life. It was women who began a livelier kind of music theatre called *Kabuki*. But its association with prostitution led to it being banned within a few years. After this *Kabuki* became, like *Noh*, an all-male art form. In style, *Kabuki* was much more flamboyant than *Noh*, with elaborate scenery, vividly painted make-up, exaggerated gestures, and a huge range of vocal effects from whispers to groans and shouts. The men who took the parts of young women were particularly celebrated, becoming the Japanese equivalent of the West's opera stars, with a huge public following.

As well as *Noh* and *Kabuki*, puppet theatre was also a thriving entertainment in Japan. Originally it was popular with the lower classes, but from the eighteenth century some of the greatest dramatists began to write for it, and it developed into a highly refined art form, *Bunraku*. The most famous writer, Chikamatsu, is known as 'the Shakespeare of Japan', particularly renowned for his tragedies of domestic life. The format of *Bunraku* lends itself to intimate, domestic stories. There is just one singer, who accompanies himself on the *shamisen* (lute), ranging from a speech-like style to more lyrical singing, depending on the action of the highly sophisticated puppetry.

South-East Asia is a huge area stretching from Myanmar (Burma), Thailand, Laos, Cambodia and Vietnam on the mainland across to the islands of Indonesia and the Philippines. From very early times the area had many contacts by land and sea, northward to China, westward to India, Persia and beyond. So the cultures of South-East Asia are very varied. However, there are musical elements that recur across the area. Singing styles often reflect the influence of China. In Vietnam, there is a tradition of women singing poetry that goes back 1,000 years, with an elaborate style that links them to China, but with choices of notes and tunings that suggest influences from India. Poems are set to a melody that is decorated with many trills, slides, vibrato and so on. The singer beats out a rhythm with sticks, and she is accompanied by a lute player.

For more than 1,000 years, until the tenth century CE, Vietnam was part of the Chinese Empire, so it is not surprising that its culture, including its music, was strongly influenced over the centuries by

China. Many of the traditional instruments of Vietnam are shared with China: zithers, lutes, fiddles, flutes, as well as drums and gongs.

It is from Vietnam that we have the earliest evidence of a kind of music-making that was to become important across South-East Asia. Sets of stone slabs have been found, dating from 7,000 years ago, which are tuned to a five-note (pentatonic) scale that has been widespread over the centuries, not only in Asia. These are, in effect, stone versions of what is known in the West as a xylophone. Over the centuries, this tradition of percussion instruments was given a boost by the arrival of bronze production. By about 500 BCE the Vietnamese were producing magnificent bronze drums, and a little later Indonesians started making bronze gongs of different sizes.

Our knowledge of the early history of mainland South-East Asian music is very patchy, partly because of the horrifically destructive wars of the twentieth century. But we know that a great empire was established in the ninth century CE, the Khmer Empire, with its capital Angkor in present-day Cambodia. Carved into the stones of its huge temples are many illustrations dating from around 1200 which show royal and military processions, with musicians carrying gongs of various sizes, cymbals, drums and wind instruments, some like trumpets and ram's horns, others probably reed instruments. The gongs indicate the sophistication of bronze technology, as in China, Vietnam and Indonesia.

In the fourteenth century, the Khmers were defeated by the Siamese, and musicians were among the workers brought to Siam (Thailand) to work for their new masters. Four centuries later the Siamese conquered Laos, and again brought the Lao court musicians to their capital, Bangkok. Over the centuries, the music of Siam was influenced by the Khmer and the Lao traditions, though it would be impossible to unpick what elements came from where.

Among these hybrid traditions that survive in modern Thailand the most important ensemble is the *piphat*, a group in which there are xylophones, gongs, drum and cymbals, and a wind instrument, the *pi*, a kind of oboe. Variations of a theme are played at three different speeds, one after the other. Within each variation, different instruments will play the melody with variations of their own, the large gongs playing the simplest version, the upper instruments a more elaborate version.

In Indonesia, the production of bronze instruments was taken to a whole new level. Gongs, chimes and metallophones (like xylophones, but with metal strips instead of wood) were made in different sizes, creating the basis, more than 1,000 years ago, of what came to be known as *gamelan*. This word describes both the set of instruments and the musical genre that is played, and it has long been the classic 'orchestra' of Indonesia, particularly of Java and Bali. *Gamelan* and its instruments have always had strong spiritual associations. Forging a gong is a solemn ritual, and there is a legend in Java that it was the god Shiva who commanded humans to create gongs. Important sets of instruments are still regarded as sacred.

Gamelan functions like a complex community, analogous to a Western orchestra, but with the contributions of each musician shared out in quite a different way. A drummer sets the tempo, which slows down and speeds up to mark different sections of the performance. There are large gongs which mark the slow rhythmic cycle that repeats throughout the performance. Above this, there are smaller gongs, metallophones and xylophones. They play patterns that are two, four or eight times the pace of the gong pattern, with the slowest forming a basic melody, and the fastest parts elaborating the melody at the top. All these patterns fit together, and in some cases two players alternate their notes with each other, so that together they produce a coherent pattern. The combination of all these patterns produces a network of layers that can be immensely complex. The complexity arises because every player knows how everything fits together. This is not an orchestra of virtuoso players, but a virtuoso achievement created by communal interaction and understanding.

Another unusual element of *gamelan* is the tuning of the instruments. Apart from the octave, it has none of the intervals derived from the harmonic series that created the tunings across most of Asia. A *gamelan* generally has two sets of instruments, which are tuned to two different sets of notes. These tunings vary, but they are fixed and carefully tuned for any individual *gamelan*. The two sets of notes, which are played simultaneously, have only one note in common. The rest jar and clash against each other to various degrees, creating a sort of floating dissonance very remote from most concepts of 'harmony'. Nobody knows how old this style of tuning is, nor where it came from, though there are theories that it might pre-date the Mesopotamian system of tuning using fifths.

Apart from the percussion instruments, *gamelan* also has a singer and a two-string fiddle player who work together, elaborating and counterpointing the melody, and there is also a separate flute which utters a sort of commentary like birdsong.

Gamelan has had many roles over its history, from small village ensembles played by local amateurs to large orchestras at court played by professional musicians, and from religious rituals to community festivals. One important art form that is combined with *gamelan* is *wayang*, puppet theatre in which the shadows of the puppets are cast onto a screen. The master puppeteer (always a man) is an important figure in the community, and the art is passed down in families from one generation to the next. The stories are taken from the ancient Hindu epics, involving battles between good and evil, and throughout the performance the *gamelan* accompanies the action, following directions given by the puppeteer in collaboration with the lead drummer. These are major festive events involving the whole community and sometimes last the entire night.

CHAPTER 7

Rhythm and Community

The Sahara has been desert for the last 4,000 years, separating the countries of North Africa from those of the south. Across North Africa, from Morocco in the west to Egypt and Sudan in the east, the predominant religion has been Islam since the seventh century. So the music of the region has formed part of that great sweep of *maqam*-based tradition we looked at in Chapter 4. To the south of the Sahara ('sub-Saharan' Africa), the continent extends for thousands of miles, with cultures that go back to the earliest days of humanity.

Sub-Saharan Africa is a very varied landscape that has undergone different histories in different areas. Long before Europeans began their wholesale plundering of Africa, many empires flourished, including, among the most substantial, Ghana (eighth–twelfth century CE), Mali (thirteenth–seventeenth century) and Benin (thirteenth–nineteenth century) in the west; Ethiopia (twelfth–twentieth century) and Aksum (first–ninth century) in the east; and Zimbabwe (fifteenth–seventeenth century) in the south. These empires had extensive trade connections, their wealth built primarily on gold, ivory, salt and slaves. As in Asia and North Africa, the spread of Islam brought with it not only the religion but also impressive buildings and scholarship. Mosques built in the seventh century still survive in the east, in Somalia and Ethiopia. Later, the most celebrated centre was Timbuktu, capital of Mali, a great focus of trade and learning. Its mosque-based university community was founded in the sixteenth century and had a magnificent collection of manuscripts.

Islam did not become as dominant in Africa as in Asia, and despite these exceptional centres of written learning, the great bulk of the population relied on their traditional oral cultures, with ancient belief in spirits of nature and of ancestors. Many of them were nomadic animal-herders or hunter-gatherers. Their cultures varied from region to region, but across Africa to a surprising extent they shared features over many centuries. This was partly to do with language.

About 3,000 years ago a language group known as Bantu began to spread from West Africa across much of the continent, so that many of the languages of Africa became related to each other. Quite how this spread occurred is debated, but it would have been partly a matter of migration in search of food, with people pushing out or combining with existing populations. Language and music are always closely related, and this spread of Bantu languages must have something to do with the fact that music across a vast area of Africa shares aspects in common.

An example with its origins in a past empire is the *jali* or *griot* ('praise-singer') of Mali. In 1353 a Muslim scholar and explorer, Ibn Battuta, visited Mali and left a description of a banquet at which a *jali* 'chants a poem in praise of the emperor, recalling his battles and deeds of valour', accompanying himself on a xylophone. This role of *jali* continued over the centuries, with every important figure employing one. With the break-up of the empire, it became a freelance occupation. One feature that connects *jalis* of today right back to the fourteenth century is that there has always been a strong hereditary tradition, with the art passed on from father to son. Since the nineteenth century there has also been an increasing number of women *jalis*. Like the bards of ancient Greece, *jalis* were not just musicians and poets, but also important in an oral culture as preservers of history. And, as with many Asian traditions, their art involved a combination of memorisation and improvisation, their singing or chanting following the rhythm and melodic shape of the words.

Two instruments are particularly associated with the *jali*: the *balafon*, a kind of xylophone with gourds as resonators, and the *kora*, a kind of harp shaped rather like a lute, with many strings stretched over a gourd. The *kora* has in recent years become famous as a solo instrument, its style of melody and rhythm still very much based on the traditional narrative style of *jali* singing.

The links between African music and language extend to purely instrumental music. In West Africa drums are used literally to speak. Many African languages are 'tonal': that is, the rise and fall in pitch are essential to the meaning. Drums which can be made to produce lower and higher pitches are made to mimic the shape and inflections of speech, so that messages can be sent over long distances. Drumming has for many centuries been important in traditional communities, the drums being regarded as the voices of ancestors, whose names are recited by drumming.

In both singing and playing instruments, there is scarcely any distinction between the concepts of 'melody' and 'rhythm'. In many kinds of African music the patterns of speech form the basis, without any need to separate its components into what we would call its 'melody' and its 'rhythm'. Because music is so closely related to speech, the range of a song, from high notes to low notes, tends to be quite narrow; there is none of the wide exploration from high to low pitches that you find in Asian music such as Arab *maqam* or Indian *raga*. This is partly because, despite the existence of solo singers, in many parts of Africa music is closely tied to communal singing, in which most of the singers are members of the community without the formal voice-training associated with those Asian genres.

Rhythmic singing and playing take many forms. One of the most unusual instruments is the *goura*. This 'mouth-bow' consists of a

large bow with a string made of sheep gut, sometimes with a reso-
nator made of a coconut shell. A quill is attached to one end of the
string, and the player puts this in their mouth and breathes in and
out, making the string vibrate. The *goura* can produce several notes
of the harmonic series, and there are reports from the early eighteenth century of three or four *gouras* being played together. At the
same time as producing a pattern of harmonics – some high, others
like a growl – the player hums a low, rhythmic chant, producing
two repetitive melodies at the same time. The *goura* is still played
by a few herdsmen of southern Africa. The effect is extraordinarily
like the didgeridoo of the Australian Aboriginal people.

In communal music-making one of the most important elements
across many African cultures is the rhythm of the body in dance.
When you see and hear African dance and music, of many different
kinds, you see and hear these two elements in combination: the
regular stepping, swaying, circling of the dance and its repetitive
rhythm, and the speech-like rhythmic melody that also goes round
in circles, but is constantly changing and evolving from moment to
moment.

In several societies in Central and Southern Africa, groups of
singers sing in different parts simultaneously, creating polyphony
(from the Greek meaning 'many voices'). This can take the form of
moving together in parallel harmony, but sometimes it is much
more complex. In one method a pattern is repeated in the different
voices, but with some starting later than others, and with variations
developing at later repetitions. Pygmy communities of Central
Africa have some of the most complex of all vocal traditions. Each
individual seems free, but co-ordinating in a web of mutually understood connections. It is like a dance in which steps are repeated
endlessly, but with every individual 'doing their own thing' – and
indeed pygmies dance in just this way while singing. The endlessly
varied repetitions have an almost trance-like effect, and such dance
and music are closely connected to the ritual of connecting with the
realm of spirits.

Some of these pygmy communities, such as the Aka, have been
nomadic for thousands of years, so they do not have large instru-

ments, singing with little or no accompaniment. It is only settled communities that have large instruments such as drums and xylophones. In East, West and Southern Africa groups of xylophone players play with complicated, interlocking rhythms. This is not like the rhythm of Western music, in which there is often one steady beat, but a much more complicated combination of different metres simultaneously. In many instances two xylophone players will play alternating little groups of notes to create a coherent musical line. Sometimes there are large ensembles of xylophones, made up of several of these interlocking pairs. In Uganda two or more players will sit either side of the same xylophone, playing complex interlocking patterns together. This means that the bass and treble of the xylophone are the opposite way round for the two groups of players. Other instruments are used to make similarly interlocking patterns, notably the *mbira* or thumb-piano, and ensembles of flutes.

Singing frequently falls into a pattern of 'call and response', in which a lead singer is answered by the whole group. Most often, the lead varies the call, elaborating the narrative and the melody, while the response is shorter and less varied. Purely instrumental music echoes this pattern, so that, in effect, instruments imitate voices. There is a strong sense that these traditions also echo patterns of African society. The importance of community is fundamental to an understanding of African culture, as expressed in religions and music over the centuries. Traditional communities were bound together by their ancestors, who remained in communication. Children were brought up to understand their role in the community, through their parents and the elders, as learning and understanding were passed on orally. Music had a part in many aspects of life, from children's games to work-songs, and involved the participation of everyone.

Where Islam took root, its authorities tended to find ways of accommodating to the old ways and religious practices. Christian missionaries, and later colonists, tended to be less tolerant. Christian teaching, where it prevailed, taught fear of the one God, and obedience to his representatives (priests and the church). This was very different from the traditional emphasis on the community and its ancestors, and it conveniently played into the hands of those who wished to subjugate the population and make them subservient to the conquerors' will. It also went hand in hand with the development of the belief that Africans were godless, superstitious people, inferior to the godly conquerors. All this served to justify first the slave trade, and later the plundering of Africa's resources.

It is partly the destruction over the centuries, partly the oral nature of the cultures, that mean any discussion of African music has to be based on surviving traditions. In cultures that have not depended on written records it is only through surviving practices that we can have some idea of how things might have been in the distant past. There is the occasional report from travellers (as in the description of the Malian *jali*), and tribes have their own legends relating to their music. One thing that is striking is that the most complex polyphonic music of Africa has much in common with the *gamelan* ensembles of Bali and Java, with layers of patterns co-ordinated on top of each other. The tunings of xylophones are also often similar to those of *gamelan*, with 'jangly' intervals as well as those that we are used to in the West. Is there a connection between these traditions, thousands of miles apart? It might seem unlikely, but there was trade between southern Africa and countries as far away as China as early as the fourteenth century, so it is quite possible that one influenced the other.

CHAPTER 8

Spirits of the Ancestors

The Americas – North, Central and South – and the countries of the Southern Seas – Australia, New Zealand and Polynesia – cover a vast area with diverse cultures and histories. But they share some important elements, which they also share with the African cultures we looked at in the last chapter. All of them were inhabited for hundreds, in some cases thousands, of years by indigenous populations, all were in one way or another, and at various dates, invaded and colonised by Europeans. All had their indigenous cultures wholly or partly destroyed, their survival depending on the extent to which they were willing to integrate with, or submit to, their conquerors. In South and Central America, as in Africa, there were mighty empires, and everywhere there were rural communities with their own traditions. As with Africa, the evidence for what went on before Europeans arrived is sparse, and we have to rely on a combination of reports by the incoming Europeans and on old traditions that have somehow survived to this day.

It is believed that the first people to inhabit North America crossed from Siberia to Alaska across the landmass that existed during the last Ice Age, at least 15,000 years ago. As they spread down through the Americas over the centuries, different cultural groupings formed. These societies were predominantly hunters, whose stone spear-heads have been found across North America. The earth mounds of settlements survive from 5,000 years ago. These were oral cultures, and the earliest written reports of them date from the appearance of Europeans from the sixteenth century onwards. The main evidence for the musical cultures of Native North Americans is the survival of traditions in modern populations, and their histories and myths passed down from generation to generation.

I touched on myths about the origins of music and its relationship to the beliefs relating to ancestors in Chapter 1. Many cultures across the world have believed in the supernatural origin of music. This is fundamental to an understanding of Native North American music. Native Americans do not consider music to be of human origin, but believe it is given to them by spirits. Various stories are told about how this happened, and continues to happen. The Blackfoot people of Canada (the Great Plains) tell how the king of the beavers visited a hunter who had collected the skins of every animal and bird. The beaver says that he will exchange each skin for a song with supernatural powers. So the hunter gives him each animal skin, and the beaver gives him the song associated with that animal together with its power. Music is widely believed to exist already in the world of spirits, and someone who creates a song is a 'song-catcher', rather than a composer.

Across the many Native North American peoples, music and dance are closely tied to religious ceremony, and to the spirits of ancestors. Singing is a vital part of all rituals, marking the changing of the seasons, warding off disease, celebrating the different stages of life from birth to death. The singing is often accompanied by rattles or drums, less often with flutes and other wind instruments. The rituals involve whole communities, though particular individuals have authority as shamans (spiritual leaders) and sometimes as exceptional singers and dancers. These include some of the most famous names in Native American history, such as Sitting Bull (leader of the Sioux) and Geronimo (leader of the Apache). Roles for men and women have traditionally been separate. The emphasis is on the community and its ancestors, and the idea of performance is not part of the tradition (though contact with Europeans inevitably introduced a performance element).

The styles of Native North American music vary from area to area, but they share many features. Rhythmic chanting is closely allied to dance, consisting of walking and trotting, jumping and stamping, often in circular formations or lines, with men and women in separate groups. The voices are often harsh, with a kind of pulsating vibrato. Falling phrases are repeated, often based on a five-note (pentatonic) scale. Various pentatonic scales are also common across eastern Asia, and since Native North Americans originally crossed from Asia many thousands of years ago, it is tempting to conjecture that this is where this scale came from. But there is no way of knowing for sure. Song of this broad kind is found from the Inuit in the north to the Pueblo in the south. Particularly in the south, incursions of Europeans produced changes in traditional North American music from the sixteenth century onwards, but otherwise there was little influence between indigenous and European musical cultures.

In Central and South America, interaction between indigenous people and European conquerors from the fifteenth century onwards was so thorough and, for the inhabitants, so catastrophic, that it is difficult to disentangle earlier history so as to understand the indigenous musical cultures. This is made even more complicated by the massive influx of African slaves from the sixteenth century onwards, which I'll be considering later. As for indigenous music of Central and South America, there is evidence, from early records, archaeology and surviving traditions, that helps us piece something together.

Before the Spanish invaded what is now Mexico in the sixteenth century, there was a highly sophisticated civilisation, the Aztec Empire, the realm of the Mexica people, established in the fourteenth century. Like Europeans, they had a society of different classes, including merchants, a ruling elite and warriors. Aztec rulers were believed to be descended from the gods. Music was an important part of all their rituals and ceremonies. There were professional musicians, the most important of whom were employed at court and in temples. Wooden trumpets were important in war and at temples, where they sounded the hours of the day and night. All Aztecs were brought up with music and dance from a young age, trained to take part in the rituals. There were instruments, drums, flutes and rattles, of which the most important were drums. Special types of drum were thought to be the embodiment of gods sent to earth, and during the most sacred royal rituals the blood of sacrificed people was poured into them. These sacrifices reached a climax during the annual festivities dedicated to the war god, Huitzilopochtli. There is evidence from stone carvings and burial sites that human sacrifices were part of Central American religious practices from 2,000 years ago, and the Aztecs' rituals were in that tradition.

After the Spanish conquest, Aztec music and dance was rapidly either suppressed or subsumed into Spanish and Christian practice. But there are reports from incoming Spaniards that reveal some Aztec traditions. Soon after the Spaniard Hernán Cortés arrived in Mexico, the Aztec emperor, Moctezuma, was taken prisoner. The population responded with music and dance in the streets and squares. According to one contemporary report, 2,000 of the highest nobles of Aztec society, dressed in their richest robes, danced a dance called *Mitotes* near the palace where the emperor was held. This was a circling war-dance (the massacre that followed belongs to a later chapter). Festivals were celebrated with carefully rehearsed singing and dancing. A missionary in the 1530s describes great festivals at which more than 1,000 dancers take part: 'the drums, singing and dancing are perfectly co-ordinated. Everything is so synchronized that one does not differ in the slightest from another, and good Spanish dancers who see them are amazed.'

A report from another Spanish writer describes how, in Mexico City in 1645, there was performed 'the dance of the Emperor Moctezuma.' Fourteen dancers in two lines were led by one representing the emperor, all dressed in ancient Mexican costume, and each carrying a gourd rattle. To one side of the flower-strewn dance floor was a drummer and a group of elders, who 'intoned the song that always accompanied the Mexican dances'. The dance began 'with slow and dignified step' and accelerated as Moctezuma took his seat on the throne, the nobles dancing for him. Then the emperor stepped down and danced with children between the two rows of noblemen. By this date the scene included a Christian altar, to which the dancers made reverence. But this was clearly a traditional, pre-Christian ceremony, which had presumably been danced not only for Moctezuma but earlier for his predecessors as emperor.

Further south in Peru, Spanish conquest of the Incas left more aspects of their culture to survive than was the case with the Aztecs. The panpipes, whose sound has become the most familiar way of evoking the Andes mountains, date back long before the Inca Empire arose in the thirteenth century – the earliest surviving examples are 6,000 years old. Unlike the flute, which consists of a single tube with finger-holes bored into it to change the note, panpipes consist of a group of several pipes of different lengths, each producing a different note. Ancient examples were made from reed or bamboo stems, bone or pottery (the people of the Andes were skilled in the production of pottery). Although they are most familiar as South American instruments, they were found across large areas of the Americas, South, Central and North, and there are equivalent instruments in Asia, Europe and Africa. Clearly, grouping tubes together was one of the basic ways of creating a wind instrument.

One feature of Andean panpipes is that they were made to be played in pairs. Each instrument had only some of the notes of the scale, the other notes being on the other instrument. So players shared the notes of a melody between them. This sharing technique is not unique to South America: I have already described similar alternating of notes or phrases in Indonesian *gamelan* and in African music.

Across South America, reports by incoming conquerors and missionaries shed light on the rituals and music of indigenous people, even though they often interpreted them as barbaric, or even satanic. Jean de Léry, a French Protestant pastor, lived with the Tupinamba people in Brazil for several months in 1557. One morning he heard a low chant being muttered by the men, which grew louder and was answered by the women, all reiterating the same syllable, 'He, he, he', in a repeated pattern of two notes. This went on with increasing intensity: 'Not only did they howl, but also, leaping violently into the air, they made their breasts shake and they foamed at the mouth.' Léry thought that they had been possessed by the devil. But then, after a pause, they began to sing again, and 'now I received in recompense such joy, hearing the measured harmonies of such a multitude … I stood there entranced. Whenever I remember it my heart trembles, and it seems their voices are still in my ears.' It was only later that he learned the significance of this chanting, which combined laments for the dead, threats against enemies, and celebration of their ancestors who survived a great flood by climbing trees.

Songs that connect people to ancestors and ancient myths are widespread across the southern hemisphere. Among Aboriginal Australians, song enshrines the memory of the 'Dreamtime', when creator-ancestors travelled across the land, creating everything and marking the trail of creation with 'song-lines'. These memories are passed on from one generation to another through rituals of dance and song. Rhythmic chanting is often accompanied by the didgeridoo, a long wooden wind instrument, up to ten feet long, which produces an imposing, low drone. The player produces shifting harmonics and rhythms to create a hypnotic pattern, enhancing the mysteries of the ritual.

This traditional chanting and playing is dominated by men. But women have special roles. One is the singing of laments. Across Australia, different Aboriginal groups have their own versions, related to the places, plants and animals of their area. These 'totems', created by the ancestral beings as they passed through the land, are evoked in the laments, with a powerful sense of longing.

Across the islands of the southern Pacific Ocean, music has taken many different forms, and several traditions involve singing in more than one part, polyphony. This was reported by European travellers to the South Seas in the eighteenth century. Captain James Cook's journal of his second voyage, 1772–5, includes a description of Polynesian polyphony: 'They sing in parts, keeping the same time and varying the four notes without ever going beyond them. The singers (that I heard) were all women. One confined herself to the Lower Note, which acted as the Drone.'

In Tonga in 1777, Cook witnessed a dance in which more than a hundred men were ranged in neatly drilled lines, moving 'as one man', flourishing wooden paddles to the accompaniment of drumbeats and a huge chorus of singers. According to Cook, the performance would have met with 'universal applause' on a European stage. And according to later witnesses, this dance also involved a rhythmic chant of four notes, endlessly repeated.

CHAPTER 9

Dance and Harmony

Thinking about the early history of European music needs an act of imagination. For many years, music historians used to write about European music as if it had begun with the invention of music notation, and as if written music was all that mattered. But European music notation didn't develop until the tenth century CE. Before that, ever since the first arrival of humans in Europe, there had been many centuries in which music was made, developed, passed on from generation to generation, by ear and voice, just as in the other parts of the world. Indeed, even after the development of music notation, for centuries most of the music that people heard, sang and played was still made and transmitted in the old way, because notating music was a rare skill. Gradually, notated music became the focus of most professional musicians, and later of amateurs too. But that was over a very long time.

Partly because of the development of music notation, the music of Europe has developed over the centuries in quite a different way from the music of other cultures. As we've seen so far, cultures where music is passed on orally have traditions that last a long time. This doesn't mean that they are fixed. Invasions, changes of religion, migrations and influences from other cultures always cause change. And everything passed on over generations by ear inevitably changes over time: the way Indian musicians perform *raga* today or Indonesians play *gamelan* must differ from the way they were performed 1,000 years ago. But the important thing is that the essential tradition remains.

In Europe the situation has been very different. For the last 1,000 years or more, European music has been in a state of fundamental change and evolution, sometimes steady, sometimes sudden and revolutionary. Any sense of a continuing tradition has sometimes been very fragile, particularly from the twentieth century onwards. This continual upheaval was shared with the other arts, and went hand in hand with changes in technology, industry and society.

Through their empires and colonies, Europeans exported these changing ideas to the rest of the world, though, as we have already seen, some cultures were more successful than others in preserving their own traditions. As for European music itself, with its complex history of change and development, it will take quite a few chapters to give even the most basic outline of what has gone on. Because of this, there's a danger that you might think that I have devoted too much space to what is usually referred to as 'the West' (Europe and North America) compared to the rest of the world. My intention is not to privilege the musical history of the West, but to convey its developing complexity. In later chapters, part of this involves the interaction of the West with other cultures of the world, which has sometimes had positive outcomes, but has also been highly destructive. Reassessing the relationship between the West and the countries which it has colonised and exploited is an important and ongoing task of our time, and music has to be part of that.

Before we get into that evolving and complex history, it is worth looking at the starting point, to try to establish how European music, before its long evolution began, compared with the music of the rest of the world. Precisely because of all the later developments, it is difficult to know very much about this early period, because so little has remained unaffected. There are only fragments of 'traditional' European music surviving.

As I have said before, there is never really a starting point. We have already seen how Mesopotamian and Egyptian musical culture fed into Greece. Greek musical ideas were to have an important influence on the development of wider European music. And there were elements from further east, specifically Jewish chant and then Christian chant, which we'll come to in the next chapter. But it took some centuries for those influences to take hold, and they created a mix with influences from many different cultures across Europe.

Not much attention was paid to the early musical traditions of Europe until the eighteenth century, when European writers began to be interested in what they called 'folk music', the music of country people. They assumed that this music, like the way of life of those who produced it, was very old, even 'timeless'. The interest in that music belongs to a later chapter, but the folk music itself is one of the possible starting points for imagining early European music.

Across Europe, from east to west and from north to south, there are surviving traditions of instrumental folk music, many of them focused on dance. How many are based on genuinely old tradition is difficult to disentangle, and there has undoubtedly been a lot of imaginative reconstruction to create the modern folk revival. But instruments that have been in Europe since ancient times include flutes and wind instruments with reeds (such as the ancient Greek *aulos*), and plucked stringed instruments including various harps and lyres. Fiddles of various kinds, small stringed instruments played with a bow, have been around since the ninth century, probably brought in from Asia. By the fourteenth century, instruments with drones had become popular: bagpipes and the hurdy-gurdy (a stringed instrument whose notes are 'bowed' by a rotating wheel). Bagpipe traditions are found across Europe, from Bulgaria to Scotland and Ireland. The Scottish bagpipe as a war instrument goes back to the sixteenth century. Noble families employed pipers, and piping families became celebrated, passing down the tradition from generation to generation. They played marching tunes, laments, tunes celebrating heroes. Families also employed generations of harp players for more intimate music-making.

One thing that is clear is that the character of folk, or traditional, music varies considerably from east to west across Europe. In the east, the border between Asia and Europe was always more theoretical than real, and the influence of Asian music cultures spread far into Europe over the centuries. The Islamic Ottoman (Turkish) Empire (fourteenth–early twentieth centuries), which bordered Europe, was often tolerant of different religions and their cultures, allowing them to thrive side by side, and this led to a rich melting pot of musical styles. To this day Eastern European traditional music shares many elements of Asian origin. It seems very likely that some of these go back long before the spread of Islam: modes with 'non-Western' tunings, Arab and Persian styles of melody adapted to other languages, and dances in complex metres. Dances with five, seven or nine beats in uneven patterns are still particularly common in Bulgaria and surrounding countries.

One feature of traditional European music that is found across the continent is the practice of singing and playing not just a single melody line, but with several lines simultaneously (polyphony), a practice that occurs in traditional music across the world. This is found in rural communities more often in Eastern Europe than in the West, and the practice varies considerably, particularly in how dissonant (clashing) the music is allowed to be. The most dissonant examples are concentrated through the Balkans – the peninsula stretching from Bulgaria on the Black Sea south through to Greece. Here, there are various genres of part-singing that delight in the voices deliberately clashing together, usually over a bass note that creates a continuous drone. Professionally trained folk choirs from Bulgaria and Albania have toured in the West in recent decades, but the strikingly dissonant, and strident, music that they sing has its origins in village communities. In ancient Greece, dissonant clashes were part of the accepted style when playing the *aulos* in pairs, so it is possible, as singers in some of these countries claim, that the surviving tradition of dissonant sung polyphony has its origins in ancient times.

Other traditions of polyphony that include clashes of harmony are found to the east in Georgia, where the styles are particularly varied and complex. They include hymns of mourning sung in three-part harmony by men, a style that is still to be found in mountain villages and is thought to be very old. Dissonant harmonies are also found across Slav countries, from Russia to Poland and the Czech Republic. To the north, in Lithuania, there is a tradition of dissonant polyphonic chanting sung by small groups of women. There are only two voice parts, but the effect is dense and complex because the parts are tightly woven together, as if battling for the same space and continually bumping into each other on dissonant intervals. This is a Westerner's way of describing it, but the Lithuanians consider these 'clashings' harmonious, not dissonant, describing the effect as like the ringing of bells. This Lithuanian tradition was one of the inspirations for Russian composer Igor Stravinsky's famously dissonant *The Rite of Spring*, a landmark of twentieth-century music, which I'll come to in Chapter 32.

Many of these traditions of polyphony must stretch back through the centuries, though little is known about their history. They were for the family and the village community, not exposed to wider public life until our modern age of communications. Some 150 years ago a singer in Lithuania told a collector of folk songs that all the mothers in his village knew a repertoire of chants that they kept secret, singing them only rarely and being careful to keep the traditional words unchanged. You can imagine this respect for inherited music being repeated across many villages of Eastern Europe, in the days before modern life began to loosen these ancient bonds.

Further west, styles of folk-polyphony tend to become less clashing, more 'harmonious', though how much this had to do with influence from composed Western music is impossible to know. Local polyphonic traditions survive in many communities scattered across France, Spain, Portugal, Sardinia, Corsica, Sicily. We are left to guess how old their styles are, but there are documents reporting similar practices in southern Europe from the fifteenth century.

There is even earlier evidence of polyphonic singing in Wales. A priest known as Gerald of Wales wrote in the twelfth century: 'When they come together to make music, they do not sing in unison like the inhabitants of other regions, but in many different parts; so that in a company of singers, which one very frequently meets with in Wales, you will hear as many different parts and voices as there are performers, who all at length unite, with organic melody, in one consonance.' He found a simpler version of the same thing in northern England. Furthermore, 'Neither of the two nations has acquired this peculiarity by art, but by long habit, which has rendered it natural and familiar; and the practice is now so firmly rooted in them, that it is unusual to hear a simple and single melody well sung; and, what is still more wonderful, the children, even from their infancy, sing in the same manner.'

Gerald also describes virtuoso polyphony played by wonderful Irish instrumentalists on harp, pipe and crwth (bowed lyre), who are so skilled 'that the perfection of their art appears in the concealment of it'. As for Irish singers, 'In their rhymed songs and set speeches they are so subtle and ingenious, that they produce, in their native tongue, ornaments of wonderful and exquisite invention both in the words and sentences. Hence arise those poets whom they call Bards, of whom you will find many in this nation, endowed with the above faculty . . .'

These traditions might have been very old when Gerald was describing them, though again we can't be sure. We can get some idea of what he means by the 'exquisite invention' of Irish singers from the surviving Irish tradition of *sean-nós*, unaccompanied singing in the Irish language. Poems are sung in a style with long and highly elaborate melodic lines. Writers have commented on the similarities between *sean-nós* and singing styles much further south and east, particularly the elaborate, melancholy song of Spanish flamenco, and even Arab styles of singing. It might seem far-fetched to suggest a connection between these traditions. But musical influences have spread extraordinarily widely over the centuries, and it is altogether possible that Irish singing was influenced from the Mediterranean and the east.

There have been bards (singing poets) in many cultures across the globe, and Europe's bards have given us some of our earliest works of literature. I have already talked about Homer, author (or at least compiler) of the ancient Greek *Odyssey* and *Iliad*. Just as we have to imagine those poems being sung, the same is likely to be true of the early epics of northern Europe, such as *Beowulf* (eighth century), the Icelandic sagas (thirteenth century) and the German *Nibelungenlied* (*c.* 1200). Those are the dates of the earliest written sources, but they all have their origins in much earlier traditions of unwritten sagas handed on orally.

Beyond the exceptional bards and professional singer-poets, we have to imagine a large, and largely forgotten, tradition of song passed down by ear through the generations, and related to important stages of life: lullabies for babies, love songs, songs of religious devotion, celebrations of the lives of saints, laments for the dead. Across much of Europe many of these were sung by women, and traces of them survive in medieval plays (which we will look at later). Like indigenous practices elsewhere, when Christianity became established these were regarded as a threat to proper ritual, and, like anything pre-Christian, were often condemned as 'devilish'. And that takes us on to the topic of the next chapter.

CHAPTER 10

Chanting in the Church, Singing in the Streets

As we begin our journey through the history of European ('Western') music, we need to start with Christianity, the great force that spread from east to west 2,000 years ago and had an immense influence on the history of European thought and society. Jesus Christ was a Jew, brought up in the ancient Jewish religion, living and teaching in what was then a province of the Roman Empire, Judaea (present-day southern Israel and the West Bank). He offered a powerful message of a god who loves each individual, of all nations and classes. This message spread extraordinarily rapidly, and within a hundred years it had reached as far as Greece and Italy. Christianity welcomed non-Jews into the new faith, and it gradually became a religion separate from the Judaism where it started. It developed into an institution, with a hierarchy of priests and bishops, and by the fourth century it was a protected religion within the Roman Empire (as was Judaism).

By this time, the Roman Empire had divided into a western empire, centred on Rome, and an eastern empire, centred on Byzantium (now

Istanbul). It was Emperor Constantine who moved his court from Rome to Byzantium and converted to Christianity. Byzantium was renamed Constantinople, and the eastern empire developed a rich culture rivalling that of Rome, with Christian worship supported by the state.

Over the centuries, there were further divisions, conflicts and shifts of authority. The eastern empire survived until it was defeated by the forces of Islam in the seventh century. In the west, Rome was attacked at various times. But the Pope (the senior bishop of the Christian Church in Rome) survived by forming alliances with important Christian rulers to the north. The climax of this power-broking occurred in 800, when the Pope anointed Charlemagne, a champion of Christianity, as emperor of a huge area of Europe, now to be known as the Holy Roman Empire. This empire survived, though diminishing in size, for just over 1,000 years, until it was dissolved in 1806.

The spread and development of Christianity had enormous consequences for music. Both in the Western and the Eastern church the focus of worship was the Last Supper, the final meal that Christ shared with his disciples before being arrested and sent to be crucified. The sharing of wine, representing Christ's blood, and of bread, representing Christ's body, formed the basis of the most important ritual, the Mass. For the celebration of the Mass, sacred texts were chanted in Latin. At first, this chanting would have closely resembled Jewish worship, in which a solo singer (cantor) is appointed to lead the congregation, who answer with responding phrases – a format that endures to this day. Over time, Christian chant diverged from Jewish chant, with a more distinct repertoire of chants for the different services and seasons of the church. As early as the fourth century, St John Chrysostom, Archbishop of Constantinople, fiercely urged Christians to avoid taking part in worship at the Jewish synagogues, and to avoid 'falling into the Jewish manner of prayer'. This presumably also included their manner of chanting. Christians had therefore already moved away from forms of worship and music that Jesus himself would have known.

This was all before the development of European music notation. Chanting was still an oral tradition, like music the world over. If you imagine a time when ear and memory were all that we had, it is obvious that the chants could never have been really fixed in the early centuries of Christianity – indeed, the very idea of fixed texts of any kind can only exist if there is an actual *text* to refer to. As chants were passed down from one person and generation to another by ear, they would have acquired variations, and chants would also have varied from one church, monastery or country to another. These regional variations persisted for several centuries. However, as the establishment of the church grew, its authorities wished to keep things firmly under control. In the seventh century, long before the development of notation, Pope Gregory headed a drive to regularise the chanting throughout the church (to this day, this kind of chant is known as 'Gregorian chant'). He sent out missions whose broad purpose was to spread the Roman form of Christianity. One member of the mission to England, known as James the Deacon, had the specific task of teaching the singing of chant 'in the Roman manner'.

The regularisation of chant was influenced by the writings of the sixth-century Roman philosopher, Boethius, who translated Greek texts into Latin. It was Boethius who systematised the modes (scales) on which chant was based, deriving them from his understanding of the modes of the ancient Greeks. Even though his ideas about Greek music were rather shaky, this didn't stop his modes becoming established as the official 'church modes' for several centuries. This did not mean a sudden break with wider traditions. In ancient Greek music, as well as Arabic *maqam* and Indian *raga*, a mode carries all sorts of associations to do with mood, character, and appropriate melodic shapes. These sorts of tradition carried over into Christian chant for some centuries, only gradually falling out of use.

As the institution of Christianity developed, it acquired set forms of worship (the 'liturgy'), organisations with a hierarchy of priests and bishops ('the church'), and buildings in which worship took place. Churches and cathedrals were built, in which priests and public came together to worship. Men and women attended, but the priests and bishops were all men. As well as these public-facing institutions, there were also self-contained communities of monks (monasteries) and of nuns (convents). It was St Basil, a bishop in Turkey in the fourth century, who first established a 'rule' for the work, prayer and obedience of monks. An Italian monk, St Benedict, based his own rule on that of St Basil when he founded monasteries in Italy in the early sixth century, and the Benedictine Order of monasteries spread across Europe over the next five centuries.

These monastic communities reinforced their relationship with God with a series of acts of worship throughout the day, beginning early in the morning and finishing late at night. Each of these services involved the chanting of prayers and sacred texts drawn both from the Jewish Bible (particularly the psalms, attributed to King David), and from the Christian 'New Testament'. Most important was the re-enactment of the Last Supper, the Mass. Some of these communities had little contact with the outside world, others were more open, holding services which were attended by the public. Monasteries and churches were often linked together, forming a religious community, and their libraries increasingly became centres of scholarship.

As the Christian church became a powerful institution in Europe, music took on a central role. As music notation developed from the tenth century, the chants of the church were increasingly written down, and this added to the sense of a formal 'repertoire' of church music.

Meanwhile outside the church, other forms of music were in general circulation, particularly songs and dances. Like early church music, these continued to be passed down by ear. When notation was developed, some examples did come to be written down – first the poems, and only later their music – and we know a certain amount about the people who produced this music.

There were many musicians who came to be known by the general term of 'minstrels', but who earlier went by various names, depending on their status. The higher-ranking musicians, widely known as 'goliards', were often educated young men aiming for a career in the church. They made up songs in Latin, the language of the church. The lower-ranking musicians, who had generally not gone to school and could not read, sang songs in the local language and played a variety of instruments. They were entertainers who danced, performed tricks and acrobatics, and juggled, hence in France they were known as *jongleurs*. Thousands of these minstrels worked across Europe, and once a year they held meetings at which they gathered to exchange songs and ideas, all by ear. Some of them were rough characters, often in trouble with the authorities. Others were more highly skilled and refined, and the most successful of them found work at aristocratic courts. This brought them into contact with a new class of high-born musicians, known as the troubadours. From the eleventh century onwards some of the troubadours' songs were preserved, in an early form of notation which gives at least an approximate idea of their music.

The troubadours arose in Provence, in what is now southern France. The earliest whose songs have come down to us was William IX (1071–1127), Duke of Aquitaine. Most others were also of noble birth, and they included several women. The subject matter of their songs ranged from war and crusades to courtly love, and the love songs echo some of the themes, and even some of the poetic styles, of Arabic songs from Spain that we encountered in Chapter 4. This raises the intriguing possibility of influence between Christian southern France and Muslim Spain. The Christian courts in southern France and northern Spain hosted Muslim and Jewish musicians, scientists and scholars, just as the courts in Muslim Spain hosted Christians and Jews. All had musicians of various ranks, from nobles to slaves. In the Arabic songs from Muslim Spain there are passages that are in Romance, a language of southern France. Reciprocally, there are snatches of Arabic texts in some of the songs of William the troubadour. But he was also a warrior, who fought against Muslims in Jerusalem, and even in nearby Córdoba, the artistic centre of Muslim Spain (which eventually fell to the Christians in 1236). William would certainly have been exposed to Arab culture, but the relationship is complex.

An important figure in the thirteenth century was Alfonso X, known as 'Alfonso the Wise', king of the Christian parts of northern Spain – Castile, León and Galicia. His court was a meeting place for scholars, artists and musicians from different cultures: troubadours from Provence, Islamic and Jewish scholars from Muslim Spain. Alfonso's interest in song had a permanent legacy. He commissioned a written collection of more than 400 songs, *Cantigas de Santa Maria* ('Songs of the Virgin Mary'), some of which he probably composed himself. These show a blend of styles, derived from troubadour song, with similar patterns of rhythm, repetition and refrain that might link them to the songs of Al-Andalus. Though they are devoted to the Virgin Mary, they are full of allusions to earthly love, and the lightness of their poetry suggests an equivalent, dancing lightness in the music (though the rhythm has to be guessed).

Royal patronage was an important way of spreading the influence of the troubadours further afield. When the Holy Roman Emperor married Beatrix of Burgundy in the twelfth century, Beatrix took to Germany a troubadour whose style greatly influenced the development of the German equivalent of the troubadours, the *Minnesänger*.

In northern France, troubadour-like figures were known as *trouvères*. These were a mixture of upper and lower classes, but with the emphasis on the lower. In the town of Arras they, together with the minstrels (*jongleurs*), formed the first known guild of professional musicians, founded in about 1175. They developed a tradition of songs over several generations, with familiar recurring themes about love and religious devotion. They also supported the poorer members in practical ways, and the members of the guild included both church and non-church people, and many women.

The influence of Muslim Spain on European culture is gradually being teased out by researchers. More definite and long-lasting was the spread of Arab instruments from Spain into Christian Europe, a result of the expertise of Arab and Jewish instrument-makers. The instruments that were most important in early European culture were stringed instruments, some plucked (lutes, harps, lyres), others bowed (fiddles, rebecs, viols, later violins and cellos). The short-necked lute, the *oud*, had become very important in Central Asia 2,000 years ago, and it has been a mainstay of Arab music ever since. It reached Western Europe via Muslim Spain, where it was the most usual instrument to accompany a singer, and the lute was a favoured instrument across Europe through to the seventeenth century.

Bowed instruments of Europe were also developed in Central Asia. Horses were important to the cultures of this landmass with its vast plains, and horsehair proved to be the ideal material for a bow. By the tenth century, bowed instruments were spreading from Central Asia in all directions, east as far as China and west via Byzantium into Europe. Muslim Spain was an important route for bowed instruments into France and Western Europe.

The more one looks at all these cross-cultural influences, the clearer it becomes that the early history of music in Europe drew on a whole web of musical cultures from a wide area. It is reckoned that, from the eighth to the thirteenth centuries, there was such mutual influence between different cultures around the Mediterranean that you could say that Arab, Jewish and Christian musicians 'understood' each other, during the centuries before Western music set off in a different direction.

CHAPTER 11

Reason It Out, Write It Down

While the Eastern church continued with its traditional chant, the Western church was developing music in new ways that would have lasting consequences. With the growth of scholarship and learning, at first in monasteries and then in universities, music became not just something to practise as part of worship, but an intellectual pursuit. Ancient Greek texts were translated into Latin from the sixth century onwards. From them Europeans acquired the idea that music was an expression of the mathematical truths of the universe – an idea that goes all the way back to the Mesopotamians and Egyptians. For Christians this meant the universe that God created. Since God is the great creator, human beings do not really 'create' anything. They are merely carrying out the creative acts inspired by God. Making music in the church was therefore seen as a matter of adhering to rules that were based in God's mathematical truths. This is not to say that music was devoid of feeling or expression. Its divine powers were recognised, and its potential misuse by humans feared.

This God-centred view of music was challenged by the discovery in the twelfth century of the writings of the ancient Greek philosopher Aristotle. He taught that human reason, rational thought, was the essential basis of knowledge. This philosophy, 'humanism', extended all the way from scientific investigation to the ethics of human behaviour. You can imagine the potential conflict of such ideas with the church authorities who considered themselves to be carrying out the will of God. Over the centuries humanism and rational thought were to have a profound effect on the way that European society evolved, setting it on a course that was distinctly different from that of other cultures. This is most obvious in a series of great shifts in European history – the Renaissance, the Enlightenment, the rise of capitalism and the Industrial Revolution, through to the modern era with its computer-driven technology. These are huge topics that affected music as they affected everything else, and we'll touch on their influence as we travel through history.

One innovation that enabled music to be developed in the West as a highly rational discipline was notation. As early as the ninth century, in manuscripts from monasteries in and around France, monks wrote markings above the words to remind them when the chant goes up or down. These are known as 'neumes', and the key word here is 'remind': These neumes are of little use to us today, because they are not enough to indicate exactly what was to be sung. They were, however, useful to singers who knew the chant, and who just needed prompts as reminders of what they had been taught. Studies of these neumes, and of writings of this period, suggest that neumes also reminded the singer how to sing the chant, with appropriate ornamental flourishes ('flowers') and expressive gestures including 'tremulous' notes. This suggests that, in the early centuries of Christianity in Europe, the manner of chanting still retained much of the character of its Middle Eastern origins, and only later acquired the plainer, unornamented style we have come to associate with Gregorian chant. This certainly makes sense in the context of the 'understanding' between Christian, Arab and Jewish musicians that I mentioned at the end of the previous chapter.

Over the next century, scribes experimented with raising and lowering the marks, to indicate the rise and fall of the chant more clearly. Then, in the eleventh century, an Italian monk, Guido d'Arezzo, introduced what we still call a 'stave', with lines indicating notes a third apart from each other. By placing notes either on a line or in the space between the lines, all the pitches of a melody were precisely defined. Early on, a stave of four lines was most common; the modern five-line stave came later.

The development of notation had two important consequences for the history of Western music, helping to separate it from the history of other musical cultures. First, this made it easier to control what was sung, by circulating copies of the music, and by referring to the notation rather than relying on memory. In the eleventh century a cantor (singer) from Rome was sent to the monastery of St Gall in Switzerland bringing a book of notated chants, from which a copy was made. This was then used to correct any 'errors' in chanting. As more copies of such notated chants were made, what had been an essentially oral tradition gradually became more fixed, with fewer variations from region to region or from generation to generation.

Secondly, over time notation made it possible to develop ever more complex methods of composing music, beyond what could be achieved by memory alone. This lies at the heart of the differences between European and other music cultures of the world. There was no sudden change: notation didn't become generally used for many centuries. Paper was not yet manufactured in Europe and didn't become widely available until the fourteenth century; parchment made from animal skins was very expensive, and books were precious luxuries. So most musical activity continued to be carried out by ear and memory, as it always had been. But in select corners of the musical world, the ability to write music down, to elaborate it on the page, and to circulate copies, was changing the course of music history.

The existence of scores also means that we have the first examples of music in which the composer is identified. Most chants were anonymous. Partly this was because the idea of a composer setting out to achieve something original had not yet entered musical thinking. Chants were made up of shapes of melody that recurred again and again, in a system of pattern-making character-istic of oral cultures around the world. But occasionally a name rises to the surface, breaking through anonymity.

One early example from the twelfth century is Hildegard of Bingen, a German abbess (head of a convent), a mystic, poet-musician and scholar, renowned as a preacher. A wide range of her sacred and secular chants and songs survive, setting her own poetry and notated in beautiful manuscripts (though, as with all music of this period, we have to guess at the rhythm). Hildegard fiercely defended the importance of praising God in music. On one occasion the (male) church authorities punished her convent for a supposed offence by instructing her to stop all singing. She dared to respond by telling them that if they insisted on this punishment, they in turn would be punished by being prevented from joining the angels praising God in heaven. It is an indication of her standing that she had the nerve to issue this threat. This is an early example of conflict between female convents and the male church authorities that was to recur time and again over the centuries, often over questions to do with music.

Around the time of Hildegard's death, an important innovation was under way as the new cathedral of Notre Dame was being built in Paris. For several centuries, it had been the custom for singers sometimes to reinforce the chants by adding other voices in parallel, often a fourth below the main chant, a style known as 'organum'. In Paris specially trained members of the choir elaborated this into more complex polyphony, in which the original chant was sustained in one voice while another voice provided a more elaborate descant. At the same time, ways were found of showing the rhythms more precisely, taking the guesswork out of reading the notation. This enabled composers to develop styles of polyphony that were as complex in their rhythms as they were in their interweaving melo-dies. We know the names of two pioneers in this new style whose compositions survive in a manuscript collection. They were both members of the Notre Dame choir: Léonin in the late twelfth century, and, building on his ideas, Pérotin in the early thirteenth century. The elaborations, in three and sometimes four voice parts, alternated with the singing of the simple chant. This combining of independent melodies together was called in Latin *punctus contra punctum*, in English 'counterpoint'.

The entry of polyphony and counterpoint into the heart of the church establishment is one of the major milestones of Western music. But not all church authorities welcomed it, even in the West. The traditional Gregorian chants were the bedrock of sung worship. Indeed, even when polyphony became well established, it was only specialist male singers who sang it, and Gregorian chant continued to dominate the music of churches and monasteries. There were those who were quick to treat polyphony as an intrusion from outside the church (as indeed it probably was, in origin), and to view it with suspicion. And there is evidence that the specialist singers of polyphony at Notre Dame were, in some cases, associated with radical groups, 'heretics', who challenged official church doctrine. But polyphony and counterpoint were here to stay in the Western Christian church. By contrast, in the Eastern church, it took another 400 years until singers in Russian churches began to improvise descants around the chant and polyphony was allowed.

The monasteries and convents were at the forefront of musical scholarship and thinking until the rise of universities in the twelfth century. As music notation and composed polyphony developed, monks and nuns began to compose new combinations of melodies and texts, often inserted into the traditional chants. For example, where a chant ended with the word 'Alleluia' ('Praise to God'), they might extend the last syllable into a long flourish. This had new text added to it, and then this new section of music and text might be separated off and turned into a separate piece, sometimes with several verses. This was a new kind of hymn, called a 'trope'. Tropes became so popular that eventually the church authorities felt obliged to impose limits on them, so as to preserve the importance of the Gregorian chants.

Another feature that became increasingly popular was the procession, for which special songs were composed. Processions had been a feature of rituals around the world over many centuries, and by the thirteenth century composers at Notre Dame in Paris were composing polyphonic processional hymns ('conductus') for up to four voices. These spread inside and outside the church, particularly in Britain. The parts tended to move all together in parallel, most often in a swinging two-beat metre suitable for processing.

Some of these tropes and processional songs had a dramatic element. An early example from the tenth century was inserted into the official chants for Easter Day. This little sequence dramatises a scene from the Bible in which three women ('The Three Marys') come to Jesus's tomb after his crucifixion and find it empty. Instead, they find an angel, who tells them that Jesus is risen from the dead. More elaborate dramatisations followed, many centring on the Easter story of Jesus's death and resurrection, others on his birth. Hildegard of Bingen wrote the earliest example of a music drama in which both words and music survive, dating from about 1150: *Ordo Virtutum*, a dialogue of struggle between virtues and the devil.

Eventually the church decreed that these dramatisations had got out of hand, and by the beginning of the thirteenth century the Pope banned their performance in church. So performance of dramas moved outside to the church steps and to the marketplace, becoming ever more elaborate, and incorporating all sorts of elements that would have been impossible in church – costume, dance, comic episodes, more instruments than allowed in church. This development is one of the most important sources of European drama, leading on to the fully fledged Mystery Plays and Miracle Plays of the fifteenth and sixteenth centuries.

With the rise of polyphony, the early habit of adding extra text to the words of the chant took a new turn. As early as the twelfth century, when polyphony was in its infancy, a second part added over the long notes of the chant would sometimes have different Latin words from the chant itself – a counterpoint of words as well as music. This developed into a highly sophisticated genre called the Motet (from the French 'mot', meaning a word). This became a popular genre in the thirteenth century, despite some objections to the combining of different texts. Sections of the set chant would be treated in this way, with two or three parts added above the slower notes of the chant, each with a different text. Often the new texts are meditations on the words of the chant, so that the three parts form an extraordinarily subtle interplay. The effect is rather like much later operatic ensembles, in which each character expresses a different point of view simultaneously. This style of motet was also popular in sophisticated circles outside the church, with common themes of love, wine and merrymaking. Sometimes the sacred and the secular were combined, with one line praising the Virgin Mary, another addressed to a lover.

This overlapping of sacred and secular might seem surprising. But we must imagine a world in which ordinary life and religious beliefs were intimately intertwined – something that links the medieval Christian world with other cultures. At the same time, we need to remember that this highly sophisticated music was not aimed at an audience, but was for worship, or for the entertainment of refined intellectuals.

Though different social levels of music must always have existed, this is a period at which we begin to get a clear sense of distinction between music for the 'common people' and music for an educated minority; and this meant not only those privileged by wealth and aristocracy, but also the many educated people in the church – priests, monks, nuns, scholars, scribes – who were themselves often from well-to-do families. In church services the predominance of Latin meant that the ordinary people in the congregation knew only what church teachers and priests had explained to them: it was not until the sixteenth century that the Bible became widely available in English or German. Most members of the congregation would therefore not have known what the words meant in an unfamiliar piece of sung music, least of all in the sophisticated, multitext motets.

For the educated, there were also simpler genres for relaxation, songs with texts of love and friendship, songs for dancing that could be either sung or played on instruments. It was thought appropriate for people of the highest rank of the nobility to compose such songs, echoing the tradition of the troubadour. And for the lower levels of society there was still the unnotated music that predominated in most people's lives: songs and dances of minstrels, and the continuing tradition of improvising extra parts to a chant.

CHAPTER 12

Old Corruption, New Thinking

Since its earliest days the Christian church consisted of groups with differing interpretations of Jesus's life and teachings. Within a few centuries the Western church had adopted a position of authority, believing that its version of the truth was from God and could not be challenged, and persecuting those who disagreed.

As we often see with governments, a rigid insistence on authority often leads to corruption, and this is what happened to the church by the fourteenth century. A prominent form of corruption involved the selling of 'indulgences'. Sinners were assured that they could lessen the punishment that they were to receive from God in the afterlife by giving money to church charities. This developed into a corrupt racket to enrich the church itself and its priests, and it was even used to persuade rulers and their armies to go to war on behalf of the church.

This persecution and corruption over the years gradually lessened the church's authority in the eyes of people of all ranks of society. Two specific events brought this decline to a head. First there was the Black Death, a plague which swept across Europe in the years around 1350, killing about half of the entire population. Many thought this was a punishment from God, but the church could do nothing to stop it or to comfort people. Then, in 1378, the weakened Western church split, in an event known as 'The Great Schism'. This resulted in there being two Popes, one in Rome and the other in Avignon in France, each claiming supreme authority as God's representative on earth.

These events encouraged a fundamental shift in society. We've already seen how the European discovery of Aristotle and other Greek philosophers in the twelfth century inspired the view that human reason should form the basis of human beliefs. As the church's hold over people weakened, this current of thinking, humanism, was given a boost, raising the importance of living our life on earth, rather than concentrating on the eternal life to come after death. There were many consequences of this shift. The patronage of art and music, which had been dominated by the church, became more focused on the royal and aristocratic courts and the civic authorities of towns and cities. These patrons tended to be more open to new ideas than the church, which tried to cling to its traditional, authoritarian ways. In 1324 the Avignon Pope, John XXII, issued a proclamation insisting that music in the church should stick to the pure Gregorian chant, banning all but the simplest organum.

The Pope and the church authorities were fighting a losing battle. Their conservatism and authoritarianism had already been mocked a few years earlier in a daring poem by Gervais de Bus, *Roman de Fauvel* ('Romance of Fauvel'). In it the Pope and his cardinals are portrayed as worshipping a horse called Fauvel. The letters of the horse's name stand (in French) for all the corruption of the church: Flattery, Avarice, Villainy, Fickleness, Envy and Cowardice.

This is an example of a work which is old and new at the same time. It is modern in its anti-authoritarian daring, but it is also in the old tradition of elaborate use of symbolism – as in the garden as a metaphor for paradise, or the harmony of the universe. These concepts were more characteristic of the older thinking than the more direct examinations of human life that came in with humanism.

There is rarely anything neat about the way currents of thought succeed each other. One of the most celebrated composers of the fourteenth century was Guillaume de Machaut, a French priest and poet. He demonstrated how it is possible to be both traditional and innovative at the same time, like many of the great creative figures of all ages. His poetry explored the old themes of chivalry and courtly love, with symbolism stretching back to the troubadours, together with formal rhyme schemes. His music, too, was very intellectual, with astonishingly complex procedures that link it back to the old notion of music as a mathematical science. But the quality that makes Machaut so important is that his music was also highly expressive in a new way. He was one of the composers who made use of sophisticated modern notation to free music from the rather rigid old rhythmic patterns. This new, freer way of thinking came to be known as *Ars Nova* ('the New Art'). Although Machaut didn't originate it, he was its most renowned practitioner not only in France, but also in Italy and England. Machaut wrote for the church, but his most important music was for the enjoyment of connoisseurs. In polyphonic music he placed a new emphasis on the highest part as the melody. This had the effect of bringing the old troubadour tradition of the melodic song together with polyphony in the interweaving of the accompanying parts. All the parts could be sung, or the singer of the top line might be accompanied by instruments rather than voices.

These musical developments were taking place against the background of a broader rise of humanism that came to be known as the Renaissance ('rebirth'). This was a great outpouring of the arts centred on, though not restricted to, the city states of northern Italy, particularly Florence. The Renaissance was to reach a climax in the fifteenth and sixteenth centuries, with many of the most famous painters, sculptors and architects. But, as we have seen, the ideas that gave rise to the Renaissance had been around for a long time, and already artists of the fourteenth century had been breaking new ground.

For the history of music, which has always been tied to poetry, writers of literature in this period took on a new importance. There had always been musician-poets, but it is in the fourteenth century that we encounter major works of poetry and prose written by named authors. Three of the great names of Italian (as opposed to Latin) literature date from this time: Dante Alighieri (usually called Dante), Francesco Petrarca (Petrarch) and Giovanni Boccaccio. They all came from Tuscany, the area round Florence, and the fact that they wrote in the local language, Tuscan, did more than anything to establish Tuscan as the basis of modern Italian. One fact to bear in mind is that books of poetry and other writings were not just for reading silently. Copies were still extremely rare, as were copies of music. Paper was only beginning to become available in the fourteenth century, printing was in its infancy, and only a few copies of a work would have existed. Most people, therefore, got to know writings by hearing them read aloud. Dante, Petrarch and Boccaccio all habitually read their works to an audience.

Dante's poetic journey through the circles of hell, *Inferno* (the first part of his *Divine Comedy*), provided great inspiration for later musicians. He also wrote lyric poems, which, according to Boccaccio, he liked to give to musician friends to 'dress' them in music. Petrarch and Boccaccio both wrote poetry intended for singing, and a few settings of their poems survive.

So how was this poetry sung in fourteenth-century Italy? Polyphonic songs of different kinds, religious and secular, survive in beautifully presented manuscripts, but outside the church few people would have seen them. As we know, informal polyphony existed at all levels of society, and continued to do so. But the most widespread songs would have consisted simply of melodies, which would have been sung with or without instruments.

A delightful source of information about song is one of the earliest substantial works of fiction, the *Decameron* by Giovanni Boccaccio, written about 1350. The book is set in Florence in 1348, when the city was devastated by the Black Death. A group of seven young women and three young men, accompanied by their maids and menservants, escape to an estate in the hills. There they spend ten days in pleasant occupations, and on every day each person in turn tells a story. All of the young people are highly educated and are accomplished musicians. The day ends with dancing and singing after supper, concluding with one of the company singing a song to the others. This is always a *ballata*, a poem sung for dancing, a genre that had been brought to Italy by troubadours. Each of the group in turn sings a *ballata* from memory while the others dance a *carole*, in which the dancers hold hands in a circle. Although the *Decameron* is a work of fiction, it seems that dancing to the *ballata* – a poem set to a single melody – was a popular pastime among the upper classes. There is a charming painting from Boccaccio's time in the town hall of Siena, in which nine ladies dance the *carole* while another sings and accompanies herself on a tambourine – very much as one can imagine in the *Decameron*.

A number of *ballate* survive in manuscripts. Typically, there is a swung, dancing metre, but the way the words are set to music is very free. The metre is stretched by flourishes of several notes on some of the syllables, giving the melody a decorative, rather formal effect, which has little to do with the spoken rhythm of the words. You might say that *ballate* have this quality in common with the music of the church, in which the music 'elevates' the words to a higher level of ritual but does not 'express' the words in any modern sense. That kind of word-setting comes later.

Meanwhile, polyphonic music continued to be written both for the church and for elite connoisseurs outside it. One feature that encouraged new ideas was the mobility of some of the most renowned composers. Machaut moved from patron to patron within France, but never visited Italy. But Italian polyphonic music in the fifteenth and sixteenth centuries was dominated by composers from northern Europe. Guillaume Dufay and Josquin des Prez were the two most famous, both from Burgundy, which in those days extended from northern France into what is now Belgium and Holland. The leading composers were able to network to their advantage, with rich patrons vying with each other to attract the best of them to their courts.

Dufay spent several periods of his life in Italy, working for some of the most prominent patrons. Then he was ordained as a priest, and served as a member of the Pope's choir in Rome. When there was revolution threatened in Rome, Dufay found himself with the Pope's establishment in Florence in the 1430s. His time there coincided with the consecration of the great dome of Florence Cathedral in 1436, designed by the architect Filippo Brunelleschi.

Dufay was commissioned to compose for the occasion a motet for four voices, *Nuper Rosarum Flores*. It is addressed to the Virgin Mary, to whom the cathedral is dedicated, and celebrates the Pope's donation of a golden rose to adorn the altar. The motet is a tour de force, bringing together the old polyphonic techniques in which Machaut had excelled with an entirely 'modern' sense of a flowing, harmonious tapestry of voices. The mathematical proportions of the different parts of the motet are meticulously calculated, but few in the congregation would have appreciated these subtleties. They would have been struck by the impact of the four harmonious voices filling the great space. Dufay's motet was the central item in a service rich with music. One of the many people who packed the cathedral left a description of the whole occasion: 'One could almost believe that the angels and the sounds and singing of divine paradise had been sent from heaven to us on earth to pour into our ears an unimaginable holy sweetness.' The motet was performed by members of the Pope's choir, including Dufay himself.

Dufay also composed music for entertainment. While he was in Florence he struck up good relations with the ruling family, the Medici. They were great patrons of music and the other arts, using them to celebrate the power and esteem of the family. Every year in the city there were carnivals which became particularly spectacular during the rule of Lorenzo de' Medici (1469–92). Members of his court and of the city guilds performed songs wearing masks in torchlight procession. Lorenzo wrote some of the texts himself and played the lute. Some of these songs had traditional mythological subjects, represented by elaborately decorated floats; others were satirical and political, sometimes obscene. Many of them were dance-songs in the line of the *ballata* of Boccaccio's day, but now with several voice parts. The voices do not sing complex counterpoint, but create chords, with very little elaboration. It is in popular part-songs of this kind that we begin to get a new sense of chords being used to move the music on from one point to another and to emphasise moments of rest or resolution, 'cadences'. It seems a small point, but it signals the beginning of a new way of shaping European music.

CHAPTER 13

Composers Spread Their Wings

Through all the changing social and political circumstances of the fifteenth century, music was evolving and the status of musicians was changing. In Italy particular composers were valued and sought after, many of them from northern Europe. But they still retained their traditional positions as members of church choirs, and were often priests. Indeed, there was no separate profession of 'composer': all church musicians who composed were also singers.

The possibility of a new status for the leading composers is shown by the figure widely regarded as the leading composer from the fifteenth into the sixteenth century, Josquin des Prez. Josquin was another Burgundian working in Italy, and he succeeded Dufay as a member of the Pope's choir. Also like Dufay, he was a master of counterpoint, interweaving the voices with harmonious complexity. But in addition his style acquired a new subtlety and freedom. He wrote the most intricate canons, in which the parts strictly echo each other, but he also favoured a much freer kind of 'imitation', in which one part would echo another, but then go its own way. This was to become such a regular feature of music in later centuries that Josquin has come to be seen as an important pioneer.

It was the natural-sounding way in which Josquin accomplished these subtleties that made him so renowned, and he further advanced the sense that the way harmonies shifted could create a sense of a musical journey, even drama. Cadences – the resting points of harmony – could plot the progress of a piece from beginning to end over a long span. The reformer Martin Luther wrote of him, 'Other composers do what they can with the notes; Josquin alone does what he wishes.' His expressive range was enormous. One of his best-known part-songs, *El Grillo*, about a cricket who sings for love in the heat, is like a lively carnival song. At the opposite extreme is the long sacred motet, *Miserere mei Deus* ('Have mercy on me, O God'), for five voices. The voices sometimes weave round each other in counterpoint with touches of imitation, sometimes singing together in chords, alternating fluidly between passages for two voices and passages for the whole choir. The voice parts are plain, without elaboration, the range of the voices restrained, and the overall mood is austere, in accordance with the words. The music unfolds with a firm sense of where the journey is going, marked by chords that create points of arrival ('cadences' again). This is a style that influenced composers right through to the eighteenth century, including Johann Sebastian Bach (whom we'll come to in Chapter 21).

The idea that a composer 'does what he wishes' is, in itself, an indication of how things were changing. We are a long way from the concept of music as a branch of heavenly mathematics, and of composers as simply receivers of God's creativity. The new idea of the artistic 'genius' was in the air, and not only in music. Great artists and sculptors, such as Michelangelo, Leonardo and Raphael, were credited with genius, even 'divine' genius. This still suggests that the talent is implanted by God, but an artist nevertheless possesses it and is marked out as exceptional. The relationship between such geniuses and their employers began to change.

In 1502, Duke Ercole d'Este was looking for a new *maestro di cappella* ('chapel-master') for his court in Ferrara. He wished to acquire one of two leading composers of the time, Heinrich Isaac, who had worked for the Medici family, or Josquin. The duke's agent advised him to choose Isaac, because he composed rapidly and was better than Josquin at getting along with his colleagues. The agent adds, 'It is true that Josquin is the better composer, but he composes when he wants to, and not when one wants him to, and he is asking 200 ducats in salary while Isaac will come for 120 – but your Lordship will decide.' The duke chose Josquin.

Josquin was also one of the composers whose work benefited from a new development: high-quality music printing. In 1501, shortly before Josquin was appointed at Ferrara, the Venetian printer, Ottaviano Petrucci, produced the first ever printed book of polyphonic music. He used a complex process in which a page was printed three times: once for the staves (lines), once for the words, and once for the notes. The result was meticulously detailed and extraordinarily beautiful, and Petrucci's series of more than sixty volumes remains an impressive achievement in the history of music printing. This laborious process meant that the books were very expensive, and they would have been acquired as single copies and collector's items, rather than the multiple copies that a modern choir would have. Each voice part is printed separately: in a song for four voices there are two parts on the left-hand page and two on the right, so that four singers could stand round the book, each reading their own part. The books are small, however, and not practical for more than one singer on each part – polyphonic music was in any case usually sung by single voices. Petrucci concentrated on the music that was most in demand among the upper classes who could afford the books: the various lighter types of polyphonic song, as well as more complex sacred music, masses and motets. The composers are overwhelmingly the French-Burgundian northerners who were in demand across Europe, with Josquin the most prominent. The distribution of Petrucci's volumes across the noble households and libraries of Europe helped to cement the reputation and influence of these composers.

But, again, it is important not to get too fixated on the music that survived in printed notation, or even in manuscript copies. The continued importance of unnotated music-making and improvisation is vividly illustrated by Josquin himself. One of his pupils remembered being taught as a boy the art of singing by Josquin, without the use of any books. He taught them 'perfect' and 'imperfect' consonances (harmonies), and how to use them to add another part in counterpoint to a chant: 'You must imagine slates with a single melody, with the master singing the melody and the pupils in turn or together improvising counterpoints of increasing floridity.' Josquin, he said, had no time for composers who had learned to write without acquiring this basic skill: 'My master Josquin thought little of them and held them as a laughing-stock, saying they wish to fly without wings. The first requirement of a good composer is that he should know how to improvise counterpoint. Without this he will be nothing.' This sort of improvising over a plainchant was expected in churches and cathedrals across Europe, in many cases well into the sixteenth century.

The basic art of singing in parts was still widely known across a broad social spectrum outside the church. There are references to it in popular plays. Here's a little episode in the Wakefield *Second Shepherd's Play*, from England around 1450, one of the popular religious dramas known as 'mystery plays'. Three shepherds sing to pass the time:

> *1st Shepherd:* By the cross, these nights are long!
>   Yet I would, ere we go, one gave us a song.
> *2nd Shepherd:* So I thought as I stood, to cheer us all.
> *3rd Shepherd:* I grant.
> *1st Shepherd:* Let me sing the tenor.
> *2nd Shepherd:* And I the treble so high.
> *3rd Shepherd:* Then the middle part falls to me.
>   Let's see how ye chant. [They sing.]

There are plenty of reports of lower-class people singing in parts. A Spanish visitor to Basel (Switzerland) in the 1430s reported that at the public baths, 'the people generally sing well; down to the common folk they sing artfully in three parts like skilled artists.' A writer on music, Tinctoris, encountered in the 1480s two blind brothers from Flanders who travelled from court to court, 'playing together on a kind of viol, one the top parts and the other the tenors of many songs, in so skilful and so pleasing a manner, that I have truly never come across greater euphony'.

At a higher social level, the tradition of improvising the singing of poetry, which stretches back to the troubadours and beyond, continued to be valued. One of the most famous musical names of the fifteenth century, Pietrobono Burzelli (known just as Pietrobono), owed his reputation to singing narrative verse and accompanying himself on the lute, on which he was a virtuoso performer. He travelled widely in Italy and as far as Hungary and England, and was praised by poets and granted many honours by the aristocracy. But not a note of his music survives, because it was never written down.

Pietrobono was based at Ferrara for a long time, so he might well have taught the young Isabella d'Este, daughter of Duke Ercole (the one who engaged Josquin). Isabella grew up to become an accomplished musician, particularly admired, like Pietrobono, for her improvised singing of poetry to the lute. She married Duke Francesco Gonzaga of Mantua, and she established herself at the court in Mantua as one of the most powerful and influential women of the Renaissance, and a leading patron of the arts.

The circumstances in which women were particularly admired for their music-making varied a great deal and were changing. Back in fifteenth-century Florence the women of the Medici household would sing and play the organ for their distinguished guests. A little lower in the social class, the daughters of well-to-do merchants all learned to sing and dance, not just for pleasure and education, but as accomplishments that would help to attract a suitable husband. There was nothing new about this: no doubt the young people in Boccaccio's *Decameron* a century earlier had been brought up to sing and dance for similar reasons, and a young lady's musical 'accomplishment' continued to be a necessary asset across Europe right through to the nineteenth century.

At many convents the music was restricted to the traditional Gregorian chant. But at the convent of Le Murate in Florence two priests were brought in to train the nuns to sing polyphony, which in churches had always been sung by all-male choirs. In 1480 an ambassador from Duke Ercole d'Este's court at Ferrara reported that their singing was as good as that of any men's choir. In the 1490s the austere monk Savonarola rose to power in Florence, preaching that everyone should repent, and demanding an end to frivolity including the carnival songs. Unsurprisingly, he condemned the singing of the nuns as 'satanic'. Across the centuries, the musical roles of women have often formed a focus for the idea of music as potentially dangerous. But as the sixteenth century wore on, there were instances of a more wholehearted acceptance of the special qualities that women could bring to music, even, to a limited extent, in public. There were orphanages in Venice at which girls were musically trained and gave concerts (one of these was to become particularly famous in the eighteenth century).

As at many other courts, there were talented musicians among the ladies at the court in Ferrara. In the 1570s a group of them came together to perform for the private concerts of the duke, Alfonso II (great-grandson of Ercole I). They were known as the *Concerto delle donne* ('Consort of Ladies'), and the court organist and composer, Luzzasco Luzzaschi, wrote new music for them to sing. Professional singers were brought into the group, and over the next twenty years they performed in private concerts at the court, in front of many important visitors. Their fame spread, both as an example of what women singers could achieve, and as pioneers of a new kind of repertoire, much of it composed by Luzzaschi, who accompanied them on the harpsichord. Books of music written for them by Luzzaschi and others were published, and the style of the music, and the manner in which it was performed, were highly influential on a new generation of composers.

This new style of composition was the madrigal, a genre in which words and music were very closely related, even though the music was polyphonic. It grew out of several sources, including the improvised singing of narrative poems, dance-songs, and the simpler kinds of polyphony that had become popular. A striking element of the madrigal was its tendency to dramatise the words, so that an ensemble of three different voices wove an almost theatrical scene. Indeed, the performances of the *Concerto delle donne* seem to have been unusually, one might say daringly, theatrical, according to a description by a visiting Roman banker: 'They moderated or increased their voices, loud or soft, heavy or light, according to the demands of the piece they were singing; now slow, breaking off with sometimes a gentle sigh . . . now with short, and again with sweet running passages sung softly, to which sometimes one heard an echo answer unexpectedly. They accompanied the music and the sentiment with appropriate facial expressions, glances and gestures.' This suggests something almost like opera, which I'll return to in Chapter 17.

CHAPTER 14

Lutes and Keyboards

When Ottaviano Petrucci published his magnificent series of printed music volumes in the early 1500s, most of them were devoted to vocal music. This is simply because, up to this point, the vast majority of written compositions were for voices. Music for instruments was rarely written down. Instruments were used to accompany singers – lute with voice, organ with several voices, and sometimes other instruments with choirs in church (though the circumstances in which instruments were allowed in church varied). Dance tunes at all levels of society were passed on by ear. Players of instruments would also play free improvisations. Lutenists would introduce a song with such 'preluding', and this style came to form separate pieces that were written down, known as preludes, fantasias or toccatas.

These lute preludes were just becoming fashionable as Petrucci was working, so it is for good commercial reasons that he included six volumes of lute music. They are particularly interesting for two reasons.

One is to do with the technique of playing the lute. Up until the middle of the fifteenth century, the strings were generally plucked with a plectrum, usually a quill, a method inherited from the older tradition of the Arab *oud*. But then players took to plucking with their fingers, making it possible to pluck several strings simultaneously so that they could begin to play the polyphonic music that was becoming fashionable. Both methods continued to be used in later centuries – to this day, guitarists play either with a plectrum or with the fingers, depending on the music they are performing.

The other feature of Petrucci's lute volumes is that, like earlier manuscript lute music, they are written not in the usual music notation, but in 'tablature'. This is a neat method in which the notation shows you where to place your fingers, rather than showing the pitches of the notes. The same principle is still used in chord diagrams for guitarists. There is a line for each string (or pair of strings on the lute), on which a letter or number indicates on which fret to place your finger. This was an adaptation of tablature that had been used for the organ as early as the fourteenth century. Indeed, it was claimed that a German version of lute tablature had been invented by the fifteenth-century organist Conrad Paumann, who was also a fine lute player.

This leads us to another of the major innovations of this period, the development of keyboard instruments. The earliest instrument to be played by depressing keys or levers was the organ. In Chapter 3, I mentioned the ancient Greeks' *hydraulis*, a sort of prototype of the organ. By the fourth century, organs blown by bellows were a feature at the court of Byzantium, and in the eighth century the Byzantine emperor sent an organ with 'great lead pipes' as a gift to Pepin 'the Short', King of the Franks (the father of Charlemagne). These were mechanical objects designed to amaze and entertain, with sliders or heavy keys to open each pipe. It was not until the fourteenth century that the organ developed into what we would recognise as a real musical instrument, with a keyboard that could be played with the fingers.

Small organs feature in many fifteenth-century paintings. There is a charming engraving by the German Israhel van Meckenem from the late fifteenth century showing an organ placed on a table. A man plays the little keyboard, while, behind the organ, his wife sits on the table, pumping the pair of bellows – at least one assistant to pump the organ was needed until the introduction of mechanical blowers in the late nineteenth century. Paintings of the fifteenth century often show angels playing such instruments, or larger organs standing on the floor. These are the sorts of organ that the ladies of the Medici family played to guests in Florence. No doubt many an angel in paintings would have been modelled on these young ladies.

By around 1400 the organ was also in use in churches, where larger, permanent instruments were being installed. The largest organs in Germany and France had two or three keyboards and a pedalboard, each controlling a different set of pipes, and setting a pattern that was repeated and enlarged in later centuries. In the fifteenth century we begin to hear of musicians being appointed specifically as organists in churches. Heinrich Isaac, one of the Burgundian composers patronised by the Medici family in Florence, was the organist at the cathedral in Florence from about 1484. But it was in Germany that organists first rose to prominence as performers, rather than simply as church musicians. And two of the most celebrated of them feature in the earliest volumes of music specifically intended for the organ.

Conrad Paumann (who possibly invented German lute tablature) was a blind organist from Nuremberg who travelled widely across Europe and was honoured wherever he went. A few of his pieces appear in the Buxheim Organ Book, from around 1470. This is the earliest substantial manuscript collection of keyboard music. Most of the music in it is based on vocal music, sacred and secular. Typically, there is a rather florid melody in an upper part, and below it one or two simpler parts in counterpoint. Paumann's pieces include a series of exercises designed to teach how to improvise such music. Improvising on a chant was a basic skill that organists were now expected to acquire, and they would play these elaborations during services, alternating with the chanting of the choir.

Another blind German organist, Arnolt Schlick, published the first treatise on organ playing in 1511, and the first printed collection of keyboard music the following year. At this date there was no clear distinction between music for organ and music for other keyboard instruments. Musicians would have played pieces on whatever instrument was at hand, though obviously there were restrictions on what was considered suitable in church.

The fifteenth century also saw the rise of stringed keyboard instruments. The two most important were the clavichord, a very quiet instrument in which the strings are struck by little metal tangents, and the harpsichord, in which the strings are plucked. The earliest known image of a harpsichord is from 1425, on a carved wooden altarpiece at Minden Cathedral, Germany. An angel plays what appears to be a harpsichord, in the classic shape that was to survive all the way to the modern grand piano: a triangle, with one side curved inwards. The triangular shape reflects the different lengths of the strings: with a range from very low notes to very high, the bass strings need to be long, the treble strings short, so it is natural to stretch the strings over a triangular soundboard.

The rise of keyboard instruments was made possible by the development of the keyboard itself. The familiar modern pattern of black and white notes goes all the way back to the fifteenth century (though some early instruments had the colours the opposite way round). The 'white' notes (as they are on modern keyboards) provided most of the notes you needed for the most common scales and chords, the 'black' notes provided all the other notes needed so that you could, in theory, start on any note and play a scale or chord in any key. In practice, tuning all the notes of a keyboard so that every combination of notes sounds 'in tune' is a subtle matter.

It was the ancient Mesopotamians who worked out how to tune their stringed instruments by using the first two intervals of the harmonic series, the octave and the fifth. If you try to do this with all the notes of a keyboard instrument, you find that it is impossible to get every interval perfectly in tune at the same time. This is because a keyboard is not something that exists in nature:

cramming all possible intervals together into the notes of a keyboard is an artificial device for the convenience of players, and it involves compromise with the natural tunings of the intervals. In later centuries, as musicians explored more and more harmonies and chords, tuning the keyboard became more and more of a problem, and it was necessary to 'bend' tunings so that all the intervals fitted together satisfactorily. These compromise tunings are called 'temperaments'. Nowadays in the West we generally use 'equal temperament', which irons out the discrepancy equally across all the notes and intervals of the keyboard. But there have been other temperaments over the centuries. In the fifteenth century, and for many years after, it wasn't necessary to have a temperament that would work across all keys: the range of harmonies in general use was quite limited, so you tuned the keyboard to suit those, and didn't worry about the excruciating mistuning of the intervals you weren't using.

There were also developments in wind instruments. One innovation was the addition of a sliding section of tube into brass instruments, to produce the slide trumpet and trombone. Without this, the tube of a brass instrument could only produce the notes of the harmonic series. The insertion of a slide into the tube enabled the player to fill in the missing notes by lengthening or shortening the tube, so producing a lower or higher note.

Another relatively new instrument was the cornett (or cornetto), made of wood but with a cup-shaped mouthpiece blown like a brass instrument. From ancient times animal horns had been used to produce notes (as in the Jewish *shofar*). As early as the tenth century, finger-holes had been drilled into them in order to produce more notes. By the fourteenth century, the principle had been used to develop the wooden cornett, with finger-holes down its length. This was to become a virtuoso instrument during the sixteenth century. Just how much skill it required was demonstrated during the first attempts to revive the cornett during the 'Early Music' movement in the 1960s. I well remember the strangulated sounds of some of these early attempts. But a decade later, some determined players had fully mastered the instrument, and the result enabled me to understand why the cornett was considered the closest of any instrument to the human voice.

Increasingly, instruments were played together in groups or 'consorts'. There were louder instruments that were mostly played outdoors, and quieter instruments for indoors. From the thirteenth century, bands of loud instruments started to appear in the towns of Europe, perhaps in imitation of the ceremonial bands that had long been a feature of the Arab world. By the fifteenth century, these often consisted of three players: two shawms (loud reed instruments) and a slide trumpet or trombone. Towns and cities employed these bands to play on ceremonial occasions and in processions on church festival days. During the sixteenth century, bands were allowed to play in the church itself, though, as you can imagine, there were objectors who thought this an intrusion into the solemnity of the church rituals.

At the opposite end of the spectrum, bands increasingly played for public entertainment. So their repertoire extended from fanfares and processions to dance music. More instruments joined these groups as time went on, and this tradition of civic music survives in the modern use of brass bands and other town ensembles across Europe. In Catalonia, bands of loud shawms, much like their medieval ancestors, continue to play dance music in the town squares for the traditional *sardana* dances.

The quieter, indoor instruments included a variety of stringed and wind instruments: viols, recorders, lutes of different sizes. The loud shawms were replaced by quieter cornetts to play with trombones in church, and for indoor processional and dance music. Apart from keyboard instruments, the other important new instrument to be developed during the early sixteenth century was the violin. Louder than fiddles and viols, it was at first mostly used by minstrels and others for dance music. Little did anyone suspect that this instrument would rise to become the supreme stringed instrument for over 300 years.

CHAPTER 15

Reforming the Church,
Educating the People

In the fifteenth and sixteenth centuries different instruments became associated with different classes. The new keyboard instruments were expensive and were therefore found in the wealthier homes and courts of the aristocracy, merchants and professional classes. Other instruments were found more at the lower end of the social spectrum – fiddles (the predecessors of violins), bagpipes, pipe and tabor, and hurdy-gurdy. The pipe and tabor were popular for dancing, at all levels. A single musician played a whistle with one hand and a small drum with the other, a classic minstrel's combination. The hurdy-gurdy is an interesting example of an instrument that had been found across a wide social range, but by the sixteenth century had fallen out of favour among the upper classes. The reasons are musical as well as social. The hurdy-gurdy is a stringed instrument like a large fiddle which is played by turning a wheel that rubs against the strings. It can only play one melody with a drone, not combine melodies in polyphony. The music increasingly favoured by the upper classes involved some element of polyphony, and the changing of bass notes during a piece. Music of the minstrels and lower social classes was still predominantly focused on a single melody, which often had no change of bass note or key. So for them instruments with drones like the hurdy-gurdy (and the bagpipes) were still appropriate.

In German-speaking countries, there was a particularly strong ongoing interest in the single-melody song among the growing middle class, a tradition that stretched back to the *Minnesänger* of the thirteenth century. Those had been German equivalents of the troubadours, many of them either aristocrats or employed by aristocrats. The new *Meistersinger* (Mastersingers) were quite different, and their rise shows how Europe had changed over the intervening centuries. These were tradesmen who met in their spare time to sing. The most famous of them, Hans Sachs, was a shoemaker (he is a central character in Wagner's opera, *Die Meistersinger*). Just as the Mastersingers' trades were organised into guilds, so their singing groups had guilds in every substantial town. There were formal contests to become a Mastersinger, in which candidates had to compose both the words and the music of a song. The movement was very important in German musical life. It set a habit of organised amateur music-making among the middle classes that was to endure in German culture right through to our own day.

In 1523, Hans Sachs wrote a poem beginning, 'The Nightingale of Wittemberg, which is heard everywhere'. This was one of a number of writings that got him into trouble with the city council of Nuremberg, because it addressed a hot political and religious topic. It was in praise of Martin Luther, the disruptive religious reformer, whose demands had brought to a head centuries of dissatisfaction with the church.

I mentioned in Chapter 12 the church's corruption, including the selling of 'indulgences'. There had been various attempts to press for reform, but so far these had been met by suppression of the reformers, many of whom were condemned to death. Now the corruption had reached new heights, with the church using the selling of 'new improved' indulgences to fund the building of St Peter's church in Rome. That was the immediate issue against which Luther protested, but his demands for reform went much further.

He was a former monk, and a professor of theology at the new Wittenberg University in Germany. He had studied the Bible in great depth, and had come to conclusions that conflicted with church teaching. The first was that forgiveness is a gift from God, not to be offered by the church, and certainly not in exchange for money. The second conclusion was that everyone should have direct access to the Bible in their own language, rather than having Latin interpreted for them by priests. Luther himself translated the Bible into German. A third conclusion was that the Bible gave no authority for the isolated life of prayer in monasteries and convents. The vows of monks and nuns were therefore invalid, and they were free to leave. They, as well as priests, could marry, which the church had prohibited.

Luther's protests and ideas spread widely and rapidly, through lectures and published booklets made available by the new, cheaper printing processes. In 1521 the Pope excommunicated Luther (in effect, expelled him from the church), and Luther publicly burned the Pope's excommunication. But Luther was already so highly esteemed across Europe that the church did not dare silence him, as it had many others. Luther's reforms took root, and across many states of Germany, and countries further afield, Protestantism (as it was called) became the official religion.

There were profound consequences for the history of Europe, including its music. One of the first musical fruits was the publication of new hymns (or chorales) for the people to sing. Luther himself composed the melodies of some and the poems of many more, and collaborated with other composers and poets. The first collected volume of hymns appeared in 1524, for use in the home and at religious meetings as well as in church. Churches held practice sessions during the week, so that the congregation could learn new hymns for the following Sunday. These hymns, published in volumes over the coming years, became very popular and were translated into other languages, including English. The early examples were published just as single-line melodies. But one of Luther's earliest collaborators, the composer Johann Walter, was the first to publish versions for several voices, usually four. The melody is in the tenor (the third voice from the top), echoing the long-standing practice of polyphonic settings of chants. Luther himself, while wanting simple and direct music for the people to sing, was a great enthusiast for polyphonic music, describing the elaboration of a chant with other voices as 'a kind of divine dance', and he particularly admired Josquin des Prez as the master of this style. You can sense this influence in Walter's hymn settings, in which the voices elegantly weave round each other, while the harmonies provide a very clear sense of direction.

There were longer-term consequences of Luther's reforms, not all of them good. Most monasteries and convents were closed in countries that adopted Protestantism. Monks had in many cases come from wealthy families or backgrounds in trade or the professions, and most were able to find new roles. It was much harder for nuns. In the Bible, St Paul had declared that women should meekly accept the authority of men and should also be silent and submissive in church. You can imagine the use that the more extreme Protestants made of this. The Scottish preacher, John Knox, argued fiercely against women in any position of authority, at a time when the thrones of both Scotland and England were occupied by women. The restriction of women to the roles of wife and mother was encouraged even in the more moderate Lutheranism, though there were exceptional women who pushed back against this expectation. Luther himself married a former nun, Katharina von Bora, from an aristocratic family, with whom he lived happily and had six children. Another former nun, Elisabeth Cruciger, was a poet and composer, who contributed to the first volume of Lutheran hymns in 1524. Christine of Hesse published her own book of sacred psalms and hymns in 1590. These were also women from aristocratic families: it was much harder for women lower in the social scale to find an outlet for their music.

Luther's reforms received widespread support. But they also led to yet further division, between rival versions of Protestantism, and above all between Protestants and the original Roman Catholic Church. This was to culminate in the Thirty Years' War (1618–48), which began as a conflict between states within the Holy Roman Empire, but drew in other great powers, resulting in massive destruction.

On the positive side, Luther's insistence that everyone should have access to the Bible in their own language led to a dramatic increase in the number of people who learned to read. This was also encouraged by the availability of printed texts, as single sheets, pamphlets and books. Printed material was everywhere, and naturally more and more people wanted to read it. From now on across German-speaking lands the German language rather than Latin was almost universally used for songs and hymns, sacred and secular. And this combination of understandable language with music that was easy to follow led to a great outpouring of German word-setting that lasted through four or more centuries.

The advance of Protestantism in England was more uncertain. Henry VIII famously broke from the Roman Catholic Church in 1534 when the Pope refused to allow him to divorce his first queen, Catherine of Aragon, in order to marry Anne Boleyn. One of the consequences of this break was the king's authorisation in 1539 of an English version of the Bible to be read in churches. But Henry was not yet a full Protestant: when the Bible's translator, Miles Coverdale, published the first English book of metrical psalms (psalms converted into hymns), many based on German originals, they became very popular. But the king was not ready to accept something so blatantly Lutheran, and had the book burned. It was not until Henry's daughter Elizabeth succeeded to the throne in 1558 that it was officially accepted. This is an early example of how, for musicians, many of whom worked for the church, life in England through the sixteenth century was a bewildering and sometimes dangerous experience. Many lost their jobs as Henry ruthlessly suppressed the monasteries and convents. This led to the destruction of long musical traditions, together with the libraries and the infrastructure that had supported learning and scholarship over hundreds of years.

Henry VIII, with his switch away from Rome, was followed in succession by monarchs who were Protestant (Edward VI), then Catholic (Mary), and then Protestant again (Elizabeth). The persecution of those who were on the wrong side varied from reign to reign, with many examples of composers working officially for the Protestant Church of England, but secretly also writing for Catholics. One composer who negotiated this minefield success-fully through a very long career was Thomas Tallis. Tallis was, and remained, a staunch Catholic. He was employed by King Henry's own chapel, the Chapel Royal, where he stayed through the reigns of the Catholic Mary and the Protestant Elizabeth. He skilfully adapted his style to the current fashions and requirements: these ranged from the elaborate polyphonic settings of Latin texts that were in vogue early in his career, to the simple English hymns needed for Protestant worship. His most famous and most complex work is his massive motet *Spem in Alium numquam habui* ('I have never put my hope in any other'), written for forty voices, arranged as eight choirs of five voices each. This is widely regarded as Tallis's masterpiece, and the grandest achievement of choral music in this period.

Music was very important to King Henry VIII, and he himself was a fine musician. He composed songs and instrumental pieces, and he also liked to improvise with other singers on popular tunes, as was the habit of the day at all levels of society. As well as this informal music-making, Henry placed great emphasis on the court's formal musical establishment. English houses displayed their status by the number of retainers, including musicians, and the king greatly increased the number of professional instrumen-talists employed at court. These included sixteen trumpeters, one of whom was John Blanke, a former African slave who came to court from Spain as part of Catherine of Aragon's retinue. He has the distinction of being the first African in England identifiable by name in a painting. The court also employed about the same number of other instrumentalists, far more than in any other grand house. They included shawms and sackbut (trombone) for the most formal dances, pipe and tabor and stringed instruments for more informal dancing. Many of these were played by minstrels who also acted in plays. Around 1540 a group of Italian viol players arrived with their instruments. The viol was a recently developed instrument in various sizes, bowed somewhat like a cello, and it soon became the most favoured stringed instrument in England.

In Scotland, a more severe form of Protestantism prevailed, which forbade all but the simplest hymn-singing in the Kirk (church) and led to the removal of many church organs. Scotland had a long tradition of composers skilled in polyphonic music, in the international style of Dufay and other Burgundians, but their activities were now mostly confined to the court and other aristocratic households. When Mary Queen of Scots succeeded to the throne in 1542, all that changed. She was a Roman Catholic, herself a fine singer and player of the lute and harpsichord, and under her the Chapel Royal in Stirling once again became a centre of high-quality polyphonic singing, as it had been before the Reformation.

Music, like many other things, was highly interconnected across Europe. Mary Queen of Scots had been married to the son of the French king Henry II, and the music sung in her royal chapel was in the international style whose acknowledged masters were Burgundians and Netherlanders. The same kind of music was sung in Henry VIII's Chapel Royal. Henry's sense of competition in the grandeur of his musical establishment was also international. When he hoped to form an alliance with Francis I of France (Henry II's father), they met in the French countryside near Calais in 1520. This meeting came to be known as the Field of the Cloth of Gold, because of the many grand tents erected to form temporary palaces, lavishly decorated with tapestries woven with gold thread. Among all the splendour and entertainment, both royal courts brought their choirs and their most distinguished composers, and music in the most sophisticated polyphonic style was sung at religious services. All the activities demanded music, from the most splendid of brass fanfares for the kings' meeting, to quieter instruments for dancing, banqueting and the entertainment of the royal party and courtiers.

Henry was well aware of the musical establishment at the court of Francis I. It included many musicians for the chapel, for ceremonies and for private entertainment, and Henry's musical establishment was partly designed to equal it.

CHAPTER 16

Conquest and Re-Conquest

Meanwhile in Spain, there were developments from the late fifteenth up to the sixteenth century that were to have lasting consequences, not just for Spain itself but for the whole world. The first was the Christian re-conquest of Spain from Muslim rule. This had been a gradual process over several centuries. In 1492, King Ferdinand of Aragon and his queen, Isabella of Castile, completed the long campaign, and declared Spain a wholly Christian country. And they meant 'wholly Christian': unlike the Muslim rulers, who had tolerated Jews and Christians and had encouraged their contribution to the culture, the new Christian regime insisted that any Jew or Muslim who refused to convert to Christianity should be expelled.

The expulsion of the Muslims and Jews meant that Spain lost some of the multi-cultural richness that had lasted several centuries. Ferdinand and Isabella's court was now more narrowly Christian. But they were enthusiastic patrons of the arts, and among the music that they promoted was polyphonic sacred music in the Burgundian style. Outside the chapel, dance songs were popular, particularly the *villancico*. Like the Italian *ballata* of Boccaccio's day, it had a repeated refrain, giving it an immediate appeal and making it easy to memorise.

It was also in 1492 that Ferdinand and Isabella sponsored an Italian adventurer, Christopher Columbus, to set sail across the Atlantic in search of a western route to India. What he found was not India but the Bahamas, off the coast of North and Central America. This didn't stop him and his successors over hundreds of years referring to the indigenous peoples of the Americas as 'Indians'. His discovery sparked off the great European grab for the Americas, with the Spanish targeting Mexico and Peru, the Portuguese Brazil, and later the English and French settling in North America. On another expedition a few years later, Columbus anchored off the island that he named Trinidad, where music was involved in a misunderstanding typical of such encounters between unfamiliar cultures. From the island, men approached in a canoe. Hoping to encourage them to come near, Columbus ordered a tambourine to be brought up on deck, and a group of young sailors danced to it. But this had the opposite of the intended effect: 'As soon as they observed the playing and dancing, they all dropped their oars and laid hands on their bows and strung them, and each one of them took up his shield, and they began to shoot arrows.' Columbus ordered his crew to fire back with crossbows, and the canoe retreated back to the island.

The Spanish were quick to exploit the Bahamas as a source of slave labour. By contrast, in Mexico the principal attraction was gold. In Chapter 8, I described the sophisticated civilisation of the Aztecs, in which music played an important part. In 1519, when the Spaniard Hernán Cortés arrived in Mexico, he came bearing a declaration, authorised by the Pope, that Spain had the right to conquer all non-Christian lands, and to require the population to convert to Christianity, on pain of war, death or enslavement. Cortés found that many of the population were eager to overthrow the ruling regime, so he was able to assemble a substantial army to advance on the capital of the great Aztec Empire. The emperor

Moctezuma, having received Cortés with gifts, was taken hostage and imprisoned in his palace. This led to another conflict in which music was involved. During the months while Moctezuma was held, outside in the streets and squares a festival was in progress. About 2,000 of the highest noblemen, dressed in their finest robes, danced a circling war dance. The Spaniards, whether alarmed or merely taking the opportunity to rid themselves of many of the ruling class, killed the unarmed dancers. This was the first of many massacres.

Plundered gold enabled the Spanish to develop and Europeanise Mexico and their other new colonies in Central and South America very rapidly. Cathedrals and churches were built, and organs installed. Christian chant and polyphonic music were introduced, and the training of choirs in choir schools helped to establish the new Christian faith among the population. The first Mass was sung in the new Mexico City (formerly Tenochtitlán) as early as 1521. Across the country, schools, monasteries and convents were established by missionaries.

An important pioneer was a Flemish monk, Pedro de Gante. He established a church and school in Mexico City teaching religion, music, art and writing, and a network of schools across the country followed. According to de Gante's own account, the people resisted his first attempts to bring them to church and teach them the Christian message: 'They fled from these things like the devil from the cross.' After three years of failure, he decided to try a subtler approach. De Gante had seen that worship in Mexican ritual consisted of 'singing and dancing before their gods', and so he composed a Christian song for them to sing and dance in their traditional manner. The song described 'how God became man to save the human race, how he was born of the Virgin Mary'. De Gante arranged for the people to wear their traditional costumes, they rehearsed for two months, and performed the ceremony in the courtyard of a monastery in Mexico City on Christmas Day 1527.

This sort of hybrid between Mexican and Christian ritual was aimed at encouraging the integration of the people into Christianity. It was also an effective tool in keeping the lingering 'superstitions' under Christian control. Nevertheless, the church authorities were nervous about these Christianised Mexican ceremonies, feeling that they could easily get out of hand unless strictly supervised.

A few years later another Spanish explorer, Francisco Pizarro, led the conquest of Peru, which was no less brutal than that of Mexico. The emperor of the Incas and his chieftains were killed, the capital was destroyed, gold plundered, and millions were enslaved. As in Mexico, the work of missionaries was vital to the establishment of Peru as a governable Christian country. Again, churches were built, choir schools and monasteries established, and the population was drawn into the study of Christian music and art.

Here is one vivid example of this drive for integration. In 1552, at the Christian festival of Corpus Christi, the choirmaster of the newly built church in Cusco, Juan de Fuentes, adapted an Inca praise-song in European polyphonic style. The verses were sung by choirboys of mixed Inca-Spanish parentage, wearing traditional Inca dress, and the other singers responded in chorus. This was performed 'to the great content of the Spaniards and the supreme delight of the Indians at seeing their own songs and dances used by the Spaniards to celebrate Our Lord's festival'. This is according to a second-hand Spanish report. It is easy to imagine that the emotions of the people at hearing their traditional music absorbed into the Christian conquerors' ritual was a great deal more complicated.

From all this destruction and forced Christianisation emerged some unique genres and styles of music over the coming centuries. In 1583 a Spanish monk in Mexico, Bernardino de Sahagún, published the first book of sacred songs in a local indigenous language, Nahuatl, with engravings of Jesus Christ and the saints. These songs were intended for the people to sing in church. No melodies were provided, and it is probable that they were to be chanted in the manner of the church's Gregorian chant, which the Mexicans had been taught to sing. De Sahagún hoped to make them forget their old songs, dedicated to their gods.

Over the next century, Christianity became firmly established across large areas of South America. The missionaries from Spanish and Portuguese monasteries were joined by teacher-priests from Italy, the Jesuits. They formed their own Christian communities, effectively ruling over the population in large numbers. In these various contexts many composers, Spanish, Portuguese and Italian, wrote music that incorporated popular elements, both from their own countries and from local traditions. At first, most of these composers had been born in Europe. Among the most distinguished are the Portuguese Gaspar Fernandes and the Spaniard Juan Gutiérrez de Padilla, who worked at Puebla Cathedral, one of the most important religious and musical centres in Mexico in the early seventeenth century.

Nowadays we talk of 'Latin American music', and its origins lie in many of the elements that came together in the century after the Spanish conquest. From Spain came the *villancico*, which was adapted in the different local languages – Fernandes wrote a large number of *villancicos* to be sung in church services. *Gitanos* (gypsies, who had only recently arrived in Spain) brought the clapping rhythms we associate with *flamenco*. But, as usual, nothing is simple. By about 1500, southern Spain had one of the largest populations of African slaves in Europe, and recent research suggests that elements of *flamenco* came from these Africans. Many African slaves were being brought to the Americas, and their music began to infuse the local popular music. So it is difficult to disentangle all the different influences. What is clear is that the coming together of indigenous South American, Spanish and African musical influences was to have immense repercussions for the future of popular music in the Americas and beyond.

The Spanish reached Florida in 1513, expanding their colonisation further across what are now the southern states of the United States, fighting off Native American tribes and attempting to colonise Virginia. But it was the English who established the first permanent settlement there at Jamestown in 1607. In 1620 the 'Pilgrim Fathers' arrived and settled further north in Plymouth, Massachusetts. Unlike the earlier Spanish and English colonists, the Pilgrim Fathers came to find a new home, away from persecution in England. They were strict Protestants who refused to accept the Church of England and had established yet another branch of Protestantism.

The musical impact of these English arrivals was quite different from that of the Spanish. The Spanish brought the polyphonic music of the Catholic Church together with popular Spanish musical elements, and made some attempt to engage with local musical traditions. The strict Protestants from England were less interested in engaging with the indigenous culture. They brought hymn settings of the psalms, which we encountered in the previous chapter. Settlers who came to the plantations in Virginia brought not only simple hymns and anthems, but also folk songs and ballads of England and Scotland. They did not set up choir schools to teach elaborate polyphonic music. Praising God in music was equally important to them, but the hymns and songs were for everyone to sing, rather than music that required formal training. And, unlike the situation in Spanish colonies, there was little integration of European music with the music of Native North Americans. There were isolated examples of integration, with some Native Americans converting to Christianity and adopting hymns. But on the whole the 'Indians' were simply a threat from whom the European settlers attempted to keep their distance.

As the southern plantations of North America were gradually populated by slaves brought from Africa, European hymns and African songs and dances had the opportunity to create new cross-cultural genres. All of this was to have a major impact on how the later music of North America developed, with its roots more firmly in popular music, less wedded to the elaboration of formal European music.

CHAPTER 17

Sing the Words, Speak the Music

While the Spanish and Portuguese were conquering the 'New World', in Italy one of the most enduring art forms of music was in its infancy. Opera was to become a grand and lavish spectacle attracting huge audiences. But its origins lie in the custom of improvising the singing of poetry to the accompaniment of an instrument, which stretches back to ancient times and across many cultures. This tradition remained particularly strong in Italy in the late fifteenth century alongside the growing composed repertoire of polyphonic music. In the intellectual circles that grew up in the Italian courts, there were poets, singers and instrumentalists who specialised in improvised song, and the patrons of the day vied with each other for their services. We met one of the most famous of these improvising singers, Pietrobono, in Chapter 13. Duke Lorenzo de' Medici of Florence was one of the most enthusiastic supporters of these poet-musicians, and he himself sang. As the new interest in the ancient Latin authors grew, the classics provided material that was both old and new. Virgil and Ovid were particular favourites, with their themes of nature and mythology, many of them drawn from the Greeks. Poets took to writing plays on themes from these authors, and these were often performed at courts, at banquets and weddings, particularly when important guests were present.

One of the most celebrated poets who wrote drama of this kind was Angelo Poliziano. His *La fabula d'Orfeo* ('The Story of Orpheus') was written for Cardinal Francesco Gonzaga, and was first performed at a banquet at the Gonzaga's family court in Mantua in 1480. The part of Orpheus, a character from ancient Greek legend, was spoken and sung by Baccio Ugolino, himself a poet, and famous for singing to his own accompaniment on the lyre. We don't know exactly how much of *Orfeo* was sung rather than spoken, but we do know that the actors would have burst into song at moments of the most heightened emotion.

In the story, Orpheus's wife, Eurydice, has died. Orpheus is so heartbroken that the god of the underworld takes pity on him and allows him to travel to the underworld and bring her back. But he must not look behind him at Eurydice as he leads her out. Of course, he does look round, and he loses her for a second time, a moment poignantly depicted at the climax of the play:

> *Eurydice:* Alas! How too much love
> Has undone both of us.
> Now I am cruelly torn apart from you,
> I am no longer yours.
> I stretch my arms to you; no use,
> I am pulled back. My Orpheus, farewell!
>
> *Orpheus:* Alas, can you be taken from me,
> Eurydice my dear one? O rage,
> O bitter fate, O cruel heaven, O Death!
> O our love so ill-starred!

We can imagine how touching this scene would have been, virtually like a scene from an opera. And yet this is more than a century before the first composed 'opera'.

Other kinds of music were becoming more dramatic through into the sixteenth century. I have already mentioned in Chapter 13 the beginnings of a new kind of madrigal associated with the Duke of Ferrara's group of women singers, the *Concerto delle donne*. This was highly influential on a young generation of Italian composers. Chief among these was Luca Marenzio, whose madrigals use a wide range of harmonies and dissonances to create subtle, and sometimes sudden, shifts of emotion. And he in turn influenced Claudio Monteverdi, generally regarded as the greatest composer of this period. Monteverdi had already published two volumes of madrigals when, in about 1590, he was taken on at the court of the Gonzaga family in Mantua, where Poliziano had worked a century earlier. Here Monteverdi was engaged as a viol player (musicians were still not employed just as composers). When he published his third book of madrigals in 1592, Monteverdi wrote a dedication to his employer, Vincenzo Gonzaga, Duke of Mantua. In it, Monteverdi compares himself to a plant: out of the flowers of his music-making for the duke he can now offer him these 'fruits'. This is an indication of how, in the century since music printing had become widespread, it was becoming important to create permanent works of music. And compositions were now being bought and distributed in much larger numbers. Monteverdi's third book of madrigals was reprinted five times within twenty years.

It was also for the Gonzagas in Mantua that Monteverdi composed his first opera, *Orfeo*, which was performed twice during the carnival season in 1607. This was the same story as Poliziano's part-sung play, now with a new libretto by Alessandro Striggio. It is significant that the surviving references to this production place greater emphasis on the poet who wrote the libretto than on the composer who wrote the music. It was seen not so much as an opera with a libretto as a play set to music. The duke, Francesco Gonzaga, ordered copies of the play to be printed, so that every member of the audience could follow it during the performance. A letter from one of them to the duke after the performance again places the emphasis on the words: 'The poem is lovely in conception, lovelier still in form, and loveliest of all in diction.' The writer praises the music for 'serving the poetry so well that nothing more beautiful is to be heard anywhere'.

This role of music as the servant of the words was central to this new art form of opera. Many in the audience at the first performance of *Orfeo* were members of an 'Accademia' of which the duke was the head, and to which the librettist, Striggio, belonged. This was one of a number of private societies for people from the highest levels of Italian society with an interest in poetry and drama. It was another Accademia in Florence that had been responsible for what is thought to be the very first performance of an opera in 1598, *Dafne*, whose music, by Jacopo Peri, has been lost.

The idea for what came to be known as opera was based on the performance of plays in ancient Greece. Research by members of the Florence Accademia had led them to believe that Greek plays were sung throughout (it is now thought that some sections were sung, others spoken). The discovery of a manuscript of some ancient Greek hymns in the Vatican Library in Rome helped them to establish that the Greeks' setting of poetry to music was based on a principle of a single line of melody, whose rise and fall and rhythm were closely related to those of poetry as it was spoken. Music was the servant of the words. They adopted this idea to create 'recitative', a speech-like singing that formed the basis of the new musical drama, opera.

It was this new recitative that Monteverdi adopted so expressively in *Orfeo* and his later operas. This was the culmination of a trend away from the intricate polyphonic counterpoint of the past, in which the complexity of the music was not designed to 'serve' or 'express' the words. This new desire to make music the servant of the words was, of course, absolutely in tune with the humanist desire to do away with obscurity and ignorance, and to reveal truth. Clarity of understanding and expression was everything, and recitative was soon adopted throughout Europe.

The stage elements of these early opera productions were less important than the words and music. But there was a long tradition of spectacular stage productions for a less specialised audience, in Italy and elsewhere. The court of the Medici family in Florence used to stage *intermedi* between the acts of plays, performed on special occasions such as weddings. These were elaborate entertainments, with music, dance, complex scenery and stage machinery to evoke storms, gods descending from the sky, and so on. Venice also staged lavish entertainments during the carnival season, so it is not surprising that it was in Venice that opera first took a more popular and lavish turn. It was in a theatre in Venice in 1637 that audiences for the first time bought tickets to attend the opera in a public opera house. One of the most successful opera composers writing for the public theatre in Venice was Francesco Cavalli, whose operas were performed at theatres across Italy.

It was not just in madrigals and opera that music had taken a dramatic turn. Cavalli had started out as a boy chorister at the church of St Mark's, Venice, where the choirmaster was Monteverdi. This grand church has two galleries facing each other. Monteverdi's predecessor, Giovanni Gabrieli, had composed works in which choirs and groups of instruments answered each other from the two galleries, creating an impressive effect in the big acoustics of the church. First Monteverdi and then Cavalli as choirmasters inherited this tradition. Monteverdi, such a dramatic and subtle composer of opera, brought the same qualities to his church music. His *Vespers* (1610) shows his command of many different musical styles, old and new. It ranges from sections that could have stepped out of an opera to traditional counterpoint based on Gregorian chants, from solo arias and duets to sections for answering choirs.

One of the most remarkable composers of this period was a pupil of Cavalli, Barbara Strozzi, daughter of a Venetian poet. In 1638 she took part in a debate at an Accademia in Venice, in which members argued about the rival powers of singing and weeping: which has the greater power to make someone fall in love? During the debate Barbara Strozzi sang laments of her own composition, which demonstrated to the members of the Accademia convincingly that a combination of singing and weeping was more moving than either on its own. Strozzi went on to publish eight volumes of compositions – madrigals, duets, cantatas for solo voice – which show her as a fine exponent of the dramatic style passed down from Monteverdi and Cavalli. Her musical reputation was very high in her lifetime, but she faced problems that no male composer would have had to encounter. She had four children with a nobleman, Giovanni Vidman, to whom she was not married. Such an arrangement was not unusual in Italian courts at this time, but it added to the struggles that even a woman of the highest talent had to face when competing with male colleagues.

Meanwhile, the Italian opera style was being exported abroad. Barbara Strozzi's teacher, Cavalli, had such a reputation that in 1660 he was commissioned to write an opera to celebrate the marriage of Louis XIV of France. But Cavalli's operas were not a success in Paris. The French had their own tradition of ballet, singing and elegant spectacle, and Cavalli's style was not to French taste.

Despite the initial failure of Italian opera in Paris, it was another Italian who was eventually to succeed there. Jean-Baptiste Lully (originally Lulli) was spotted by a French aristocrat at the age of fourteen performing with his violin in the streets of Florence during carnival. He was taken to France, where, through a combination of talent and luck, he attracted the attention of the fourteen-year-old king, Louis XIV, and at the age of twenty was appointed as royal composer for instrumental music. As for stage music, Lully first rose to fame writing incidental music for Molière, the leading writer of comic and satirical plays. And then, in 1672, he was granted a monopoly for opera productions, both royal and public. For fifteen years Lully staged almost an opera per year at the Académie Royale de Musique, which later became the Paris Opéra. Lully set the model for French opera right through to the eighteenth century. His recitatives and 'airs' are closely tied to the styles of French poetry, just as composers in Italy tied their music to the style of Italian poetry. And Lully exploited the French love of formal dance, each act ending with a 'divertissement' of ballet and chorus.

CHAPTER 18

The Appeal of Dramatic Music

The Italian influence spread to Germany and England. Luther's Reformation had already emphasised the principle that music should serve the text, and the tradition of the single-line song had been kept in vogue by the Mastersingers. So Germany was open to the idea of Italian recitative. With the new Italian styles in fashion, Italy became a magnet in the seventeenth century, and young German composers would travel there in order to learn with the best Italian masters.

Heinrich Schütz worked with the two composers who most strongly represented the currents of Italian music. First he went to St Mark's church, Venice, and studied with Giovanni Gabrieli, master of sonorities and grand effects. Later, he studied with Monteverdi, leader of the new operatic style. Schütz brought these two influences powerfully together. He composed the first German opera, to the same libretto as the earliest Italian opera, *Dafne* by Jacopo Peri. But Schütz's *Dafne*, like Peri's, is lost, and we know little about it. It was in Schütz's religious music that he created the most successful synthesis of the two Italian styles, the recitative-based music of Monteverdi, and the bold sonorities of Gabrieli, combining them with the thoroughly Protestant influence of Lutheran hymns.

Schütz composed 'passions', musical settings of Christ's last days leading up to his crucifixion. The tradition of dramatising episodes from the life of Christ goes right back to the Miracle Plays of the fourteenth century, and the little church dramas before that. But it was Schütz who brought the resources of the new Italian styles to bear on this old tradition. How he wrote these modern church dramas was partly determined by the circumstances. At the court of Dresden, where he worked for many years, no instruments were allowed during Holy Week, the week leading up to Christ's crucifixion and Easter. So when Schütz composed passions for Holy Week, they were *a cappella* (sung without instrumental accompaniment), with solo singers representing Christ and other people, the story narrated in unaccompanied chant, and passages of chorus. The overall effect is austere. By contrast, Schütz's *Christmas Story* (1660) is much closer to Monteverdi: he has two violins to accompany an angel, recorders with the three shepherds, and trumpets for King Herod. The story is narrated by a tenor singing Italian-style recitative.

In England, the Italian influence arrived by another route, and had rather different consequences. During the long reign of Elizabeth I (1558–1603) religious music was expected to conform to the requirements of the Church of England which, though not quite fully Protestant, rejected anything that smacked of Roman 'popish' ideas. But a blind eye was turned to Catholic composers who continued to write privately for Catholic clients. Thomas Tallis and his pupil William Byrd were, despite being Catholics, both leading members of the queen's Chapel Royal, and in their official capacities composed anthems and other music for Church of England services. But they also set Latin words in the Catholic tradition. I have already mentioned Tallis's mighty forty-part motet, *Spem in Alium numquam habui*. Byrd set the English words from the authorised Book of Common Prayer in his 'Great Service', but he also composed Latin Masses for use in private by his fellow Catholics. It is an indication of how highly the queen regarded Tallis and Byrd that, despite their Catholicism, she awarded them an exclusive licence to print music for twenty-one years.

Italian influence spread into matters of behaviour. In 1561 an English translation was published of Baldassare Castiglione's book on how to behave at court, *Il cortigiano* (translated as *The Book of the Courtier*). It was widely read in English upper-class circles throughout the following decades. Among the qualities required in a male courtier, it lists dancing, singing while playing the lute, and playing the viol. A woman courtier should also dance and sing, though only after being persuaded reluctantly and without showing off.

And then in 1588 a collection of Italian madrigals, was published: *Musica Transalpina* ('Music from across the Alps'). These were newly set to English words, with madrigals for four, five and six voices, mostly by Italian composers including Marenzio and an Italian composer resident in England, Alfonso Ferrabosco. Ferrabosco had worked at the court of Elizabeth I for several years, and it was his madrigals that had introduced the English to the genre. But *Musica Transalpina* set off a positive craze among the English educated classes, and over a period of forty years English composers responded to the Italian challenge with a flow of madrigals of their own. The range and quality are extraordinary. There are 'ballets', like Italian dancing songs, with a refrain of 'fa la la' (by Thomas Morley and William Bennet). There are poignant songs of frustrated love and death, full of an English version of the twisting and clashing harmonies popularised by Marenzio (by John Wilbye, Orlando Gibbons and John Dowland). And there are extended settings of intellectual texts, with complex interweaving of the voices (by Thomas Weelkes and Gibbons again).

Collections of these madrigals were published in beautifully printed and expensive volumes. The four or five voice parts were sometimes arranged over a double-page spread, each part facing outwards in a different direction, so that it could be placed on a table, and a group of singers could sit round it and sing. As the popularity of the lute increased, an accompanying lute part was included underneath the top voice, which was by now always the principal melody part. Many madrigals could therefore also be sung as solo songs with lute accompaniment, performed by either one or two people.

Indeed, the lute song took on a life of its own, nowhere more vigorously than in the work of John Dowland, a virtuoso lutenist. He encapsulates not only many of the musical qualities of Elizabethan music, but also the international, political and religious challenges that a musician might face. Brought up in the Church of England, in 1580 he went, as a brilliant teenager, to work for the ambassador to the French court, where he converted to Roman Catholicism. Back in England, he was refused a post at the royal court, and Queen Elizabeth is reported to have said that he 'was a man to serve any prince, but was an obstinate papist' (Catholic). This is odd given that, as already noted, Elizabeth tolerated several Catholic musicians at court. Dowland went to work as lutenist to the King of Denmark in Copenhagen, where he stayed for several years. This is also odd, since Denmark was by then firmly Protestant, and Danish Catholics were not allowed to hold prominent offices. It was only in 1612 that Dowland was finally appointed to the English royal court, now under Elizabeth's successor, James I – who was also a Protestant – and Dowland remained at court for the rest of his life.

When you hear his music, you can imagine how difficult it would have been to deny Dowland work. His songs and lute solos range, like the English madrigals, from cheerful to sad. But Dowland at his most characteristic has a vein of melancholy which he sustains through harmonic twists and the interweaving of inner parts – quite a challenge on the lute. One of his most famous works began as a lute solo, the *Lachrimae Pavan*, which he reworked as a song, 'Flow my teares' ('lachrimae' is the Latin for tears, a pavane was a slow dance). He then developed it into a longer set of variations, called *Lachrimae, or Seven Tears*. The set is written for lute, but also has single-line parts for five instruments, 'viols or violins', as it says on the title page ('violins' meaning also viola and cello). This is in keeping with the fashion in England for playing as well as singing in groups, 'consort' music, and it was common for a composer to describe a volume of madrigals as 'apt for voices or viols'.

At the opposite extreme from private madrigals and lute songs, James I and his queen, Anne of Denmark, were enthusiasts for the musical entertainments known as masques. These were on a grand scale, akin to the *intermedi* and other entertainments at Italian courts. A focus for them was the new Banqueting House built between 1619 and 1622 next to the Palace of Whitehall in Westminster by the architect Inigo Jones. Jones had travelled widely in Italy, absorbing the architectural styles of the Renaissance, and particularly the classical buildings of ancient Rome. His Banqueting House is modelled on these principles, with its carefully arranged proportions and placing of columns. Jones brought similar care to his designs of stage scenery and costumes for the royal masques, which were also heavily influenced by Italian taste. He often collaborated with Ben Jonson, one of the finest playwrights of the day. Masques were a regular feature of royal court life, and in poetry, dance, music and spectacular scenery and costumes, they glorified the rulers of the newly united England and Scotland. The emphasis was on, first, spectacle, second, poetry, and third, music. Musicians often formed part of the action. In the final scene of *Caelum Britannicum* ('British Heaven') two clouds descended, in which were placed singers representing Religion, Truth, Wisdom and other virtues.

Masques could last three hours or more. Like court entertainments in Italy and France, they were an opportunity to display the splendour of the court to important visitors. The king and queen together with other senior members of the royal household often took part, in suitably dignified poses. Sometimes the entire production, with its scenery and costumes, would be transported in procession through the streets to the City of London, and re-erected in one of the great guild halls for another performance.

Professional troupes of actors performed the plays of Shakespeare, Ben Jonson and others, both at court and in the new public theatres. But in the plays, unlike in the masques, music played only a small part, with the occasional song or dance. The more substantial singing of drama, as in Italian opera, did not come to England until later in the century. This followed years of political and social upheaval. Civil war culminated in the execution of Charles I in 1649 outside the Banqueting House. There were then eleven years of Puritan (that is, strict Protestant) rule under Oliver Cromwell, a period known as the Commonwealth, during which theatres were closed. A prominent poet, Sir William Davenant, came up with the idea of getting round the regulations by setting much of the drama to music, so that it did not count as a play. He obtained permission from Cromwell to perform *The Siege of Rhodes* 'in recitative musick', converting a room of his house into a little theatre. The all-important vocal music was written by two of the leading composers of the day, Henry Lawes and Matthew Locke, with other composers adding dances and more instrumental music.

That was as far as opera and 'recitative musick' went in England, until, with the restoration of the monarchy in 1660, and the more relaxed reign of Charles II, the theatres reopened and England sprang to artistic life again. But still the musical dramas that were favoured were not quite opera. Matthew Locke was one of the first to write the music of what came to be known as 'semi-operas'. These were, in effect, plays with a lot of incidental music, like those that Lully and Molière wrote together in France. The most successful was an adaptation of Shakespeare's play, *The Tempest*, by the poets William Davenant and John Dryden, with music by Locke and others. The diarist Samuel Pepys went to its premiere at Lincoln's Inn Fields in London, and reported, 'the house mighty full' with 'a great many great ones', including Charles II and members of his court.

There are two real English operas from this period: *Venus and Adonis* by John Blow, and Henry Purcell's *Dido and Aeneas*, both composed in the 1680s. *Venus and Adonis* is charming, but *Dido and Aeneas* is both charming and convincingly dramatic. Purcell, like Blow, deploys real Italian-style recitative. The succession of choruses, duets and solo arias culminates in Queen Dido's tragic lament, one of the most enduring moments in all opera. Purcell did not follow this up with other operas, but with semi-operas. These included

King Arthur, with words by Dryden, and *The Fairy Queen*, an anonymous adaptation of Shakespeare's *A Midsummer Night's Dream*. Purcell also wrote a large amount of incidental music for plays. And the style of his music for the stage was, like that of Matthew Locke, more French than Italian in influence, echoing Lully particularly in the dances.

It seems that the English love of spoken plays was such that they had no desire to import Italian opera wholeheartedly. But this is one of those poignant moments in music history where it is easy to imagine that things might have turned out differently. Purcell, the leading English composer of his day, died tragically young at the age of thirty-six. He was a master of church as well as stage music, and what he achieved is impressive enough. If he had survived, he might in time have built on *Dido and Aeneas* to lead the development of English opera. But it was not to be.

The staging of masques, operas and semi-operas at court was, of course, aimed at an audience at the highest level of society. But the growth of the public theatre in England opened opportunities for people lower down the social scale to enjoy the same music, and for composers and musicians to earn money beyond the traditional high-class patronage. London was a focus for the growing public of theatregoers. And they didn't just go to the theatre: they also acquired an appetite for singing and playing the theatre music themselves. Purcell and others who wrote for the theatre supplied music that would appeal to this new market. And the most famous singers helped to popularise the songs, and to attract the crowds. Publishers were quick to capitalise on this new fashion, and volumes of theatre tunes and other popular songs were printed and sold in large numbers.

CHAPTER 19

Instruments and the Rise of the Orchestra

Instruments have been important in the history of music for many thousands of years. Different cultures across the centuries have developed different ways of using instruments, with or without voices. By the seventeenth century, instruments had become particularly important in Europe. And the way they were used illustrates the gulf that had by now opened up between European music and the traditions of the rest of the world.

By the seventeenth century a piece of European music, say a dance tune, could be played on a keyboard instrument or a lute. Or it could be played on a group of instruments, each playing a single line, and together creating the same succession of combined notes and chords as on the keyboard instrument. The word 'chord' is crucial here. In most musical cultures, the idea of a chord scarcely exists. If several musicians play (or sing) together, they either play variants of the same melody, or a different melody that fits with the others according to the conventions of the culture. As we've seen, there are varying traditions of what is harmonious or dissonant, and some musical cultures encourage more dissonance than others. But anything we might think of as a chord occurs as a consequence of the interaction between the different voices.

By the seventeenth century in Europe, chords as entities in themselves had acquired a vital role in how music was created. Chords were no longer just the result of polyphony but were fundamental to creating the 'structure' or 'journey' of a piece through its sequence of harmonies. And they played an increasing part in determining the mood of a piece, most obviously by the difference between 'major' and 'minor' chords. The succession of chords proceeded from one resting point ('cadence') to another, and this partly determined the way in which melodies and polyphony interweaved through a piece. These continually changing chords and harmonies set European music apart from the rest of the world. In rural 'folk' music, and in other cultures, harmonies do not continually shift. Admittedly, in Arab *maqam* there is a way of shifting from one mode to another, but even here you do not find the restless exploration of harmonies that had, by the seventeenth century, become essential to European music.

One of the consequences of this new emphasis on continually changing chords was the custom of using a chord-playing instrument – keyboard instrument, lute or harp – to play the bass notes and the chords associated with them throughout the piece. Often they would play along with another bass instrument such as a cello, viol or bassoon. This was called 'basso continuo' ('continuous bass') or 'continuo' for short. The practice developed of giving the continuo player just the bass line, sometimes supplemented with numbers indicating the chord to be played ('figured bass'). So the player worked out an appropriate way of playing the chords, without having it all written out on the score – a sort of semi-improvisation. These figured-bass parts are found in all sorts of ensemble music, ranging from part-songs and madrigals to consorts of viols, to pieces for one or two voices or instruments over a 'basso continuo'. In complex operas and extended church pieces the continuo player keeps up the thread of chords throughout, sometimes accompanying recitative, sometimes filling out larger ensembles.

Playing an instrument to a virtuoso standard was also becoming a serious aim in itself. Solo keyboard pieces were increasingly popular, but printing keyboard music was still complex and expensive, so players would have acquired their music mostly in manuscript copies. An indication of what was in circulation in the early seventeenth century in England is shown by *The Fitzwilliam Virginal Book*, a manuscript collection dating from around 1614 and named after the aristocrat who acquired it. The virginal was a small, rectangular version of the harpsichord, but the pieces could be played on any keyboard instrument. The collection contains nearly 300 items, most of them dances and arrangements of vocal pieces, including many by composers whom we have already met as writers of madrigals and songs (Byrd, Dowland, Morley and others). Some are short, but others extend to lengthy sets of variations full of running passages and ornaments. These are early examples of the delight in virtuoso keyboard playing for its own sake. *Parthenia*, a small, printed volume of keyboard music published around the same time, is devoted to music by Byrd, Orlando Gibbons and John Bull, reputed to be one of the most brilliant keyboard players of his time. The title page proudly declares *Parthenia* to be 'the first musicke that ever was printed for the virginalls', and it was indeed the first in England.

We encountered one of the first celebrity organists, Conrad Paumann, back in the fifteenth century. Now in the seventeenth century, with the proliferation of music printing and developments in organ-building, there was a great increase in composed organ music. Specific 'schools' of organ-building, organ-playing and composing rose to prominence. The most important pioneering organ composers in the early seventeenth century were an Italian and a Dutchman.

Girolamo Frescobaldi was the organist at St Peter's, Rome, for more than thirty years and published several volumes of organ music. These give a good idea of the range of pieces that would have been played in the early seventeenth century before, during and after Mass: toccatas and preludes that one could imagine being improvised, and more formal contrapuntal pieces, showing that the old art of interweaving several voices had not been ousted by the Italian fashion for recitative and dramatic song.

The influence of Frescobaldi spread north into Germany, partly through his publications, but also through German organists travelling to Italy and learning the latest methods and fashions. But it wasn't necessary to travel to be influenced by composers in other countries. The Dutchman, Jan Pieterszoon Sweelinck, seems to have spent most of his working life in Amsterdam, travelling only locally to play the organ and try out new instruments. But his music shows that he was well aware of the latest developments in other countries: France, England, Germany and Italy. Like Frescobaldi, he wrote pieces that alternated prelude-like passages with sections of intricate counterpoint. Indeed, Sweelinck was one of the first to write what came to be known as 'fugues', in which an entire contrapuntal piece for several 'voices' is worked out from one or two short fragments of melody. He made free use of the pedalboard, operated by the feet, as well as the keyboards played by the hands. Through Sweelinck's pupils these developments were taken up by what came to be known as the North German Organ School, which was to reach its climax in the work of Johann Sebastian Bach.

This flourishing of organ music was accompanied by developments in organ-building. The organs of Germany and Holland from this period are still admired as the pinnacle of what is thought of as 'classical' organ-building, and the names of the principal makers still resonate, among them Arp Schnitger and Gottfried Silbermann. They specialised in constructing an assembly of stops (ranks of pipes) that together created a brilliant and clear tone, suitable for the complex counterpoint which was then in fashion. This is quite different from the way that the organ developed in France, where the emphasis was on strongly contrasted tone-colours. These distinctions were to carry on into the succeeding centuries.

One aspect of this boom in music for instruments was a surge in the publication of instruction books for enthusiastic amateurs. An important English publication was Christopher Simpson's *The Division Viol* (1659), which was bought in large numbers across Europe. It teaches how to improvise 'divisions' (that is, variations) over a repeating bass line, with one or two viols together – another reminder that the art of improvisation continued to be valued despite the increase in the availability of printed music.

The instrument that made the biggest impact on the development of music history from the seventeenth century onwards was the violin, and its larger relatives, the viola and cello (though these sizes were not standardised for a long time). The violin was not new: it had evolved from various earlier bowed instruments, many of them of Arab origin. In Muslim Spain many of the most skilled instrument-makers were Jewish. When the Jews were expelled from Spain in the 1490s, a number of Jewish instrument-makers fled to Italy, and worked with Italian craftsmen, including Andrea Amati, the first of a famous family of violin-makers. The newly developed construction of the violin gave it much greater power and more concentrated tone-quality than the earlier stringed instruments. In its various sizes it was soon the most highly favoured stringed instrument in Europe, gradually ousting the older family of viols, though often played together with them.

In 1560 Andrea Amati supplied a set of violins, violas and cellos to the French court, and this was to form the basis of the earliest ensemble that we can really call an orchestra. Of course, large ensembles of various kinds had existed for many years across the world. In Europe, large bands of string and wind instruments would be assembled on grand occasions at court or in towns. What was new in the French court was to group together a substantial ensemble of similar instruments of different sizes, so that the effect was a homogenous blend rather than a combination of contrasted sounds.

By the time that Jean-Baptiste Lully was appointed director of the king's music at Louis XIV's court in 1661, the king's orchestra of stringed instruments, the *Vingt-quatre Violons du Roi*, was long established. Lully took it to a new height of refinement and discipline. As well as playing on their own, the *Vingt-quatre Violons* were combined with the wind instruments from the royal stables, and this enlarged orchestra played on ceremonial occasions and for the royal opera and ballet. Lully's successor at the French court,

Michel Richard de Lalande (or Delalande), composed hundreds of dances and stately overtures that were grouped in suites and published as *Simphonies pour le souper du Roi* ('Symphonies for the King's Supper').

The French orchestra was the envy of European courts, just as the grand Palace of Versailles was imitated on a smaller scale all across Europe. Charles II of England, who had spent years of exile in Paris and would have heard Louis XIV's orchestra, enlarged the English royal ensemble of 'violins' to twenty-four, combining with wind instruments for theatre work, and for grand royal pieces. Henry Purcell composed 'Birthday Odes' for the king, with overtures and dances that are very much in the French style.

As for the violin, both as solo and orchestral instrument, the next important developments took place back in Italy, where the violin had been perfected. Arcangelo Corelli established a reputation as a violinist and composer in Rome in the 1670s. His sonatas and concertos were immensely successful, continuing to be distributed across Europe into the early eighteenth century. Consisting of several contrasting movements, they were used as models by the next generation of composers, including Vivaldi in Italy, J. S. Bach in Germany and Handel in England.

Some of Corelli's works were designed for performance in church during Mass, and were more serious in tone, with movements in which the lines weave round each other in counterpoint. Other pieces were for playing at home, and were in effect suites of dance movements, influenced by French models. Corelli himself was a fine violinist, and, like Lully, a stickler for precision and discipline. He would usually have in Rome an orchestra of a dozen or so, but on grand occasions he had fifty or more, and once, for a concert for a visiting ambassador, 150 musicians. So there was no fixed size for an orchestra at this time. All of Corelli's concertos were scored for two groups: a solo group of two violins and cello, with continuo (usually harpsichord or organ), and a larger group of strings as the main orchestra. The two groups sometimes play together, at other times alternate, a style derived from Italian church music in which different choirs alternate (as at St Mark's,

Venice). This was the beginning of the concerto for instruments, which later evolved into the concerto for a single instrument and orchestra.

None of this would have happened without the development of the violin, with its marvellous tone-quality and power, and its possibilities for agile display. Corelli clearly delighted in its character. One feature of his music, and of others who imitated his style, is the elaborate ornamentation of the melody in the slow movements of his sonatas. Some of this was written in the score, but a lot was left for the player to make up. There is a particularly striking example in an edition of his last set of sonatas for a single violin, Opus 5. The publisher included versions of the slow movements which he says are 'as Corelli played them'. We can't know if that is true, and there is no reason to suppose that Corelli would always have played them the same way. But they show an extraordinarily free elaboration of the melody, with many running flourishes. Despite all the printed compositions becoming available at the time, the art of improvisation was alive and well.

And what about that most universal instrument, the human voice? While violinists were beginning to make their names with their virtuoso command of their instrument, vocal stars were reaching a larger public, both in churches and in the increasing number of opera houses. But this deserves a separate chapter.

CHAPTER 20

Star Singers and the Opera Market

From the seventeenth to the early eighteenth centuries there were enormous changes in the relationship between musicians and their audience, and in the way that music was financed. I have already touched on some of the broad changes in society that had been taking place ever since the rise of humanism and the Renaissance: the decline of the power of the church, the shift to patrons outside the church, particularly the aristocratic courts, and then the rise of merchant and professional classes, and the growth of public theatre and concerts to entertain them. This wasn't a straightforward shift: the church and the aristocracy continued to wield immense power, with musicians coming and going between the available patrons.

One important element was the rise of star singers, around whom the opera world came to revolve from the seventeenth century. And here we encounter a phenomenon that, from a twenty-first-century perspective, seems one of the most grotesque in the entire history of music. Many female roles in opera were taken by men, singing soprano and alto. These male sopranos were *castrati* (plural of *castrato*), men who had been castrated before their voices broke at puberty. This meant that they kept their boy's treble voice, but greatly strengthened it as they became adults, developing qualities that made them quite different from female voices.

Castrato voices had been prized for many centuries in Byzantium, but in Western Europe they first rose to prominence in Spain in the sixteenth century, and then became known in Italy. A castrato would typically begin in a church choir as a boy treble. If he had exceptional talent he was operated on, and helped into a career as a castrato by wealthy patrons. For the first performance of Monteverdi's opera *Orfeo* in Mantua in 1607, Orfeo was sung by a male tenor, but several female roles were sung by male castrati including Orfeo's wife, Eurydice. Fifty years later, most of the important roles in Italian operas were sung by castrati, and the singers became international stars, commanding high fees. The profits and success of theatres came to depend on them.

An anecdote gives an idea of the status they had acquired by the eighteenth century. In 1719 the German composer George Frideric Handel was at the court in Dresden, a great centre for music. A series of lavish entertainments had been planned to celebrate a royal wedding, with a new court opera house built for the occasion. Handel had been commissioned by an opera company in London to engage top-quality singers for their next season. Among those in Dresden were several of the leading Italian singers, including the castrati, Senesino (Francesco Bernardi) and Matteo Berselli. Rehearsals were under way for an opera by the court's composer, Johann David Heinichen. The opera was in Italian, but the two castrati complained that Heinichen did not know how to set Italian to music. The row reached a climax when one of them tore up the aria they were rehearsing and threw it at Heinichen's feet. The opera was cancelled, and Senesino and Berselli were then free to accept Handel's offer to go to London.

Why was Handel based in London in the first place? Because London had become a major focus for Italian opera. This was partly because it was the capital of the British Empire and was by now a very wealthy city. An opera house was just the sort of prestigious enterprise that the rich liked to promote. You might think this craze for opera unlikely in England, which had preferred 'semi-opera' in English to the Italian genre. But the growth of the commercial theatre meant that any sudden success could change public taste rapidly. Handel, like many a German, had absorbed the Italian style during a lengthy stay in Italy, and had gone on to score a major triumph in Venice with his opera *Agrippina* in 1709. Word spread rapidly, and he was soon in demand. He was invited to compose an Italian opera for the King's Theatre in London, and *Rinaldo* was the first newly composed Italian opera ever staged in London, in 1711. It was a triumph with the public and was frequently revived. The success, partly achieved by the leading alto castrato, Nicolò Grimaldi, encouraged Handel to move to London permanently the following year, and he stayed there for the rest of his life.

The writer Joseph Addison ridiculed the idea of English audiences sitting through a whole evening in a foreign language: 'We no longer understand the language of our own stage,' he complained. This was a sign of the troubles that were eventually to mount against Handel, but for several years he rode a wave of public success, supported by the aristocracy. In 1719 a group of aristocrats founded a new opera company, the Royal Academy of Music, putting up the equivalent of about £2 million today. Handel was engaged as the leading composer for the enterprise, and was also responsible for directing the orchestra and booking the best singers (such as the castrati he brought back from Dresden).

The castrati did not, however, have the field all to themselves. By Handel's day there were also women opera stars. This was part of women's long struggle to be heard in a world dominated by the male authorities of church and state. Only men sang in church choirs. In Catholic countries, attempts to clean up the abuses of the church had included discouraging nuns in convents from singing anything other than chant. But in practice several convents in Italy and France continued to be renowned for their singing of polyphony. In Venice there were orphanages where girls were taught to sing and play to a high standard – the composer Antonio Vivaldi taught at one of them from 1703 for thirty years. The success of the *Concerto delle donne* in Ferrara and of Barbara Strozzi had raised interest in women as singers of madrigals and 'chamber' music. It was the opening of the first commercial public opera house in Venice in 1637 that brought women to prominence as singers on the stage.

In England, women had not been allowed on the public stage until 1661, with the restoration of the monarchy and the beginning of Charles II's reign. But by Handel's day they were welcomed enthusiastically. From his trip to Dresden, Handel brought to London not only castrati, but also two of the leading Italian women singers, Faustina Bordoni and Francesca Cuzzoni. They often appeared on stage together in operas, and a fierce rivalry developed among the public between supporters of one or the other, climaxing in actual fighting at a performance in 1727. They, and the castrato Senesino, each earned more from the opera than Handel did.

As for the music that Handel wrote for his stars, this reflected a change away from the earlier Italian emphasis on recitative. As Addison correctly pointed out, most of the English audience would not have been able to appreciate the finer points of Italian word-setting, so endless recitative would have gone over their heads. No doubt it was partly for this reason that Handel concentrated on a predominantly song-like style in which he was supreme, capturing the appropriate emotion for the dramatic situation: by turns plaintive, defiant or joyful. The action was still partly carried by recitative, but the principal vehicle for these emotions was the 'da capo' aria, 'da capo' meaning 'from the beginning'. After a middle section, the whole of the first section was repeated, giving the singer the opportunity to elaborate and decorate the melody expressively. The great stars were renowned for their skill in doing this.

Handel dominated the London opera scene for a few years. But rivalries and competition were as fierce offstage as they were onstage. In 1733, Handel and the great castrato Senesino fell out, and Senesino joined a newly formed rival company, the Opera of the Nobility. This had been set up by another group of aristocrats in 'a spirit got up against the dominion of Mr. Handel', as their spokesman put it. But the fact was that the London audience for opera was not big enough to support two top-class opera companies paying exorbitant fees to their stars, and it wasn't long before both companies went bankrupt.

One of the pressures leading to this crisis was another shift in public taste. In 1728, *The Beggar's Opera* was staged, and went on to run for sixty-two performances, unprecedented at the time in London. This was the first and most successful example of a 'ballad opera'. It was a satire aimed at politicians, the divide between rich and poor, and the injustices of society in general, and it mocked the craze for Italian opera. Its cast consists of poor people, thieves and prostitutes, and its chief character is a highwayman, Macheath. It is all in English, the dialogue is spoken, not sung in recitative, and the music consists of a succession of short songs. The words by John Gay are set to existing well-known tunes: folk songs, hymns, popular arias and songs by Handel, Purcell and others, arranged by Johann Christoph Pepusch, another German-born composer who had settled in London. Although *The Beggar's Opera* and other satirical ballad operas attracted criticism from establishment quarters, and often ran into threats of prosecution and censorship, they were immensely popular with audiences. The lead female singer of *The Beggar's Opera*, Lavinia Fenton, not only became a celebrated star, but ended up eloping with her married lover, the Duke of Bolton, whom she eventually married.

With Italian opera facing difficulties, rivalled by more straightforwardly tuneful stage music, where would Handel turn next? He was already renowned not only for his operas but also for his church music. This included his anthem *Zadok the Priest*, written for the coronation of George II in 1727, and sung at every British coronation since. The massive first entry of the chorus in *Zadok the Priest* is a vivid example of the sense of drama that Handel brought to his religious music. So perhaps it's not surprising that, as the staging of opera became more problematic, he turned back to a genre of non-staged dramatic music known as oratorio. This was most often to religious texts, based on episodes from the Bible.

Religious musical drama had taken various forms over the centuries, from the early Miracle Plays to the Passions and *Christmas Story* by Heinrich Schütz. Oratorio arose in Italy in the seventeenth century. Handel himself had composed oratorios in Italy before he came to London. Now he took to composing them with English words, and they proved very successful.

Handel very skilfully brought together all his experience at writing both opera and church music, deploying a set of ingredients in varying proportions: recitative, now often accompanied by orchestra, not just by continuo, solo arias, but not so often 'da capo' as in opera, choruses, and orchestral effects and interludes. The most enduring of all his oratorios is *Messiah*, first performed in Dublin (Ireland was then under British rule). In the intervals between the sections of his oratorios, Handel used to perform concertos composed by himself. At first these were organ concertos, and they proved so successful that Handel composed a brilliant set of twelve *Concerti Grossi*, Opus 6, for string orchestra, modelled on Corelli's recently published set.

In his operas, oratorios and concertos, Handel freely reused his own and other composers' music. He had a genius for reinvention, turning an aria into an instrumental movement, adapting a love duet by giving it religious words, and lifting an idea from another composer to make a theme for a fugue. Nowadays, we might think this laziness or plagiarism. But Handel was just an extreme example of common practice in the eighteenth century. There was no expectation of 'originality' as we now conceive it, and there were no copyright laws. Everyone shared and understood the same musical language, and material was passed around more or less freely.

Handel's popularity extended beyond the formal opera house and church. This was the era of the pleasure gardens of London, notably Vauxhall Gardens, at the centre of which was an elegant Rotunda for concerts and other events. Late in his career, Handel was commissioned by George II to write a grand work for wind instruments to celebrate the end of yet another war in 1748 (the War of the Austrian Succession). It was to be accompanied by a firework display. The performance was spoiled by rain, but the rehearsal in Vauxhall Gardens was a great occasion. It was estimated that 12,000 people flocked in, each paying half a crown, and causing a three-hour traffic jam of coaches over London Bridge.

Half a crown was the equivalent of about £50 today, so it is not surprising to read reports that the visitors were 'well dressed'. Handel's Music for the Royal Fireworks is in the grand French style, like Lalande's 'symphonies' for the French king, and is scored for a huge wind band including twenty-four oboes.

And what happened to the castrati? The fashion gradually declined, but there were still some around into the nineteenth century. The practice of castrating boy singers was not formally banned in Italy until 1861. A few castrati lingered on in the Vatican Choir, and one, Alessandro Moreschi, survived to make some solo recordings in the early years of the twentieth century. Very weird and haunting they are too.

CHAPTER 21

A Composer's Life at Court and in the Church

Two other famous composers were born in 1685, the same year as Handel: the Italian Domenico Scarlatti and the German Johann Sebastian Bach. These three composers illustrate how varied musicians' experience could be in the changing musical world of the early eighteenth century, with its combination of traditional patronage and new markets.

Handel was at one end of the spectrum: a brilliant musician and opportunist who exploited to the full the possibilities of the new audiences and markets of his time. Scarlatti was at the other end of the spectrum, with almost no contact with the modern market, and very limited audiences. Bach was, for most of his life, a traditional employee of the Lutheran church in Germany. He was an organist and composer whose main focus was on church music, though he had a strong sideline in instrumental music outside the church.

Domenico Scarlatti was the son of a successful Italian opera composer, Alessandro Scarlatti. Domenico began by following in his father's footsteps and composing operas, but without great success. It was instead as a harpsichord player that he excelled, described by a visiting Englishman as if 'ten hundred d—s [devils] had been at the instrument'. There's a report that Handel and Scarlatti, both in their twenties, met in Rome, and were persuaded to play on harpsichord and organ in front of an audience as 'a trial of skill'. The consensus was that Scarlatti was an 'exquisite' player on the harpsichord, superior to Handel, but that Handel was the more impressive organist. A few years later, Scarlatti was engaged by the King of Portugal as music tutor for his daughter, Maria Bárbara, a highly talented ten-year-old. In 1729 she married the heir to the Spanish throne, and Scarlatti went with them to Spain. Her husband became Ferdinand VI, and Maria Bárbara was his queen. Scarlatti remained with the royal family for the rest of his life, until his death in 1757.

During all these years, Scarlatti composed a stream of more than 500 sonatas for the harpsichord. These were all single movements, unlike the multi-movement sonatas of Corelli. Only a few of them were published in his lifetime, most importantly a volume of thirty 'Exercises', as he titled them, published in London in 1738. These were admired for their brilliance, which included unusual passages in which the hands cross over each other, a technique that was a speciality of Scarlatti's style. But the ambition of these sonatas was limited, as Scarlatti's preface to this volume states plainly: 'Reader, do not expect, whether you are a dilettante or a professor, to find in these compositions any profound intention, but rather an ingenious banter in the art to exercise you in rigorous play of the harpsichord.'

Scarlatti was already aged fifty-three, a ripe old age in those days. But he had many years of development to go, and these Exercises only show a small part of what he could achieve. The greatest number of his Sonatas were composed in the last few years of his life, and they show depth as well as brilliance. Scarlatti was, of course, an Italian, but he had absorbed the sights and sounds of Spanish life and brought them into his music very vividly. Above all, there is the influence of flamenco, with its persistent clapped and stamped rhythms, and harsh, lamenting song. Often he suggests the sound of a guitar, spiced with the dissonances beloved of flamenco guitarists. This was the music of the poor, brought into sonatas composed for the highest in the land. Scarlatti could have had a great influence on other composers of his day. But these late sonatas were virtually unknown outside the immediate court circles, and they were not published in a complete edition until the twentieth century.

This puts Scarlatti in an interesting position from the point of view of a historian. We tend to place most emphasis on composers who had the greatest effect on those around them and on those who came after them. Where do you place an isolated figure like Scarlatti? Historically, you might say he was unimportant. But he composed works of striking originality that, once they became known, were highly valued by musicians and audiences through to our own day.

Johann Sebastian Bach provides another striking comparison with Handel. Handel held various church appointments, but his public career was far more important. For Bach, the church was the centre of his activities for most of his working life, as it was for many composers in both Catholic and Protestant countries. He had a period of six years (1717–23) when he was employed as a court musician, by Prince Leopold of Anhalt-Cöthen. The prince was an accomplished musician, and Bach composed some of his best-known instrumental music while he was with him, including his Brandenburg Concertos (dedicated to the Margrave of Brandenburg). These concertos show how Bach had mastered the Italian style popularised by Corelli, and he brings his own unique insights to the genre. The groupings of instruments are unusual. In No. 1 the solo group includes two horns, three oboes and a high-pitch violin, in No. 2 the soloist is a stratospherically high trumpet (nobody knows whether any trumpeter in Bach's circle could play it). Nos 3 and 6 are for strings only, No. 4 has a pair of recorders and a virtuoso violin soloist; and No. 5 includes a long flourish of a cadenza for solo harpsichord, which Bach would have played himself at early performances. The variety in these concertos shows how he was constantly stretching the possibilities of the styles handed down to him.

Bach was one of the great organists of his time, renowned as an improviser. His organ works exploit to the full the sonorities of the magnificent organs that were built in the eighteenth century in Germany and Holland: powerfully dramatic preludes, like improvisations, each followed by a steadily evolving fugue; and gentle 'chorale preludes', meditations on the Lutheran hymns that were at the centre of church music.

After he left Anhalt-Cöthen, Bach took up the post of music director at the Lutheran church of St Thomas, Leipzig. Here he was in charge of the music at three churches, of which St Thomas was the most important. During his twenty-three years in Leipzig, Bach composed the great choral works for which he is most famous: the Passions according to St Matthew and St John, the Magnificat, the Christmas Oratorio, and the Mass in B minor. Apart from these major works, he also amassed over the years three sets of shorter church cantatas for performance at each Sunday and feast day in the church's calendar, more than 200 cantatas in all.

In Lutheran worship, music was an aid to religious meditation and cantatas were an important expression of that. They had been developed in the early eighteenth century, bringing together recitatives and arias (elements from Italian opera) with Lutheran hymns (chorales) to make a genre that was both dramatic and pious. Bach was a master of this new genre. His Christmas Oratorio is a sequence of six cantatas. His Passions, developing the pioneering examples by Heinrich Schütz, tell the story of the events leading up to Christ's crucifixion. They are like greatly extended cantatas, incorporating choruses that represent the voice of the people, almost as in ancient Greek tragedy.

With all his other duties, you might imagine that some of these works were composed in a hurry. But Bach rarely seems anything other than thorough in the careful working out of his material. Thoroughness does not mean routine or dullness. It is difficult to think of another composer who combines such meticulous attention to detail with a sense of emotional purpose. In his big works, particularly the Passions, there is outright drama, which at least one contemporary accused of sounding 'like opera'. And in his

cantatas there are startling moments of joy, or of sad contempla-
tion, conveyed by strands of melody that intertwine in the most
intricate tapestry, but at the same time are beautifully shaped in
themselves. One of the most beautiful cantatas is No. 82, *Ich habe
genug* ('I am fulfilled'). It is a meditation on lines from the Bible
known as the *Nunc dimittis*. They are the words of Simeon, an
elderly Jew who was in the Temple when Jesus's mother, Mary,
brought the baby to be blessed. Believing that he had seen God's
chosen one, who will redeem humanity, Simeon says that he would
now be able to die in peace. Bach's singer is accompanied by an
oboe, whose gradually evolving melody expresses wonderfully a
sense of peaceful and serene resignation.

While Bach's life was centred on the churches in Leipzig, he was
also involved with a Collegium Musicum, one of many music societies across Germany that brought together musicians to perform
chamber and small-scale orchestral music. In Leipzig the society
consisted of around forty instrumentalists and singers, including
university students and professional musicians, and they gave free
concerts every week at a coffee house, outdoors in the summer.
The works that Bach wrote for them included two violin concertos
and a double concerto (for two violins), and probably many others
that have been lost. He also pioneered the harpsichord concerto,
which, though it never really took off more widely, laid the basis
for the later piano concerto.

Apart from these works written for an obvious purpose, Bach
made a habit of constructing collections of music that seem to
explore all the possibilities of a genre, perhaps as a teaching model.
When he died in 1750, he was working on *The Art of Fugue*, a long-
term project of great complexity. In it he takes a single theme and
explores many different ways of combining and developing it, in a
series of twenty or so fugues. This giant work of counterpoint
seems to have more in common with the pre-Renaissance view of
music as a way of expressing the complexity of God's universe,
rather than with any of the more humanistic concerns of the eighteenth century. But for Bach the working out of counterpoint is not
just an intellectual exercise. His finest fugues have as strong a sense

of human drama as any instrumental music of the time, with a great feeling of arrival and achievement when you reach the end.

The same applies to two other monumental works. Bach's *Goldberg Variations* for harpsichord is a set of variations on a theme, incorporating almost every conceivable style of the time, including a series of canons (rounds), a challenge of which Bach was particularly fond. The *Well-Tempered Clavier* (meaning a keyboard instrument tuned so that it can be played in any key) consists of forty-eight preludes and fugues, two in each major and minor key. Bach would have been amazed at the way these works are now performed complete in concert. He would have conceived them as resources to explore for the illumination of different styles and techniques, one piece at a time.

Later musicians came to regard Bach and Handel as the founding fathers of a great line of German music that then stretched from Gluck, Haydn and Mozart by way of Beethoven and Schubert, Schumann and Mendelssohn, to Brahms and Wagner. Bach and Handel were indeed composers with extraordinary imaginations, who pushed the boundaries of the musical language of their time in unique ways, and their music is still treasured. That is why I have devoted so much space to them. But their music owes as much to Italian and French musicians as it does to Germans, as we have seen. The idea of them as founding fathers of a 'German line' was the result of intense lobbying by later writers with a strong sense of German nationalism.

CHAPTER 22

Enlightenment and Revolution

As the eighteenth century wore on, there were new ideas and new turbulence in the air. The emphasis on human reason as the basis of society gave rise to a philosophical movement known as the Enlightenment. This was centred on France, but rapidly became international, drawing in thinkers in Germany, England, Scotland, North America and Russia. Its great central project was the writing of a multi-volume encyclopaedia, *L'Encyclopédie*, designed to cover systematically all 'the sciences, arts and crafts'. But its entries spread widely across all aspects of human knowledge to include areas of belief, politics, anthropology and philosophy, providing a focus for the great debates of the time. Many of the principal writers were vehemently critical of the church, deploring what they saw as its use of superstition to exercise power and control. They similarly deplored the infringement of liberties by autocratic rulers and governments. These challenges to authority were to explode in revolution in the last quarter of the century, first in the British colonies of North America and then in France, with reverberations across Europe.

What did all this have to do with music? We have seen through the centuries how music and musicians find themselves responding to the current forces of power and society. Now, in the mid-eighteenth century, the new debates and rumblings began to have their effects on musicians. These ranged from discussions about the science of music, by way of arguments about sophistication versus simplicity, to conflict with authorities about librettos of operas and what was and was not allowed.

It was in France that arguments about the science and sophistication of music were most heated. The initial spark was a work of music theory published by the French composer Jean-Philippe Rameau in 1722, *Treatise on Harmony, Reduced to Its Natural Principles*. It was the first major attempt to explain the principles of harmony as it had developed in Europe, and to relate it to the basic natural phenomenon of the harmonic series, and the mathematical relations between different notes. His approach was in the spirit of writings on mathematics and scientific reason, and it formed the basis for later writings on music theory.

This might seem like dry stuff, but Rameau soon found himself at the centre of a very public argument about the direction of French music. At this point in his career Rameau was known as a composer of harpsichord pieces and church music. But he was (like Domenico Scarlatti) a late developer. In 1733, when Rameau was fifty, his first opera, *Hippolyte et Aricie*, was staged in Paris. Superficially, it followed the model set by Lully, with plenty of dance in the French courtly tradition dating back to the days of Louis XIV. But its harmonies and orchestration were far more complex than earlier French opera, with clashing dissonances that never occurred in the music of Lully. The audience and critics were sharply divided. Some found it refreshingly original and thought it showed the way forward; others saw it as a betrayal of the elegant French tradition established by Lully. This argument grew more heated over the years. And even when Rameau's reputation had been established with his later operas, an even greater argument blew up.

The spark this time was a visiting Italian theatre troupe, who in 1752 performed a one-act comic opera by the Italian Giovanni Battista Pergolesi, *La Serva Padrona* (The Servant as Mistress) in the grandest opera house in Paris. The delightful simplicity of this little opera caused influential writers to compare it with the elaborate complexities of current French opera, particularly Rameau. Leading the charge was the philosopher Jean-Jacques Rousseau. He admired the melodious simplicity of *La Serva Padrona*, which he contrasted with French music, with its 'barking' voices and 'brutal' harmonies. Rousseau was something of a musician himself and wrote both the words and music of a simple little one-act opera, *Le Devin du Village* (The Village Soothsayer), which was performed in Paris two months after *La Serva Padrona* and was admired by the king. As for Rousseau's condemnation of French musical ugliness and complexity, it all seems rather out of proportion until one realises that Rousseau had more profound reasons for admiring simplicity and distrusting complexity.

His most important writings are to do with human nature and human society, how they have developed, and what has been lost or gained. He came to the view that modern humans had lost touch with their original natures. 'Primitive' humans, in his view, led lives of simplicity, but this essential quality had gradually been drowned in a destructive flood of sophistication and complexity – what we call 'civilisation'. Rousseau's yearning to regain simplicity led to the concept of the 'noble savage', the uncivilised human being who has retained the innocence of primitive life and is therefore to be admired.

This was part of a debate about other cultures that was growing among European thinkers. Ironically, it was the 'over-sophisticated' Rameau who had first evoked other cultures in music in *Les Indes Galantes* (The Amorous Indies), staged in Paris in 1735. This 'opera-ballet' followed the usual French format, with a rich mixture of arias, choruses and ballets. But here each act is set in a different exotic location – Turkey, Peru, Persia and North America – and centres on amorous encounters and rivalries involving both natives and Europeans. Rameau and his librettist drew on published descriptions that had been flooding in from travellers in recent years. But one scene was inspired by a more direct encounter.

In 1725 six Native American chiefs from Illinois (then a French colony) were brought across the Atlantic to France in order to meet the king, Louis XV. When they did so, a letter was read out declaring their allegiance to the French crown. Later, in a theatre in Paris, the chiefs danced three of their traditional dances, the like of which had never been seen in Paris before. It was this that inspired Rameau to write his dance 'Les Sauvages' (The Savages), first as a harpsichord piece, and then as part of the last act of the opera. This is an early example of the 'exotic' being used as spice to enhance the flavour of opera. The basis of this fashion now strikes us as highly problematic, with its obviously racist ingredients. But eighteenth-century audiences did not have modern sensitivities, and the fashion continued right through into the nineteenth century.

Was there any sign that Europeans were seriously interested in the music of other cultures, beyond the spice of the exotic? The history I have outlined over the preceding centuries makes it clear that Europeans almost entirely turned their backs on the music of the rest of the world, developing a new language of harmony that took European music further and further away from its global roots. As Europeans began to re-encounter the music of other cultures, through colonisation and the reports of travellers, there were some limited signs of re-engagement, though the general attitude was more often indifference or hostility.

By 1765, the British ruled Bengal, the richest province of India, through the East India Company and its army. Bengal's first governor, the ruthless Robert Clive, was succeeded by Warren Hastings, a man who grew to love India and its culture. He spoke several Indian languages, attempted to sing Indian songs, and encouraged translations of Indian sacred texts. But the British, including Warren Hastings, were in India to exploit its people and resources in the pursuit of profit, and such appreciation of Indian culture was a rare sideline. Hastings's rival for power in Bengal,

Philip Francis, viewed the Bengalis as 'ignorant and unimproved', summing up in a nutshell the language with which colonisers the world over asserted their own superiority.

If colonial rulers could not be relied upon to appreciate the culture of their subjects, missionaries, writers and philosophers could sometimes take a more sympathetic view. In 1768, Rousseau published his *Dictionary of Music*. In a broad-ranging entry on 'Music', he includes (in European notation) 'A Chinese Air', 'A Persian Air' and 'A Song of the Savages in Canada'. Rousseau declares that, across all the centuries that people have cultivated the fine arts, 'Every people on earth have a music and a melody [but] . . . the Europeans alone have a harmony of concords.' The fact that only Europeans have harmony leads him to a surprising conclusion. Since the music of the eastern peoples and the Greeks had 'such prodigious effects without [harmony], it is very difficult not to suspect that all our harmony is but a Gothic and barbarous invention, which we should never have pursued if we had been more sensitive to the true beauties of art, and of truly natural music'. As we have seen, music in many cultures of the world has developed polyphony, but Rousseau is correct that the European system of harmony and chords is unique. He uses this to attack the complexity of French harmony, particularly Rameau, in favour of the simplicity of Italian music. However, he himself did not go so far as to compose music without European harmonies: his *Le Devin du Village* is thoroughly modern, like a simplified Lully.

It is missionaries who supply some of the most detailed information about the music of other cultures in this period. A French Jesuit priest, Jean Joseph Marie Amiot, spent more than forty years as a missionary in China from 1751. As part of his wide-ranging studies of Chinese culture, he wrote *Memoir on the Music of the Chinese, Ancient and Modern*. He writes how he formed the desire to understand Chinese music in depth, its rules and its theories, its importance in Chinese life and ritual, and its ancient history. He examines the Chinese approach to the nature of sound, their scales and their instruments. It was another Jesuit, Jean-Baptiste

Du Halde, in his 1735 description of China, who noted down the Chinese tune that Rousseau quotes in his *Dictionary*.

Sir William Jones, an English lawyer in India, wrote an essay 'On the musical modes of the Hindus' in 1792, and compiled a collection of 'Hindustani Airs'. The governor, Warren Hastings, declared them to be authentic Indian melodies. But there is an inescapable problem: European notation cannot convey the subtleties of tuning and rhythm in the music of Indian, Chinese and other cultures that do not conform to European conventions. So such transcriptions could never be really 'authentic', however well meant.

The effect of these publications on European composers was very limited. Indian and Chinese music could be a topic of interest to the curious, but generally European composers made use of this information only when an 'oriental' flavour was required. The oriental was also fashionable in art and architecture. Frederick the Great, King of Prussia, built a Chinese Tea House in the grounds of his palace at Potsdam. Round the outside of the building there are statues of figures in Chinese dress and hats, but the faces are more European than Chinese. Vauxhall Gardens in London featured a Turkish Tent. In modern times, we have come to acknowledge the problems with this kind of 'orientalism'. Like other forms of the 'exotic', it tends to reduce foreign cultures to objects of curiosity for Western audiences and viewers, with an emphasis on their strangeness. But European audiences and viewers in the eighteenth century were not in the habit of questioning such attitudes.

It was poets who began to take a serious interest in other cultures. The German poet Johann Wolfgang von Goethe engaged with both Chinese and Persian literature. He was fascinated by the poems of the fourteenth-century Persian, Hafez, whose *Diwan* (a collection of short poems) had recently been translated into German. Goethe responded with his own collection, *West-Eastern Diwan*, in which he echoed the themes of Hafez: the torments and ecstasy of love, the beauties of the dawn, gardens, flowing wine, all traditional themes of Arabic and Persian poetry that we encountered in Chapter 4.

But poets didn't need to look so far afield in search of 'the other', people whose lives and culture were remote from their own. While Goethe was looking east, the English poet William Wordsworth was turning his attention to the lives of ordinary working people in the English Lake District, a class which had generally been ignored in the arts of the privileged. He published poems about shepherds and other country people, expressing in unusually simple language the hardship of their lives and their relationship with nature. Wordsworth's 'anti-elitist' sentiments went hand in hand with his enthusiasm for the French Revolution and its early promise of freeing ordinary people from the tyranny of the ruling classes. Wordsworth spent some time in France during the Revolution and later wrote, 'Bliss was it in that dawn to be alive, / But to be young was very heaven!' As the Revolution descended into violence, and Wordsworth aged, he rather turned away from these radical sentiments. But the valuing of ordinary people was a powerful new element in literature which had a wide influence. Even Goethe (an aristocrat by birth) wrote simple poems that were mistaken for folk songs. And the Scottish poet Robert Burns achieved international fame with his evocation of the lives of poor Scots in poems written in Scots dialect.

What was the effect of all this in music? We have already seen the success of *The Beggar's Opera* in London in 1728, which included popular folk songs. It was in 1778 that the German philosopher Johann Gottfried Herder published pioneering volumes of folk songs – indeed he coined the term 'Volkslied' (folk song). This set off a fashion for folk songs, and their publication became a profitable business. English and Scottish songs were particularly successful. George Thomson of Edinburgh oversaw a project to publish a great collection of the folk songs of Scotland, and engaged the most famous composer of the day, Joseph Haydn, to provide accompaniments for piano, with optional parts for violin and cello. As there was a limited supply of 'genuine' folk songs, new songs (including many by Robert Burns) were slipped into the collection to satisfy the market. When Haydn died in 1809, Thomson persuaded Beethoven to continue the task.

This signalled not so much a new interest in the lower classes, but a fashion for something home-grown and mildly 'exotic' among the growing middle class. There was nothing rough and ready about Haydn and Beethoven's accompaniments. You might say that the songs had been domesticated, like servants trained how to behave in their new uniforms. Although folk songs were certainly performed in public, as in *The Beggar's Opera*, the main target for the publishers was the respectable home, in which women increasingly sang and played the piano.

CHAPTER 23

African Slaves and Fashionable Europe

My discussion of Europeans' engagement with other cultures has left until now a major and inescapable topic: slavery. I have mentioned it from time to time in earlier chapters, in the context of war and colonisation. Slavery has been a feature of human society since ancient times and across many parts of the world. As I write, there is a rising tide of awareness in the West about the trade in African slaves, on which much of the prosperity of our people and cities has been built. This trade reached a climax in the eighteenth century, on a scale that deserves to be called industrial. You might think that this brutal treatment of fellow human beings would have been incompatible with the eighteenth-century drive against prejudice and superstition, and towards scientific knowledge and 'Enlightenment'. But what we now call 'science' is not so easy to separate from ingrained attitudes.

The eighteenth century was the great era of classification, in which researchers attempted to arrive at universal truths underlying the variations in plants, animals and, of course, humans. There were studies of human anatomy that revealed differences between groups, and particularly between Europeans and Africans. These were all too easily used to confirm the prevailing view of Africans as 'inferior' to Europeans. Even some of the most radical thinkers of the Enlightenment failed to see the falsehood in this attitude: the philosophers Voltaire and David Hume, both clear-thinking in so many other ways, accepted the view of Africans as inferior to Europeans. There was a religious dimension to this, which tended to colour the science. The belief that God had originally created perfect species, including humans, and that they had degenerated over time, fed into what we now think of as racial discrimination. There had been opponents to this discrimination for many years, and a campaign against slavery developed into the nineteenth century. But it was to be a very long battle – and it is not over yet.

The Portuguese had been taking slaves from Africa to Europe since the fifteenth century. The Pope authorised the buying of non-Christian slaves from the Portuguese, and they were soon to be found in large numbers in Italy and Spain. Many former slaves were employed as servants in England and Germany. They appear among musicians, particularly as drummers and trumpeters (we met Henry VIII's trumpeter John Blanke in Chapter 15). Britain had sugar plantations worked by slaves in Barbados by the seventeenth century. Over the eighteenth century, Britain transported about three million Africans to forced labour in plantations in the Caribbean and the Americas. The French were next, with about one million. The consequences were immense, in deaths on the voyage across the Atlantic, further death and appalling treatment on the plantations, and the profound effect on society in Africa.

The trade in slaves, and in the plantations that they worked, was hugely profitable. I mentioned in Chapter 20 that London was a wealthy city in the early eighteenth century, with its theatres and opera houses, and much of this wealth came from the slave trade. Several of the principal investors in the Royal Academy of Music, for which Handel worked, were shareholders in the Royal African Company and South Sea Company, both of which traded in slaves. Handel himself acquired shares and annuities in these companies.

One by-product of the slave trade was that large numbers of Africans were brought to Europe. There were perhaps 15,000 in England in the 1770s. Many led impoverished lives at the bottom of society. In both Britain and Germany, Black servants were fashionable, acquired from slave-owners. They were collected as curiosities, along with exotic animals and plants. Eighteenth-century family portraits show African servants looking up adoringly at their masters and mistresses, sometimes echoing the similar expression of the family's dogs. A few rose to prominence, particularly as the campaign against slavery began to gather pace. Several former slaves wrote books, describing their terrible experiences, and these were powerful ammunition in the anti-slavery campaign.

One who became famous was Ignatius Sancho, whose letters were published in 1782 after his death. He was brought to London at the age of two, was employed as butler to the Duchess of Montagu, had his portrait painted by Thomas Gainsborough, the leading portraitist of the day, and was befriended by Laurence Sterne, author of the novel *Tristram Shandy*. Sancho wrote to Sterne, urging him to campaign against slavery, and Sterne replied sympathetically, with this succinct summary of slavery and its consequences: ' 'tis no uncommon thing, my good Sancho, for one half of the world to use the other half of it like brutes, and then endeavour to make 'em so.'

Among his accomplishments, Sancho became skilled in the fashionable music of the time. Three volumes of minuets and other dances by him were published around 1770, for harpsichord with additional parts for horns, flutes, mandolin and violins. These volumes are dedicated to Lord Montagu, the husband of his employer – an aristocratic household of that kind would routinely have had musicians available for dances. The composer was given on the title page as 'An African', without naming Sancho. But he was named in a later volume of simpler pieces for the harpsichord, *Twelve Country Dances for the Year 1779 set for the Harpsichord*. By this date he had left the Montagu household and was running a grocer's shop in Westminster. He was famous, so his name would have helped sell the dances. Like those in the earlier volumes, these have fashionable titles – 'Lady Mary Montagu's Reel', 'Strawberries and Cream', 'All of One Mind' – and they are set in a simple style that could be managed by any reasonably accomplished harpsichord player. The volume's dedication to 'The Right Honourable Miss North' reminds us that, within the household, such harpsichord players would usually have been the women of the family. At the bottom of each dance is given the sequence of appropriate dance steps: this was music for use in the drawing rooms of England, rather than for performing in concert.

Sancho composed domestic music as a sideline. By contrast, Joseph de Bologne, Chevalier de Saint-Georges, was a professional composer on a far grander scale. His mother was an African slave in the Caribbean, his father the white French plantation owner (many mixed-race children were born from such encounters). At the age of seven, Joseph and his mother were taken by his father to France. The father, being a highly established figure, was able to make sure that the boy got a good education. Like Sancho, Joseph thrived, and he became brilliant in two fields. He was an exceptionally talented fencer, beating one of the top fencing-masters in France while he was still a teenager. And he also became an outstanding violinist, though nothing is known about his musical training.

When Saint-Georges was in his twenties, one of France's leading composers, François-Joseph Gossec, dedicated a set of trios for violin, viola and cello to him. Three years later, in 1769, Saint-Georges joined a new orchestra that Gossec led and directed (this was in the days before modern-style conductors). Four years after that, when Gossec left to lead a rival orchestra, he chose Saint-Georges as his successor as the leader for his orchestra, which was then called Le Concert de la Loge Olympique after the masonic lodge with which it was associated. Under Saint-Georges's leadership, this became one of the most disciplined and admired orchestras in Europe. It is an indication of its status that Joseph Haydn wrote six symphonies for them.

In 1776, when the directorship of the Paris Opéra fell vacant, Saint-Georges was the obvious choice to succeed. But four leading ladies of the Opera petitioned the queen, Marie-Antoinette, to spare them the humiliation of having to submit to the orders of a man of mixed race. Saint-Georges withdrew, to avoid embarrassing the queen. As well as his career as a violinist, he was also a highly esteemed composer. He wrote six operas, but only one survives, *The Anonymous Lover*. He also composed chamber music, violin concertos and several *Symphonies Concertantes* – large-scale concertos with more than one soloist, a French speciality. One of them, for violin and viola, composed in 1778, has some phrases that are very similar to a few in Mozart's much better-known *Sinfonia Concertante* for violin and viola, composed the following year. That is probably not a coincidence: Mozart was in Paris for three months during 1778, and very likely heard this work or saw the score. We'll come to Mozart in the next chapter.

Of course Sancho and Saint-Georges succeeded in their music because they mastered the prevailing European musical style. Sancho wrote charming little pieces, Saint-Georges composed substantial works with a fine command of the European international style of the day. There is nothing in their compositions that identifies them as African. If we search for evidence that any Europeans were interested in African music in the eighteenth century, as opposed to Africans who had mastered European music, we find very little, and what there is comes from visitors to Africa rather than those encountering the slave populations. There are descriptions of African instruments from late seventeenth-century missionaries. And in the early years of the eighteenth century there is a detailed account by Peter Kolb describing the society of the Khoekhoe (known to colonists as the Hottentots) of South-West Africa. Kolb was a German astronomer, commissioned to make observations of the African skies as part of the search for a way to calculate longitude – a characteristic Enlightenment enterprise. He spent eight years in southern Africa, and he describes dances, polyphonic singing, and the playing of instruments including the *goura* (mouth-bow) that I mentioned in Chapter 7.

The music of the enslaved Africans was largely ignored by Europeans until well into the nineteenth century. When we consider how much our modern music owes to Africans (as I'll discuss in

Chapter 34), this might seem shocking. But slavery was a distorting glass through which Africans were generally seen and judged. Indians, Chinese and Native North Americans, who were not routinely enslaved, excited more curiosity about their music, though few people made any serious attempt to engage with it. European society had already 'classified' Africans as inferior in order to justify enslaving them. Even in North America and the Caribbean, where there were so many African slaves, next to nothing was written about their music. The white people overseeing the plantations must have been continually exposed to African singing and dance. But the overriding concern was to keep the slaves under control, so their music, with its insistent rhythms and dances, was likely to be perceived as a threat. It would be a century or more before Europeans, and white Americans, began to hear what African music had to offer.

There were obviously immense obstacles in the way of Black musicians trying to make a name for themselves in Europe. Sancho and Saint-Georges were fortunate in having people in high places to push their cause. But they had one other great advantage: they were men. No woman, not even a white woman, could have led an orchestra at public concerts in eighteenth-century Paris. You'll have noticed how few women composers have featured in this book so far, and those that have appeared were all exceptions in their day. There will be a few more as we move into the nineteenth century, but it was difficult for women musicians to make their mark in public, however gifted. And those that did succeed have tended to be ignored by later historians. I'll have more to say about this contentious topic later.

CHAPTER 24

Storms, on the Stage and in the Mind

I've talked in earlier chapters about the steady rise of instruments and the development of a repertoire of music for instruments alone. This carried on through the late eighteenth century into the nineteenth, with the growth of concerts and of music in the home. There was a demand for orchestral music for public occasions, and 'chamber music' for the more private ones: trios and quartets for stringed instruments or mixed strings and wind, works for keyboard instrument with one or two other instruments. There was also a growing repertoire of music for solo keyboards, at first harpsichord or clavichord, later the piano. Some of this was for playing at home by amateurs, some was aimed at the increasing number of virtuoso performers.

The music itself was changing in character. It tended to become more dramatic, with contrasts of mood within each movement, and an increasingly powerful sense of a 'narrative' drawing the music forward to the end. This sense of narrative had been gradually developing ever since the days of Josquin in the early sixteenth century. Now it took on a new dramatic intensity, with several currents of influence coming together from different sources.

One important source of change in music for instruments filtered through from changes in opera. In the 1750s and 1760s there was a widespread feeling that the emphasis on the virtuosity of the star singers had gone too far, obscuring the drama of opera for the sake of mere display. Comic opera took a turn for greater simplicity, as we saw with Pergolesi's *La Serva Padrona*. There were other composers of comic opera who began to concentrate on the dramatic interaction between characters, with ensembles heightening climactic moments. In serious opera too, with its plots often drawn from classical myths, there were calls for a more natural emphasis on the drama and on the expression of the emotional force of the words through the music. This was, in effect, a call for a return to the first principles of opera, as it had been devised a century and a half before, with its roots in ideas about Greek drama.

The composer who came to be seen as the leader of this movement for reform was not an Italian, but a German who studied in Italy and spent most of his working life in Vienna and Paris: Christoph Willibald Gluck. His first great triumph, *Orfeo ed Euridice* (Orpheus and Eurydice, yet another retelling of the ancient myth), premiered in Vienna in 1762, and still holds the stage to this day. Its climactic aria, *Che farò senza Euridice* ('What shall I do without Eurydice'), has long been admired for its tragic simplicity. Gluck declared that his aim was to make the music serve the poetry and the 'situations of the story', without interrupting the action or stifling it with a useless excess of ornaments'. He wanted to do away with the sharp distinction between recitative and aria, so as not to 'upset the force and heat of the action'. And he felt that the overture 'ought to alert the audience to the nature of the action that is to be represented and to form, so to speak, its argument'. Some of Gluck's ideas were drawn from French opera, particularly the French love of ballet. Gluck sought to reform this too, making ballet, like everything else, serve the drama, and not just be bolted on as a separate element. Above all, Gluck was devoted 'to seeking a beautiful simplicity'.

This reforming spirit carried over through Gluck's pupils and followers to later generations. He came to be seen by composers and writers in German-speaking countries as the reformer who 'saved' Italian opera from its absurdities. This played into the rising sense of German national identity, which was to have such far-reaching consequences. More immediately, it was Gluck's dramatic effects that aroused the enthusiasm of audiences. One of these was a 'Dance of the furies' that first appeared at the climax of his ballet, *Don Juan*, in 1761, when Don Juan is dragged down to hell. This was so successful that, when Gluck revised *Orfeo ed Euridice* for performances in Paris in 1774, he added this dance for the scene in which the furies refuse Orpheus entry to the underworld. When Orpheus is finally admitted, the music melts into a new 'Dance of the Blessed Spirits', with a serene flute solo.

There had been powerful instrumental passages in opera before. Decades before Gluck was writing, the French specialised in tempests in operas, echoing the taste for storms in landscape paintings of the day. Handel and Vivaldi had incorporated many 'tempest arias' into their Italian operas, in which singers battled against real or imagined storms. Famously, Vivaldi brought a storm into his set of violin concertos, *The Four Seasons*. It was this new sort of instrumental drama that proved infectious for writers of orchestral music. Opera overtures were already played separately in concerts: they were often miniature symphonies in several movements. Now, the element of drama began to change orchestral writing fundamentally.

Several of the most important composers in this new, dramatic genre were associated with the powerful breed of orchestra that had sprung up. We have already encountered Saint-Georges's orchestra in Paris, Le Concert de la Loge Olympique, one of two in the city that had a high reputation. Their speciality was a fierce opening attack, with all the bows precisely co-ordinated. Composers were careful to give the strings the opportunity to show off this effect, such as Haydn in his Symphony No. 82 and Mozart in Symphony No. 31, both composed for Paris.

The other centre that became famous for orchestral playing was the court at Mannheim in Germany. The Mannheim orchestra was highly disciplined, and it too had dramatic specialities. These included the trick of starting a passage very quietly and gradually getting louder and louder to a great climax – the 'Mannheim Crescendo'. The first leader and composer to introduce these effects was Johann Stamitz. He spent a year in Paris in the 1750s, and ideas certainly passed continually between Paris and Mannheim. All these dramatic possibilities influenced the next generation of composers. I have already mentioned Mozart's *Sinfonia Concertante* with solo violin and viola, composed after a visit to Paris. This has one of the finest of all Mannheim crescendos, rising over a series of trills just before the soloists first enter.

The new, dramatic style seeped into smaller-scale music too. One of J. S. Bach's sons, Carl Philipp Emanuel Bach (known as Emanuel), composed church music, symphonies and chamber music. But his largest and most important output was a great number of sonatas for keyboard. These include relatively simple pieces, some specifically published as being 'for the ladies', at a time when playing a keyboard instrument was a regular part of a well-to-do young woman's education. Many others are advanced, not just technically, but in the sense that they explore all sorts of dramatic turns and changes of mood. In the music of his father, J. S. Bach, there is a great deal of drama in some of the preludes and fantasias, and some of his melodies have an extraordinarily expressive freedom. His son Emanuel took this in a new direction, with an almost operatic style brought into instrumental music, full of twists and surprises.

Nowadays, if we think of dramatic keyboard music, we might imagine the modern grand piano, with its huge range of volume and tone. In Bach's day, when the piano was only just becoming available, and was much smaller and quieter than the modern piano, the usual keyboard instrument for intimate drama was the clavichord. This is a very quiet instrument, designed for private use, or for playing to very few people gathered close by. But its mechanism allows a great range of expression on a small scale. When you press a key, the other end rises to hit the string with a tiny metal tangent. The harder you press, the louder the sound.

The tangent stays against the string until you take your finger off the key. This means that you can produce a little 'vibrato' by moving your finger up and down. So, within this intimate scale, there is great opportunity for highly expressive playing. Emanuel Bach's music is wonderfully tailored for this intimate expression.

His own approach to playing keyboard instruments was set out in his book, *Essay on the True Art of Playing Keyboard Instruments*, which covers many aspects of musicianship. He stresses the importance of feeling the emotions in the music: 'Since a musician cannot move others unless he himself is moved, he has to feel all the passions that he hopes to arouse in his listeners.' Mozart is reported to have visited Emanuel Bach at Hamburg, where he worked in the last years of his life. Bach, then in his seventies, improvised for Mozart several times on his Silbermann piano. At a soirée, Mozart was asked by the host what he thought of Emanuel Bach's playing: 'The great man replied with his characteristically Viennese candour and directness: he is the father, we are the children. Those of us who know anything at all learned it from him; anyone who does not admit this is a – ' (we are left to imagine this word). This underlines, once again, that the art of improvising continued to be important. The English historian Charles Burney left a more detailed description of Emanuel Bach, whom he considered 'not only one of the greatest composers who ever existed, for the keyboard, but the best player, in point of *expression*'. Burney heard him improvise for several hours, while in Germany: 'During this time he grew so animated and possessed, that he not only played but looked like one inspired. His eyes were fixed, his under lip fell, and drops of effervescence fell from his countenance.' Bach's *Essay* was widely admired for many years: for Joseph Haydn it was 'the school of schools', and for Beethoven it was the book that piano pupils needed to acquire before he would teach them.

This new 'sensibility' fed into music from several different directions. I have already mentioned the fashion for storms in paintings, and there was also a fashion for intimate domestic scenes. Poets were seeking new, more direct, means of expression. Emanuel Bach was in contact with the poet Friedrich Gottlieb Klopstock, who wanted a new freedom in poetry, analogous to the sort of expressive freedom and surprise in Bach's music.

As for the 'inner storm' of the human emotions, this reached a climax in literature in the 1770s. I have already mentioned Goethe, with his interest in Persian poetry and folk song. He was to become one of the dominant figures into the nineteenth century. As a young man, he published in 1774 a novel, *The Sorrows of Young Werther*, in which a young poet is tortured by love for a married woman and ends up committing suicide. Based partly on Goethe's own experience as a rejected lover, this had a tremendous success, initiating a series of tragic figures drawn from ordinary life. It was one of the key moments in the development of the movement that came to be known as Romanticism.

A fundamental restlessness was at the heart of Goethe's writings, and he declared that the secret of life was continuous change: 'The principle of metamorphosis is the key to all of Nature's signs.' The physical, mental and spiritual were in constant flux, and Goethe expressed this philosophy in a huge range of work over a long life (he was eighty-two when he died in 1832). At one end of the spectrum were little poems expressing a moment caught on the wing – set to music by many composers over the coming decades. At the other end was his massive drama reworking the old legend of Faust, the doctor who sells his soul to the devil in exchange for experiencing complete knowledge. Goethe is one of the figures who links the philosophy of the Enlightenment, with its examination of the rational, to that of Romanticism, with its opening up to the world of the spirit and the unknown.

Music is not literature, and it is naive to look for exact equivalents. But if we want to find musical developments analogous to all this expressive freedom and 'inner storm', the best place to look is Vienna in the last decades of the eighteenth century and the opening of the nineteenth. Here three of the giants of music overlapped and created something new: Joseph Haydn, Wolfgang Amadeus Mozart and Ludwig van Beethoven.

CHAPTER 25

Becoming 'Classical'

In the eighteenth century, Vienna was the capital of the Holy Roman Empire, ruled by the German-speaking Habsburg family. It stretched from Bohemia in the east (part of today's Czech Republic) across to Belgium in the west, and from the Baltic Sea in the north down to the Mediterranean in the south. Vienna was an immensely wealthy city, and a centre for German culture, attracting artists and musicians who wished to reach the top of their professions.

From the late eighteenth century through to the early nineteenth, so much important music was centred on Vienna that later historians took to referring to this as the period of the 'Viennese Classics', focused on three of the acknowledged great composers, Joseph Haydn, Wolfgang Amadeus Mozart and Ludwig van Beethoven. But 'classic' is a rather dry label to give these energetic thinkers. The manner in which they all pushed the expressive boundaries of the music of their day makes it more appropriate to think of them as early 'Romantics', if indeed they need a label at all. They were the heirs of the new dramatic style developed by the orchestral composers of Mannheim and Paris, and by Emanuel Bach on the keyboard. And they learned a great deal from each other. But their different experiences of the culture and society of the time also show how things were changing.

As boys, Joseph Haydn and his brother Michael (also a composer) were choristers at St Stephen's Cathedral in Vienna. After being thrown out for bad behaviour, Joseph spent a few years working in various households until he landed permanent posts, first with a count, and then with a prince. The prince was the head of one of the wealthiest families in Austria, the Esterházys, with palaces in Vienna and Eisenstadt. In the 1760s they built a new summer palace in the Hungarian marshes that included a theatre in which plays and operas were staged. Haydn stayed with the family for thirty years as their director of music (Kapellmeister). He was in charge of the court orchestra, leading it from the violin or keyboard instrument, and supervised the annual season of opera productions, which included more than a dozen composed by himself. He also wrote small-scale chamber music and church music including splendid settings of the Mass for singers and orchestra – Austria, unlike most German-speaking states, had remained Roman Catholic. Haydn's employer for most of this period, Prince Nikolaus Esterházy, was an enthusiastic music-lover and amateur musician who gave Haydn free rein to compose.

The prince held the right to all of Haydn's compositions, but his music circulated widely in manuscript copies, and was published from time to time. Eventually Haydn was allowed to write for outside commissions and to sell to publishers. The result was that he soon became the most famous composer in Europe, even though he was isolated in the Esterházy palaces. Haydn himself acknowledged that being 'cut off from the world' had its advantages. With the support of the prince, and the freedom to experiment and refine his style and technique, Haydn said 'there was no one to confuse or torment me, and I was forced to become original'. The climax of his career came in the 1790s when, after the death of Prince Nikolaus, Haydn was allowed to travel to London, where he was greeted as a great celebrity.

During his long life Haydn wrote a huge quantity of music, but he became particularly famous in two genres, one small-scale, the other large-scale. The small-scale genre was the string quartet (two violins, viola and cello). Haydn is traditionally called 'the father of the string quartet', though he didn't exactly invent it. It had long been the habit for people to come together to make music in various combinations, playing whatever instruments came to hand, and stringed instruments were particularly popular. Haydn had composed his first quartets in Vienna in the 1750s for just such a haphazard group of amateurs. From the success of this experiment, Haydn went on to demonstrate over the years the full potential of this ensemble.

The string quartet is a grouping that opens up all sorts of possibilities. Four stringed instruments can supply full chords, without the need for a keyboard instrument. The cello gives a strong bass line, the first violin can play solo melodies, or the two violins can play in duet. The viola has a fluid role, sometimes filling in the notes of chords, sometimes echoing the melodies of the violins. Viola and cello can duet together below the violins in counterpoint. And the cello too can sometimes play a melody – this was a time when the cello was first being explored as a virtuoso instrument. If there is a single word to sum up the appeal of the string quartet at this time, it is musical 'conversation'. Indeed, when Haydn's very first quartets were published in Paris in 1764, the title page described them as 'quatuors dialogués' ('conversational quartets'). Haydn's quartets were taken up enthusiastically by the Viennese, and increasingly by music-lovers across Europe.

Haydn had made a close study of traditional counterpoint techniques and the intimate dramatic compositions of Emanuel Bach. But he was also a man of great wit and imagination. Now his quartets combined the learned with the dramatic and witty. Even a fugue could become dramatic, its working-out creating tension as part of the developing narrative. When Charles Burney was in Vienna in 1772, he went to a concert at the residence of the British ambassador in Vienna, where he heard 'exquisite quartets, by Haydn, executed to the utmost perfection'. These might well have included some from his set of six quartets Opus 20, which Haydn composed that year. These were the works in which Haydn fully developed the art of dramatic conversation in a string quartet.

Equally, Haydn traditionally has the title 'father of the symphony'. Again, he didn't invent the symphony. As I mentioned earlier, it emerged out of the opera overture, performed as a separate piece. Johann Stamitz, director of the Mannheim court orchestra, was writing four-movement symphonies by the 1750s. Haydn took this idea and developed the symphony into one of the most important and durable of genres in music, to the extent that we still refer to large orchestras as 'symphony orchestras'. Haydn wrote over a hundred symphonies, ranging from early works that are little more than opera overtures lasting ten minutes or so, to substantial pieces lasting half an hour.

This was not just down to Haydn's imagination, but also depended on the orchestra and audience for whom he was writing. The private orchestras of Haydn's employers increased from a dozen or so players to about twenty-five by the 1780s. Then Haydn was invited to compose six symphonies for an orchestra in Paris, where his music was already well-known. These were to be played by the orchestra that Saint-Georges led, Le Concert de la Loge Olympique, which included forty violins and ten double basses. The success of these symphonies (Nos 82–87) was so great that Haydn was asked for three more (Nos 90–92). A Paris critic was particularly struck by the way 'this great genius . . . is able to make so much of a single subject, to draw out such rich and varied developments'. This was indeed one of the novel features of Haydn's style. He often works up a whole movement from very little material, creating a tight argument, highly dramatic in its effect – a method that was to influence the young Beethoven (whom we'll come to in the next chapter).

Haydn's writing of symphonies reached a grand climax in the 1790s with his two visits to London. This was the result of an invitation from a German violinist living in London, Johann Peter Salomon, who ran an important series of public concerts there. He offered a lucrative contract for Haydn to travel with him to London, and to compose six new symphonies for his series.

Haydn's music was, as in Paris, already famous in England, and he was received with rapture. While Salomon led the orchestra from his violin, Haydn, according to Charles Burney, 'presided at the piano-forte: and the sight of that renowned composer so electrified the audience, as to excite an attention and a pleasure superior to any that had ever, to my knowledge, been caused by instrumental music in England.' Burney stresses 'instrumental' music: only opera had aroused such passions before, and it was Haydn more than anyone who brought instrumental music to rival opera in audiences' affections. By the time Haydn had returned to Austria after a second visit, he had earned 24,000 florins, roughly half a million pounds today.

Wolfgang Amadeus Mozart was twenty-three years younger than Haydn, but despite the age difference, the two composers became great friends, and they influenced one another in their music. Haydn was a composer of enormous range, from joyful exuberance to dark tragedy. Mozart was too, but what distinguishes his music from Haydn's is the way he tinges the mood with suggestions of other emotions under the surface.

Finding the character of Mozart as a man is tricky. His letters to his family are full of crude jokes, with many 'farts' and 'shits' and the like. In the play and film *Amadeus*, writer Peter Shaffer uses these to portray Mozart as a childish buffoon somehow gifted with musical genius, to the frustration of the distinguished court composer, Antonio Salieri. But such crude private jokes were common in German children's rhymes and popular sayings of the time, and particularly in Salzburg. Mozart's mother, who was brought up in Salzburg, had almost as rich a vocabulary as Wolfgang in her letters. Of course, we can't know how much of this spilled over into Mozart's behaviour. Mozart's sister-in-law once described his character: 'even in the best of moods, he remained very pensive, always looking you keenly in the eye, replying in a considered way to everything, whether it be happy or sad, and yet he always seemed deep in thought and appeared to be working on something quite different'. Often his music seems like that too, giving the impression of someone who understands all the subtleties of the emotional landscape.

Wolfgang Mozart's father, Leopold, was a distinguished violinist, employed in the court of the Prince-Archbishop of Salzburg, and famous as the author of a treatise on violin-playing. When he discovered that he had two exceptionally gifted musicians as children, he seized the opportunity to capitalise on the possibilities. Wolfgang's elder sister, Maria Anna ('Nannerl') was four years older than Wolfgang, and showed great musical talent. Wolfgang and Nannerl were aged only seven and eleven respectively when their father organised a grand tour of the capitals of Europe. The children caused a sensation wherever they went. Wolfgang played and composed, developing in skill as the tour progressed, and learning from the musicians and composers he met on the way. How much more talented he was than his sister is impossible to say. Her father took the conventional view of the day that, as a girl, she could not be destined for a public career. Her talent, however great, was simply required to take a back seat to that of her brilliant young brother. Not a note of music by Nannerl survives.

For some years, Mozart was, like his father, employed at court by the Archbishop of Salzburg, but he hated the limited role he was given. In the end, he broke away and settled in Vienna, with no promise of regular employment. From time to time through his life he approached the most important courts of Europe in the hope of being given a post. But although his music was admired wherever he went, nothing came of these attempts. Perhaps after all there was something about his character that made it difficult for him to break into the formalities of court. In order to live, he relied on the support of individual patrons, and what he could earn from concerts, teaching and publications.

Mozart developed a particular reputation as a pianist: one contemporary described him as playing with 'a sensitivity that went straight to the heart'. Drawing on the example of Emanuel Bach, Mozart was one of the first players to understand the full expressive possibilities of this fairly new instrument, and he wrote a series of twenty-seven piano concertos, most of which he performed himself in concert. He also composed forty-one symphonies which, like the piano concertos, cover an enormous expressive range. In his late works, he created a uniquely subtle and powerful style – though these 'late' works were those of a young man. He died at the age of thirty-five, and it is poignant to think what he could have achieved if he had lived as long as Haydn.

One of the secrets of Mozart's success as a composer of music for instruments is the fact that, like Haydn, he was also an opera composer. His great operas – *Don Giovanni, Così fan tutte, The Marriage of Figaro, The Magic Flute* – encompass an extraordinary depth of emotion. You might expect that in a tragic opera, but it is particularly striking in the comic opera *The Marriage of Figaro*. This is based on a subversive comedy by the French playwright Pierre-Augustin Beaumarchais about servants outwitting their lecherous master. In the hands of Mozart and his librettist it becomes a deeper human drama, in which the characters experience a full range of emotions from anger and despair to joy and fulfilment. It is this operatic palette that Mozart brings to his instrumental music, as if it is populated by real characters, each with their entrances and exits, their achievements and their disappointments.

Mozart learned from Haydn the art of composing conversational string quartets, and he added a second viola to create a string quintet, bringing an extra richness to the conversation. On the last day that Mozart and Haydn spent together before Haydn left for London in 1790, the two friends played Mozart's quintets together, each taking one of the viola parts. The following year, while Haydn was away in London, he heard the news that Mozart was dead. He had died leaving his widow Constanze heavily in debt, was given only a basic funeral, and was buried in a common grave. Haydn was by now the most famous composer in Europe, and rapidly becoming one of the wealthiest. So it is touching to read what he wrote about Mozart to a mutual friend: 'For some time I was beside myself about his death and could not believe that Providence should so quickly have summoned such an irreplaceable man into the other world ... Friends often flatter me that I have some genius, but he stood far above me ... Posterity will not see such a talent again in a hundred years.'

CHAPTER 26

The Artist as Priest and Visionary

If there is poignancy in the short life of Mozart, there is struggle and tragedy in the life of Ludwig van Beethoven. He was born in 1770, fourteen years after Mozart, and like Mozart was a virtuoso on the piano. He was fortunate to rise to fame at a time when the new pianos were developing rapidly. Haydn had already encountered powerful pianos built by John Broadwood in London, and took advantage of their sonority in the sonatas he wrote late in life. Beethoven was an exceptional pianist and improviser, and stretched the instruments of his day to their limits. In some of his sonatas, he seems to be thinking and feeling well beyond the capabilities of the piano. Those who heard him play agreed that he was at his greatest when improvising. But even with a room full of aristocrats and patrons, he would only improvise if he was in the mood. If he did consent, he would often reduce the company to tears, and then laugh in their faces for their weakness.

He was a difficult man. But 'difficult' doesn't begin to describe the misfortune that afflicted him at the height of his powers. He was only thirty-two when he had to face the terrible realisation that he was going deaf. He hadn't even completed his second symphony. By the age of forty he, one of the greatest performers of his age, could no longer play the piano in public. Life became increasingly hard for him, and his truculent character became more and more difficult for his friends and supporters to handle. And yet, despite this tragedy, and maybe partly because of it, Beethoven battled his way through the difficulties to produce a stream of powerful and highly original works.

His sketchbooks and drafts are full of a confused scrawl of second and third thoughts, fierce crossings-out, with ideas for several different works jostling side by side. He had learned from Haydn the technique of trying to base a piece on little more than fragments, creating a logical and dramatic structure that would hold together precisely because of its reliance on so little material. Sometimes this is obvious: the first movement of his Fifth Symphony, with its arresting four-note motto-theme, is utterly uncompromising in its severe concentration on this idea, and echoes of it recur through all the four movements. In the Seventh Symphony, there is similar concentration on little ideas, but now the mood is predominantly joyful, and the energy of the concentration is irresistible, from a dancing first movement through to a whirlwind of a finale. The mighty Ninth Symphony, with its choral finale and its exceptional length, seems to spread its wings much more, with a great range of moods and material. But even here, all the themes are linked, jagged themes and calm themes alternating, until in the climactic 'Ode to Joy' the calm element triumphs.

When Beethoven moved to Vienna at the age of twenty-two, he was fortunate to be able to find his feet as a freelance musician. 'Freelance', however, did not mean quite what it would today. It meant attracting wealthy patrons who supported him with income and opportunities to perform, who found servants who could tolerate working for him, and who gave him the space to compose without the obligations of a traditional court post. This was what Mozart had attempted, with only patchy results. Beethoven was more successful, even though he was often rude and disrespectful to his patrons.

As well as truculent, Beethoven was also immensely high-minded. In the aftermath of the French Revolution, Napoleon Bonaparte rose to power as head of the French Republic. He promised to lead the struggle against tyranny and oppression across Europe and beyond, and the result was a decade of war. At first, Beethoven was an enthusiastic supporter of Napoleon, believing in his promise to free ordinary people. He intended to dedicate his Third Symphony, the 'Eroica', to him. But when he heard that Napoleon had proclaimed himself Emperor of France, he was enraged, and tore up the dedication.

Beethoven's one opera, *Fidelio*, is a heroic story of triumph against oppression, set in a jail full of political prisoners. Characteristically, it took him ten years to achieve its final form, after an unsuccessful production and lengthy rewriting. He was often dissatisfied with his work and would return doggedly to it again and again. But you might say he had the luxury of being able to do that. A composer employed by a court or church was obliged to produce music, and could not spend too much time revising. J. S. Bach or Joseph Haydn would not have lasted long in their posts if they had composed as slowly as Beethoven.

Partly because of his music, and partly because of his character and life-story, Beethoven became an iconic figure for later generations. His influence as a role model was mixed. On the one hand it is obviously a good thing if musicians, like Beethoven, have high aspirations. But belief in the importance of one's art can easily slip over into an arrogant belief that one is accountable to nobody. For a generation of musicians, poets and painters – the 'Romantics' of the early nineteenth century – the role of the artist took on something of the role of a priest. The understanding of creation, of the spirit, of what came to be known as the unconscious, had become a matter for artists as much as for conventional religion. Among composers, Beethoven was the first who insisted on his own stature as an artist, and whose music declared the importance of the task. This declaration can be felt echoing down the generations, encouraging composers to strive to express bigger and bigger ideas, and to think that they must constantly push ahead into new territory even if the audience is not ready to follow them.

For Haydn, Mozart and Beethoven, it was not just a matter of striding forward into the future. The past was immensely important to all of them. Two composers who had fallen out of fashion loomed large again: Johann Sebastian Bach (father of Emanuel) and Handel. Mozart mentions in a letter of 1782 that he went with a group of musicians every Sunday to the house of Baron van Swieten, the Vienna Court librarian, and they played from his collection of music by Bach and Handel. This had a profound effect on Mozart's style. His music took on an added richness because of a new, subtle attention to how all the parts interweave in counterpoint. Beethoven learned Bach's Forty-Eight Preludes and Fugues as a student. He too got to know Baron van Swieten's collection in Vienna, and he continued to study the scores of Bach and Handel all his life.

Beethoven's mighty Mass in D, the *Missa Solemnis*, shows the most obvious influence of the grandeur of Handel's oratorios and of Bach's Mass in B minor. You might expect that in a choral work. More surprising is the way that the spirit of Bach and Handel permeates Beethoven's late piano sonatas and string quartets, when, sunk in deafness, he struggled to preserve a sense of the sublime. He composed his Piano Sonata in A flat, Opus 110, at the same time as he was working on the *Missa Solemnis*. In the two slow movements, he quotes a sorrowful aria from Bach's St John Passion, sung at the moment of Jesus's death. And the sonata ends with two attempts at a fugue, the first of which falls back into the darkness of Bach's aria, and the second of which culminates in a climax of the utmost confidence and splendour, like a declaration of faith in an afterlife. Beethoven's late string quartets similarly have a sense of Bach-like spiritual serenity achieved through determined struggle.

Beethoven has become such a god-like figure that it sometimes seems as if all his music must be regarded as beyond criticism. But there is sometimes clumsiness amid the sublime, as his contemporaries acknowledged. His now-famous Symphony No. 3 (the 'Eroica') was reported to have struck most of its early audience in 1805 as 'too heavy and too long' and one reviewer found in it 'too much that is glaring and bizarre'. A composer of the next generation, the nineteen-year-old Franz Schubert, wrote in his diary in 1816 that he regretted 'the eccentricity that is common among most composers nowadays, and which is due almost entirely to one of our pure German artists; the eccentricity that combines and confuses the tragic with the comic, the agreeable with the ugly'. He means Beethoven, of course.

The really telling thing is that, as he matured as a composer, Schubert too found himself unable to resist the challenge of Beethoven. His late works, such as the Ninth Symphony and the String Quintet in C major, develop Beethoven's sense of determined persistence to produce enormously expanded musical journeys. But he does it in a way that is so utterly his own that we treasure it as Schubert, not as the echo of Beethoven. And one of the secrets of this is that Schubert found a way to combine the ambitious reach of Beethoven with the intimate, multi-layered melancholy of Mozart in order to create his own uniquely lyrical style.

By instinct, Schubert was a composer of songs above all else. He wrote more than 600, including two song cycles – *Die schöne Müllerin* (The Miller's Beautiful Daughter), and *Winterreise* (Winter's Journey). He was only seventeen when he composed one of his greatest songs, to words from Goethe's *Faust*: 'Gretchen at the spinning-wheel'. The intense, lyrical power of this song is breathtaking, and doubly so from a teenager. It conjures up vividly the young girl who has fallen under the spell of Faust but will be betrayed by him. That sense of the potency of song would remain with Schubert for his entire composing life, and it permeates his instrumental music as well as his songs. Unfortunately, he lived for even fewer years than Mozart – thirty-one – and who knows how different the music of the later nineteenth century would have been if he had lived into old age.

A little younger than Schubert, Felix Mendelssohn and Robert Schumann were the composers who were most seen as keeping the 'classical' flame of Haydn, Mozart and Beethoven alive into the next generation. Both were, like Schubert, major song composers. Mendelssohn's songs tend towards an intimate, comfortable melodiousness that was much appreciated in the drawing rooms of the cultured middle and upper classes. Schumann, though also a great melodist, had a darker side to him, which gives psychological depth to his songs. Their instrumental music differs in a similar way. Mendelssohn's finest works, from his brilliant teenage Octet for strings to his mature symphonies and Violin Concerto, have a spirit of glorious sunshine, with only passing clouds. Schumann wrote symphonies and concertos which are more troubled and struggling than Mendelssohn's. But it is in his solo piano music that Schumann is at his most complex and fascinating. His sets of pieces veer wildly in tone from energetic to contemplative, from anguished to serene. He was much inspired by the eccentric Romantic novelists, E. T. A. Hoffmann and Jean Paul, and named his own divided impulses as if they were characters in a novel: the inward-looking Eusebius, and the confident, outgoing Florestan.

Mendelssohn's and Schumann's music largely reflected their own personalities. Mendelssohn was an energetic and outgoing character. He founded a new music conservatoire in Leipzig. And he was one of the first of a new kind of orchestral conductor, who used a baton to guide orchestras through the increasingly complex modern scores. Schumann also attempted a career as a conductor, but he was too withdrawn and undiplomatic to make a success of it. Soon after giving up, his mental health collapsed and he ended his life in an asylum. It was his wife, Clara, who carried on pursuing a distinguished career as a pianist. We'll come to her in Chapter 28.

CHAPTER 27

Grand and Light, Sublime and Witty

One of Schubert's last songs is 'Der Doppelgänger' ('The Ghost-double'), a setting of a poem by Heinrich Heine. In it a young man revisits the house of his former sweetheart at night, to find a ghost of himself gazing up in anguish at her window. It is a terrifyingly simple setting, with a slow and relentless succession of dark chords. Ghost stories became a popular genre in Germany around 1800, and several were translated into French and English. It was some of these that inspired Mary Shelley to write her novel *Frankenstein* in 1816, about Dr Frankenstein's creation of a human being from dead body parts, reanimated by electricity. It was a story as much moral as horrifying, about the responsibility of the creator towards his creation.

The supernatural became a theme running through this period, and it entered opera with a bang in 1821, with Weber's *Der Freischütz* (The Marksman). Witches and sorceresses had long featured in opera, such as Handel's *Alcina* and Purcell's *Dido and Aeneas*. More recently Mozart, in his opera *Don Giovanni*, had portrayed a statue of a knight that comes to life and drags his murderer (Don Giovanni) down to hell. Weber brings a new, scary intensity to the stage, as magic bullets are forged with the help of the devil. This famous scene, set in the 'Wolf's Glen', takes previous methods of evoking storms or fear in opera to a new level, with sudden changes of pace, stabbing accents and shuddering chords. It evokes the sensation of being confronted with powers beyond our understanding, which the German philosopher Immanuel Kant had identified as the sense of the 'sublime'. It had an enormous influence on composers, not only of opera but also of instrumental music. One who seized on its possibilities was the virtuoso pianist Franz Liszt, who built overwhelmingly dramatic piano pieces from much the same musical elements as Weber in *Der Freischütz*.

Amid all this German-centred activity, the line of Italian opera was still going strong. The work that brought Mozart the greatest success of his short life was *The Marriage of Figaro*, an opera in Italian: in fact, not just *in* Italian, but deeply rooted in the tradition of comic opera that Mozart had first encountered during his tours in Italy as a boy. Haydn too wrote Italian comic operas. Only Beethoven, with his high-minded disdain of anything that he thought trivial, turned his back on the Italian opera tradition. And the most successful living composer in the early nineteenth century, financially as well as in popularity, was an Italian composer of comic opera, Gioachino Rossini. A wit, pragmatist and successful wheeler-dealer, Rossini was in some ways like an Italian echo of Handel (a German master of Italian opera). Rossini had an unfailing eye and ear for what people would like, and how to provide them with it. He saw off the competition effectively, and he, like Handel, made extensive reuse of his own material in different operas, sometimes adapting for a comedy an overture originally composed for a tragedy.

Although Rossini wrote tragic operas, it was the comedies that took the world by storm. *The Barber of Seville* was based on the play by Beaumarchais that preceded *The Marriage of Figaro*, and it gave the Italian comic tradition a fresh lick of paint. Rossini's genius was to combine the comedy with the Italian tradition of *bel canto* (beautiful song), a manner of singing that combined grace with elaborate ornamentation. You can hear echoes of both the wit and the *bel canto* right through nineteenth-century comic opera, from Donizetti's *Don Pasquale* in 1843 to Puccini's *Gianni Schicchi* in 1918. If Rossini was never taken quite so seriously as a composer of tragic opera, he did however surprise everyone by ending his career with an opera in French on the grandest scale, *William Tell*, staged in Paris in 1829. It is a serious drama about a Swiss peasants' revolt against Austrian tyranny. It lasts four hours, and owes as much to Weber's *Der Freischütz* and to French opera as to Italian models.

William Tell set in train the vogue for 'grand opera'. Chief among its composers was Giacomo Meyerbeer, a German composer who rose to fame in Paris. His operas are rarely staged nowadays, but in his day he was a great success, outdoing Weber in his sensational effects. In *Robert le Diable* (Robert the Devil, 1831), nuns rise from their graves, and are bewitched into dancing a devilish erotic ballet. In *Les Huguenots* (1836), there is a bathers' chorus, and in the final scene of *Le Prophète* (1849) the palace is consumed by flames.

Other composers who aspired to grand opera included the French composer Hector Berlioz. Unlike Meyerbeer, Berlioz had little success with opera in his lifetime: his grandest project, *The Trojans*, was not staged complete until long after his death. His vivid *Memoirs* reveal a larger-than-life figure, witty, passionate and ambitious, unwilling to be tied down to orthodox ways of doing things. It is his orchestral writing that is most characteristic, one moment delicately coloured and blended, the next bold and stark.

Meanwhile, Italian opera continued to flourish both in Italy and in Paris, with the work of Vincenzo Bellini and Gaetano Donizetti. It was in their operas that the Italian tradition of *bel canto* reached a climax, combined with the French taste for high drama. It takes singers of exceptional agility and finesse to negotiate the complex lines while remaining elegant and expressive – they have to sing like ballet dancers. These operas are particularly notable for their heroines: In Bellini's *Norma* (1831), the title role is the high priestess of the Druids under Roman occupation. Like many operas of this period it combines historical myth with personal tragedy, the music for the voice treading a fine line between elegant decoration and emotional depth. Donizetti's *Lucia di Lammermoor* (1835) is based on Walter Scott's historical novel *The Bride of Lammermoor*, featuring another tragic heroine. Forced to desert her lover and marry against her will, she ends up killing her husband on their wedding night. In the famous mad scene, Lucia appears in front of all the wedding guests in her nightgown covered with blood. Donizetti creates a touching effect by the contrast between this horrific situation and the elegant music which Lucia sings, culminating in a decorative duet with a solo flute – a favourite device of *bel canto*.

In the next decade, a new star rose to fame who was to dominate the world of Italian opera for the next fifty years. Giuseppe Verdi established his reputation with a series of operas on biblical and historical themes, beginning with *Nabucco* in 1842. The plot centres on the defeat of the Jews by the king of Babylon, Nebuchadnezzar, and their struggle for freedom is interwoven with a story of rival lovers. This was one of the operas that Italian audiences saw as echoing struggles of their own time. Northern Italy was ruled by the Austrians, and Verdi found himself elevated to a figurehead in the campaign for Italian freedom and unification. Over his long career he refined the elements of *bel canto* and grand opera to create increasingly powerful and subtle dramas. His international reputation was cemented with the operas he wrote in the 1850s, *Rigoletto*, *Il Trovatore* and *La Traviata*.

Bellini and Donizetti's operas are all about the voice, and the orchestra has little more than an accompanying role. Verdi was a master of the orchestra as well as the voice, but still his aim was to express the drama through the great tradition of Italian singing. Richard Wagner, an exact contemporary of Verdi, developed a very different approach to opera. He saw himself as a reformer, like his fellow German Gluck in the previous century, and aimed to save opera from what he saw as the corruption of the Italians and the French. He is another of those characters who, like Beethoven, seemed to later generations to represent a culmination and a turning point in the great line of German music. Wagner was always keen to demolish the reputation of his rivals, and declared Meyerbeer's operas 'monstrous', no more than a 'dramatic hotch-potch'. But he certainly picked up a few tricks from Meyerbeer: his grand four-opera cycle, *The Ring of the Nibelung*, begins with three maidens singing while they swim in the river Rhine, and ends with the palace of the gods consumed by flames, echoing two of Meyerbeer's most celebrated scenes.

Wagner, like Beethoven, took his role as an artist extremely seriously. He declared that it was the purpose of art 'to save the spirit of religion'. This echoed the words of his fellow disruptor, the pianist-composer Franz Liszt, who had said, 'when the altar is cracked and tumbling ... art must emerge from the temple [and] say, "Let there be light"'. Together Liszt and Wagner proposed what came to be known as 'The Music of the Future', which would build on the ground-breaking achievements of Beethoven (particularly his massive Ninth Symphony), and strive to fulfil the Romantic aspiration of expressing the inexpressible.

To achieve this, Wagner and Liszt developed a way of writing highly fluid music, loosening the old formal procedures to produce a more 'improvisational' style. To retain some sense of structure, Liszt had developed the 'transformation of themes', whereby themes not only reappear, but are also transformed, by being slowed down or speeded up, given different harmonies or rhythms, and so on. This was not new – Liszt's prime inspiration for the idea was Schubert. Wagner in his later operas took this to its logical extreme, giving every character or concept in an opera its own *leitmotif* (guiding motif), representing Siegfried, The Sword, Death, and so on. These motifs provide the listener with a constant supply of recognisable reference points, creating an impression of coherence through an enormously long span. *The Ring of the Nibelung* is Wagner's most massive work, consisting of four operas (*Das Rheingold, Die Walküre, Siegfried, Götterdämmerung*), and it was first performed complete in 1876. *Götterdämmerung* (The Twilight of the Gods) lasts four and a half hours. Wagner's aim was what he grandly called a *Gesamtkunstwerk* ('complete artwork'). This concept returned once again to the source that had inspired the first operas, ancient Greek tragedy, with its unique blending of poetry, music and choreography.

Wagner's intention was to make the force of the words stand out, avoiding anything that would obscure their meaning. The singers therefore sing almost always one at a time, not in duet or ensemble, so that their words are clear. Only rarely are there choruses – except in *Die Meistersinger* (The Mastersingers), where the people of Nuremberg play a major role. The predominant style is a kind of stately recitative, which would be monotonous if it were not for Wagner's command of the orchestra. It is the orchestra that plays all the motifs, which are hardly ever sung, and these are woven into an ever-changing tapestry. In his earlier operas, he wrote beautiful and satisfyingly moulded arias, such as Wolfram's hymn to the evening star in *Tannhäuser*. There is nothing as formally constructed in Wagner's late operas, the *Ring* cycle or his last opera *Parsifal*. He reserves anything really 'song-like' for rare, climactic moments, where they have an overwhelming effect: the moment in Act I of *Die Walküre* where Siegmund and Sieglinde declare their love, and the god Wotan's farewell to his daughter, Brünnhilde, in Act III of the same opera.

One of the ways in which Wagner had a major impact on music history was his enormous range of harmonies. When he evokes the depths of the river Rhine at the opening of *Das Rheingold*, he builds sweeping arpeggios on a simple, unchanging chord. By contrast, *Tristan and Isolde* begins with a prelude whose harmonies twist and turn without ever finding resolution, a powerful way of suggesting the anguish of the two lovers. This huge range of harmonic styles struck later composers very forcefully. Should they adopt this method, take it further? Gustav Mahler, who expanded the symphony as Wagner had expanded opera, also has a huge range of harmony, from the simplicity of folk song in his Fourth Symphony to tortured darkness in the Ninth Symphony and *Das Lied von der Erde* (The Song of the Earth). Richard Strauss later took Wagnerian dissonance to an extreme in his operas *Salome* and *Elektra*, in both cases evoking an atmosphere of fevered intensity and violence. Arnold Schoenberg went even further to what he saw as a logical extreme, abandoning conventional ideas of harmony altogether.

Wagner supported those who wholeheartedly adopted his point of view, including Anton Bruckner, whose naive worship of Wagner fed into his monumental symphonies. But composers who were opposed to his and Liszt's New Music were treated by Wagner as enemies. Johannes Brahms had unwisely published a 'manifesto' against the New German School in 1860, making him Wagner's main target. His First Symphony was dismissed by Wagner as 'little chips of melody like an infusion of hay and old tea leaves'. Brahms was to become the leading German composer of more traditional symphonies, concertos, sonatas, string quartets and songs. He admired Wagner up to a point, but Wagner's antagonism ensured that the public perceived them as rivals in a war for the future of German music.

In France, there were devotees of Wagner, such as César Franck and his pupils, who created a dense and rich version of Wagnerian harmony. But there were other French composers who took a sideways course away from Wagnerism. Charles Gounod was best known for his opera, *Faust*. He retained the clarity of traditional harmonies and was most admired for his gift of lyrical melody. Georges Bizet's opera *Carmen* is a story of doomed love between a fiery gypsy girl and a young soldier. Bizet uses an almost Wagnerian range of harmony, but with an appealing directness and simplicity that makes *Carmen* one of the most enduringly popular operas.

Wagner's and Liszt's use of *leitmotifs* and transformation of themes was taken up by countless later composers, including many of those mentioned in the previous paragraphs. By the late nineteenth century almost all major composers had absorbed what they found useful of Wagner's ideas. But they were able to do this while maintaining their individual, and national, characteristics. Among the composers who accepted some Wagnerian influence while maintaining a safe distance were Verdi, Tchaikovsky, Smetana,

Dvořák, Musorgsky, Rimsky-Korsakov, Puccini and Debussy. We'll meet them all in later chapters.

Meanwhile there was an eager market for 'lighter' music in more informal venues. Vaudeville, musical entertainment catering to a wide audience, had been popular since the eighteenth century, incorporating everything from popular songs and dance tunes to parodies of famous scenes from operas. In the 1850s this developed into operetta, light opera with spoken dialogue. Jacques Offenbach established his own theatre for comic one-act pieces in Paris in 1855. His first fully fledged operetta *Orpheus in the Underworld* (1858) was a huge success. Then the operetta spread to Vienna, the centre of the international craze for the waltz. The chief composer of waltzes, Johann Strauss II, realised the potential of his dance music to capitalise on Offenbach's success with operetta. Strauss's *Die Fledermaus* (The Bat, 1874) became the most frequently performed operetta worldwide.

CHAPTER 28

Women Playing at Home and Abroad

The lives and works of the composers who have come to be regarded as 'great' have dominated most histories of Western music. But there has always been a whole world of music-making below this elite and public level, and I have tried to pay attention to it through this book. It is much more difficult to get hold of because the evidence is scattered. But scholars find out more and more about this vanished world as time goes by, and by the nineteenth century we can have quite a good idea of what was going on.

This was the last century before the arrival of recordings and broadcasting. People never heard music unless they were in the presence of musicians or were making music themselves. There was therefore, as there had always been, an almost universal need to make music oneself, or to find people who were making it.

There was a huge demand for musicians among all classes. At lower levels of society there were street musicians and popular entertainers. With the rise of the middle and professional classes over the eighteenth and nineteenth centuries, there was surging demand for music to play or sing at home and the instruments on which to play it. The piano, which at first was very expensive, was increasingly affordable, so that ordinary homes aspired to have a little piano in the living room. Piano manufacture boomed across the Western world. At the top end, Viennese and English instruments were particularly esteemed, but there were local makers supplying the domestic market in many countries. In Russia the Empress Catherine the Great had ordered a piano from London as early as 1774. By 1860 there were thirty manufacturers of pianos in the Russian cities of Moscow and St Petersburg, supplying homes of the rapidly increasing population. Similarly, in the United States the piano was the most popular instrument by the late nineteenth century.

But the market for pianos did not exist in isolation. It was supported by publishers, who produced sheet music of everything from the latest popular songs and dances to piano arrangements of symphonies and opera arias. Even the most esteemed composers devoted time to this amateur market. Haydn wrote piano trios for the domestic market, Mozart and Beethoven wrote some relatively easy piano pieces. Robert Schumann wrote not only virtuoso music but also albums 'For the Young'; some of Mendelssohn's *Songs without Words* and some of Chopin's shorter pieces require only a modest technique. Piano music was published in regular monthly magazines: Tchaikovsky composed his suite *The Seasons* for one in Russia, published in twelve monthly instalments. Brahms published his Waltzes in two editions, one simplified for the less accomplished performer, and Edvard Grieg wrote sets of *Lyric Pieces* for people to play at home. Orchestral works were arranged for piano duet. It was in this form that people first got to know the latest symphonies, when opportunities to hear them played by an orchestra were few and far between.

The level at which people played and sang varied enormously, from that of hesitant beginners to a virtually professional standard. Amateur musicians would collect large quantities of sheet music – some printed, others copied out by hand – and bind them together. The family of the novelist Jane Austen possessed many volumes of music for piano, harp and voice, and domestic music-making features in her novels written in the early years of the nineteenth century. Similar volumes were popular in the United States too among the well-off white population. A few examples have even been found of freed Black young women who were fortunate enough to have such collections, and the time to play them.

Music was, of course, only one of several pastimes habitually carried out in the home. Reading was important too. In the nineteenth century it was still the custom for people to read out loud. There are many paintings and descriptions of domestic scenes in which someone is reading to members of the family. This is often a woman reading to other women, but it could also be the head of the household reading to the whole family, most often from the Bible. People were appointed to read aloud to servants, soldiers, and workers in factories, and reading the Bible at mealtimes had been a custom in monasteries and convents for many centuries. This habit of reading aloud is an important context to bear in mind. Today, music at home mostly means recorded music played through loudspeakers or headphones, just as reading usually means reading silently to oneself. The age-old habit of singing and playing to each other went hand in hand with the timeless custom of reading to one another.

The piano was widely regarded as the most suitable instrument for a girl or young lady, and playing it was one of the accomplishments that would help to attract a husband. Some young women were put to hours of reluctant practice, others took real pleasure in music and attained a high level. Unlike a violin, the piano could be played modestly, without distortions of the body or unseemly movements of the arms. To guide young players, there were instruction books which sold in large numbers, and there were many teachers. These were not just musicians but, in effect, educators of young women in etiquette and deportment. This is the latest example of the linking of music and etiquette that we encountered in Castiglione's *Book of the Courtier* three centuries earlier, but now it has trickled down to the newly 'respectable' middle classes.

Society across Europe and North America still discouraged even the most talented women from pursuing a public career as performers. And because their playing was restricted to private circles few of them would have had access to the highest level of music tuition. The new music conservatories admitted some women, but they were not generally given the same level of training as the men, because they were expected to become teachers or amateur musicians; few rose to be professionals on the public stage. But there were examples across the nineteenth century of women who made an exceptional mark as pianists, and even some who broke through the barrier to public performance which was overwhelmingly dominated by men.

Already at the end of the eighteenth century, Mozart and Haydn had written some of their most demanding piano music for women pianists. Haydn's most difficult piano sonatas were composed for Therese Jansen, a pianist he got to know in London. She was one of the best pupils of Muzio Clementi, a celebrated pianist, composer and manufacturer of pianos. Jansen never pursued a public career as a performer, but she had a great reputation as a piano teacher. In France, Hélène de Montgeroult, a pianist from an aristocratic family, narrowly escaped execution in the French Revolution, and was appointed the first ever woman professor at the newly founded Paris Conservatoire in 1795. Renowned as a pianist and teacher, she published one of the first progressive piano courses in 1816. It was republished across Europe over many years. Frédéric Chopin, one of the most famous composer-pianists of the next generation, certainly knew it: one of his most famous studies (the 'Revolutionary') echoes one of Montgeroult's studies very closely. Another woman pianist-composer who influenced Chopin was Maria Szymanowska, a fellow Pole, who wrote studies, mazurkas, waltzes and preludes that are like simpler prototypes of the pieces that Chopin composed twenty and more years later.

The most famous woman pianist in the nineteenth century was Clara Schumann, wife of the composer Robert Schumann. Her father, Friedrich Wieck, was a leading piano teacher, and when he realised what talent young Clara had, he pushed her into the public realm rather as Leopold Mozart had done to Wolfgang and Nannerl Mozart. Unlike Nannerl, Clara Schumann had a public career for over sixty years, from her debut with the Leipzig Gewandhaus Orchestra at the age of nine. She was the only woman pianist to rival in fame the male nineteenth-century virtuosi of the day. Once she had married, she abandoned brilliant display pieces to concentrate on music of emotional depth, from J. S. Bach and Beethoven to her husband Robert Schumann. She matured into an elderly, highly respected figure with a serious demeanour and a great reputation as a teacher, described by Liszt and others as a 'priestess' of music. In her early years she composed beautiful piano and chamber music. But her husband, Robert, made it clear at their marriage that her primary duty would be to home and family (they had eight children), and she gradually lost heart in her ability to compose. She did, however, continue playing and touring, in between giving birth, and was the main breadwinner of the family while her husband descended into mental illness.

One thing that links Clara Schumann, Maria Szymanowska and Hélène de Montgeroult is the importance of the 'salon', the gatherings of musicians, poets, artists and patrons that formed a vital support system for musicians from the mid-eighteenth to the early twentieth century. Today, if a young pianist rises to the point of pursuing a public career, there is an international network of concert halls, festivals and concert agents and promoters to help arrange performances and tours, and there are international competitions to bring young pianists to attention. In the nineteenth century, the supporting of performers was a matter of word of mouth, connections between connoisseurs and patrons, and informal 'networking'. None of these methods has gone away, but in those days it was vital to find an entrée into the society in which such people were to be found, and one of the prime methods of doing so was through the salons. Many of them were presided over by wealthy women, often high-born, and sometimes truly knowledgeable connoisseurs of music. Some were performers themselves: Montgeroult ran an important salon in Paris. Szymanowska and Clara Schumann were able to arrange their concert tours through networks of salons hosted by people who put their own money into promoting their favourite performers.

In Germany and Austria, string-playing in groups, mostly carried out by men, was a particularly treasured pastime. Players in these countries were acutely aware of the great German legacy of string quartets from Haydn to Beethoven and Schubert, which continued through the nineteenth century to Mendelssohn, Schumann, Brahms and others. In Beethoven's day, the string quartet was still a genre principally for private enjoyment, though it was sometimes played in concerts of mixed repertoire. When Beethoven wrote his String Quartet in F minor, Opus 95, in 1810, he included a note: 'N.B. This Quartet is written for a small circle of connoisseurs and is never to be performed in public.' It was only in 1823 that the very first series of concerts dedicated to string quartets was inaugurated in Vienna, by Beethoven's friend the violinist Ignaz Schuppanzigh. This marked a significant move out of the home, and gave the first public voice to Beethoven's even more difficult later quartets.

Around the same time there are reports of the musical evenings that gathered round the composer Franz Schubert. He was much less widely known than Beethoven in his lifetime, and his own playing was mostly carried out in private circles. Amid a group of friends he would sing his songs, accompanying himself on the piano. Then there would be food and drink, followed by dancing, for which Schubert would play the piano (it is difficult to imagine the fiery Beethoven playing for dancing). This is the most informal end of a spectrum of dance activities that were extremely popular in the nineteenth century. At the upper end of society dancing-masters had been engaged for centuries, teaching the latest dances as they emerged, often from France, spreading across Europe and crossing the Atlantic. Now, at home, the ladies who learned the piano played for family dancing, and in grander households and at formal events there would be a group of instrumentalists or even a small orchestra.

The great new dance craze of the nineteenth century was the waltz, whose popularity extended from modest households all the way to the top of society. As I have already mentioned, Vienna became famous as the centre of this waltz craze, and its composers used waltzes and other popular dances as the basis of spectacularly successful international careers. Pre-eminent in this field was the Strauss family. The elder Johann Strauss formed his own dance orchestra in 1825, and quickly established a reputation at the annual carnival in Vienna. Soon he was touring to other countries with his orchestra. Johann Strauss II, son of the elder Johann, took over the business, becoming even more famous than his father, and touring with his orchestra further and further abroad. But that takes us to a whole new topic: mechanical transport, and the Industrial Revolution that made it possible.

CHAPTER 29

Finding the Audience

At the end of the eighteenth century and the beginning of the nine-teenth, the development of machines made it possible to produce goods quickly and in large quantities by centralising labour in facto-ries. The poor flooded into cities to find work, creating an industrial 'working class' in which life was very different from that of the tradi-tional rural poor. There might be a steadier income to be earned as a worker in a factory, but the hours were brutally long. The vast profits from all this industrial activity went not to the workers, who were paid very little, but to the factory-owners and shareholders, who grew rich. The need for managers, lawyers and others to support the new industry led to a steady growth in the urban middle classes, and the towns and cities increased enormously in size. We have already seen how music and other entertainments fed the needs of the middle class with opera, concerts, and music at home. Now in the nineteenth century the 'music industry' became bigger and more established, with permanent opera houses, orchestras, music colleges (conservatoires) and music publishing on a greater scale than ever before.

Conservatoires to teach musicians to a professional standard proliferated. There was a new emphasis on instruments, and the training of orchestral players. I've already mentioned the pioneering orchestras of Paris and Mannheim. In most European countries it was opera houses that employed the greatest number of orchestral musicians. As the nineteenth century progressed, opera orchestras increasingly gave concert series, and 'symphony orchestras' were founded as separate institutions. The Leipzig Gewandhaus Orchestra was unusual in having been a regular concert orchestra since the 1780s, rising to fame when Felix Mendelssohn took over as its conductor in 1835. It was during the nineteenth century that many of the famous orchestras of Europe and North America were founded, in Vienna, Berlin, Amsterdam, New York, Boston and Chicago.

The audiences for orchestral concerts were generally middle- to upper-class. But as well as what we would now call 'classical' concerts, there were also programmes of lighter orchestral music through the nineteenth century, and these attracted a broader range of social classes. The composer Philippe Musard had immense success with these popular concerts in Paris in the 1830s. The audience was free to walk around, take food and drink, and even dance to the quadrilles and other dances that were played together with a selection of light classics and new pieces. The pattern was copied in London, in effect bringing indoors the long-standing tradition of concerts in pleasure gardens. This gave rise to the 'Promenade Concerts' that continue, on a much grander scale, to this day. There were similar popular concerts with cheap tickets in Berlin.

Series of orchestral concerts generally took place through a season extending from autumn to spring. Over the summer, musicians found work in the spas, hotels, seaside and lakeside resorts scattered across Europe, in which many groups and small orchestras played for the entertainment of guests. There were also music festivals. In England, ever since the success of Handel's oratorios, amateur choral societies had flourished. The biggest musical events of the year were the choral festivals lasting several days, at Leeds, Sheffield and Birmingham, and the Handel Festival at London's Crystal Palace. Major new works were composed for these festivals by the leading composers of the day. And one of the most striking features of these festivals was that the upper chorus parts were sung by women. The church choirs were all male, and always had been. The choral societies presented women with new opportunities for public music-making. However, it was not until the twentieth century that women were admitted to professional orchestras.

The prize for the most ambitious festival must go to Wagner, and his establishment of the Bayreuth Festival dedicated to perfor-mances of his own operas. Having settled on Bayreuth for his new opera house, he needed to raise a huge amount of money. This was just at the time that the various German states had come together into a unified Germany in 1871. Wagner was able to represent his project as a great German enterprise, and set up Wagner Societies to raise money for it in major centres. King Ludwig II of Bavaria, who had for years been devoted to Wagner, provided a large loan to make the enterprise possible, and the first festival in Wagner's new theatre took place in August 1876. Despite the artistic and social success of the festival, it lost so much money that Wagner was not able to repeat it for six years. The second festival took place only a few months before Wagner's death, with the premiere of *Parsifal*.

All this musical activity meant that there were more ready-made venues and organisations that could give opportunities to composers, so they could plan major works with more confi-dence than before. The grandeur of orchestral projects reached a climax with Gustav Mahler, most of whose symphonies are on a massive scale. Mahler was a great conductor, as Wagner had been, and was for several years the music director of the Vienna Opera, transforming its standards of performance. He was able to mount successful performances of his own works in Vienna and other cities in Austria and Germany. From 1902 he regularly conducted his works in Amsterdam with the Concertgebouw Orchestra, whose conductor, Willem Mengelberg, was a great enthusiast for Mahler's work.

The Industrial Revolution led to new techniques for constructing instruments, from which composers benefited. By around 1850, trumpets and French horns in most orchestras had acquired valves, which enabled the player to add extra lengths of tubing. This meant that they could play any note at will, not just the notes of the harmonic series. This fed into the brass band, in which the new, easily played instruments led to a great surge in the number of bands associated with the military, town authorities and the factories and mills. Flute, clarinet, oboe and bassoon had improved systems of keys for the fingers. Changes to stringed instruments and their bows made them more powerful. Indeed, the whole trend of the orchestra was towards greater and greater power.

Meanwhile, the mechanisation of organ-building led to new styles of instrument in which the selection of pipes, and therefore volume and tone-colour, could be varied at will. Aristide Cavaillé-Coll in France and Henry Willis in England were leaders in this new technology, and their splendid instruments are still to be found in many of the major churches and cathedrals of France and Britain.

Travelling to different cities to conduct, play or sing was made much easier by the development of railways across Europe and North America, and musicians also crossed the Atlantic more and more frequently on steamships. Previously, orchestras rarely played outside their own cities. But now travelling by train meant that whole orchestras could tour. The Meiningen Court Orchestra was the first symphony orchestra to tour regularly, travelling from Germany by train and ship as far as London and Copenhagen. Sometimes, complete opera productions with their sets would be transported by train.

Among smaller ensembles, it was Johann Strauss II, the 'Waltz King', who grasped the new opportunities. In 1847–8 he and his orchestra spent six months in Hungary and Romania. Then they were invited to Russia by the newly established railway company of St Petersburg to play during the summer of 1856. Their visit was such a success that they returned every summer for the next nine years. Strauss's most famous waltz, 'The Blue Danube', was premiered during another tour at the Paris World Fair in 1867.

Many of the musicians who took advantage of the rail network were famous individual performers, particularly the new breed of virtuoso pianists. They benefited from several consequences of the Industrial Revolution: the train made international travel possible; the audiences in the growing cities were large enough for musicians to make good money from public performances; and the instruments on which pianists played were undergoing change. From the 1850s, grand pianos increasingly had iron frames, which meant that they stayed in tune longer. Strings could be thicker and pulled to higher tension, making the instrument louder and more suited to large concert halls and the strings less likely to break. The most famous virtuoso of them all, Franz Liszt, who pioneered the public recital, had toured before this, playing on the wooden-framed pianos. It was routine for a spare piano or two to be kept ready for when Liszt's powerful playing caused the strings to start breaking. If you listen to his flamboyant virtuoso works – concertos, Hungarian Rhapsodies, phenomenally difficult studies – it is easy to imagine the scene.

Liszt's contemporary, Frédéric Chopin, also travelled extensively by rail. He was a very different character and player from Liszt. Though he also played on the older, wooden-framed pianos, his style of playing was much more intimate, without outward show. He was reserved and aloof by temperament, and his health was frail. So he preferred to play in salons and other small venues. His playing was subtle and lyrical, and his music reflects this. He shows a wonderful understanding of the possibilities of piano sonorities, from the delicacy of his mazurkas, waltzes and nocturnes to the intense drama of his ballades.

The overwhelming majority of travelling virtuosi were, of course, men. But there were a few women who toured and became famous. One of the most remarkable was Maria Szymanowska, a Polish pianist and composer, whom I mentioned earlier as a composer who influenced Chopin. She was lucky to have a wealthy and artistic family who supported her in her ambition to play in public – indeed, she could not have pursued her touring career without them. When her husband opposed her public career, the couple divorced. Maria's parents looked after her children, and she embarked on an astonishing international career, drawing on networks of musicians, aristocrats and their salons to smooth her entry to centres across Europe. This was in the 1820s, before the development of railways in Europe, so she had to travel everywhere by horse-drawn coach, accompanied by her brother and sister who took care of all the practical and social arrangements. Her first tour lasted four years, taking in Germany, France, England, Italy and finally Russia.

I have already mentioned pianist and composer Clara Schumann. She was only twelve when her father, the piano-teacher Friedrich Wieck, took her on tour in 1831, again before the advent of the railways. During her marriage, she travelled with her husband Robert, in between giving birth to eight children. Then, after his death in 1854, she toured in her own right again, using her extensive connections with friends and admirers across Europe. By now there were many centres that could be reached by train, enabling her to play concerts in different cities a few days apart, rather than a few weeks. She continued travelling and teaching into her seventies.

Many singers and conductors took to the railways and the trans-Atlantic steamships. One of the most celebrated was the Swedish soprano, Jenny Lind, known as the 'Swedish Nightingale'. In 1850 she crossed the Atlantic, and gave concerts as far north as Canada, and as far south as New Orleans and Cuba. A private railway coach was specially arranged for her, and she was such a star that Jenny Lind merchandise was on sale – scarves, handkerchiefs, even sausages.

Also touring North America in the 1850s was a former slave, Elizabeth Taylor Greenfield, who came to be known as the 'Black Swan' by analogy with the 'Swedish Nightingale'. She is reckoned to be the first African American singer to achieve fame both sides of the Atlantic. In England she sang to Queen Victoria at Buckingham Palace. Her repertoire included opera arias, but also more homely songs that were popular in the United States, such as Stephen Foster's 'Old Folks at Home'.

There was by the mid-nineteenth century a thriving appetite in North America for both classical European and more home-grown lighter music. It was at the domestic end of the musical spectrum that a specifically 'American' music was developing. This included the songs of Stephen Foster and others, many inspired by the 'Negro spirituals' of African Americans. At the level of formal concerts, it was more difficult for American composers to break through the predominance of European, and particularly German, taste: it was not until the twentieth century that American works were routinely included in orchestral concerts in the United States.

This makes all the more remarkable the achievements of Amy Beach. She began to make a name for herself as a pianist in Boston in 1883 when she was only sixteen. But when she married two years later, she agreed with her husband to limit her appearances to two charity concerts a year. This did not stop her composing, and she wrote a large quantity of music which is only now becoming widely known. An important landmark was the premiere of her Gaelic Symphony, performed by the Boston Symphony Orchestra in 1896 to great acclaim. It was the first large-scale work by a woman composer to be performed by a major symphony orchestra in the United States. Beach was immediately welcomed into the company of fellow Bostonian composers, including George Chadwick, Horatio Parker and Edward MacDowell, who, with the addition of Beach, became known as the 'Boston Six'. If their names are not as well-known as they might be, it is because, like Beach, they wrote in a fairly traditional European style that was soon to seem old-fashioned, as the twentieth century brought in new and radical ways of making music.

CHAPTER 30

Longing for My Own Country

The idea of bringing 'folk' music into formal compositions goes back a very long way. But the broader idea that music can have national characteristics is something that rose to prominence in the nineteenth century, hand in hand with the rise of political nationalism. As the century wore on, composers were looking for styles that belonged specifically to their native country. And for this they looked to music that seemed to have been there for ever: the music of rural communities and the ancient music of the church.

The Polish composer and pianist, Frédéric Chopin, whom we met in the previous chapter, first made a name for himself with music deeply infused with national spirit. In 1831 he was in Paris when he heard that the Russians had crushed a Polish uprising, and he realised that he could not return home to Poland. He spent the rest of his short life in exile, composing and playing music which is full of nostalgia. Sometimes, as in his polonaises, it has a strong patriotic spirit. More often, it seems to exude the longing of the exile, remembering the songs and dances of his country, and using them to express delight in something much loved and lament for something lost. His mazurkas, based on various traditional Polish dances, are wonderfully varied between these two extremes, sometimes combining both in the same piece.

But Chopin was not just a patriot. He had been brought up loving Italian opera – Rossini, Bellini, Donizetti – sung with expressive freedom by the great Italian singers. And he had been struck by the power of the virtuoso Italian violinist, Niccolò Paganini. In his piano music, Chopin combines Italian expression and virtuosity with the traditional Polish elements in a unique way.

Meanwhile, a young Russian composer was heading in a more radical direction. Mikhail Glinka had been brought up studying the German and Italian classics, as was usual in Russia. In the early 1830s he spent three years in Italy. But his attempts to write in the Italian style felt unnatural and awkward. As he wrote, 'We inhabitants of the North feel differently. With us it is either frantic jollity, or bitter tears . . . A longing for my own country led me gradually to the idea of writing in a Russian manner.' Glinka took characteristics of Russian folk song – repetitions, terse phrases, insistent rhythms, hints of Asian scales – and created a musical expression of what he saw as the Russian character. Glinka's chief works were two operas, *A Life for the Tsar* and *Ruslan and Ludmila*. With their vivid effects and daring contrasts, they provided a model for later Russian composers of opera. But one of the next generation, Pyotr Ilyich Tchaikovsky, said that if you wanted to understand the importance of Glinka all you needed to hear was his little orchestral piece, *Kamarinskaya*. This is a simple set of variations on a fast Russian folk song. All Glinka does is repeat it again and again, changing the instrumental colours, harmonies and counterpoints at each repetition, a technique inspired by the traditional Russian bands that played at weddings.

In the next generation, the composer Mily Balakirev gathered round him a group of young composers that included Modest Musorgsky, Alexander Borodin and Nikolai Rimsky-Korsakov. Inspired by Glinka, Balakirev encouraged them to use folk (or folk-like) material in constructing large-scale works. Russian composers varied in their approach to this material. Musorgsky was the most daring, using stark and wild effects. And he also developed a distinctive way of setting the rhythms of Russian speech, most notably in his monumental opera *Boris Godunov*. At the opposite extreme, Tchaikovsky distanced himself from Balakirev's group by saying, 'though born Russians, we are at the same time even more Europeans'. He particularly admired Mozart and Mendelssohn, and you can hear their influence in the lightness and elegance of Tchaikovsky's ballet scores, *Swan Lake*, *The Sleeping Beauty* and *The Nutcracker*. But there is still enough of the flavour of folk music for Tchaikovsky to sound distinctly Russian.

This range of Russian approaches persisted right the way through into the twentieth century. At the stark and uncompromising end, there is Stravinsky's *The Rite of Spring*, which caused uproar at its premiere in Paris in 1913. It is built almost entirely from little folk-like (and actual folk) elements, which pile up relentlessly. At the most 'Western' end, there is Sergei Rachmaninoff, who wrote symphonies and piano concertos. His sombre melodies owe as much to the chanting of the Russian Orthodox Church as to folk music. And between those two, Prokofiev and Shostakovich drew on all the tradition of Western symphony-writing, but with a distinctly Russian hard edge.

The idea of developing a national voice was particularly strong in countries under the Austrian Empire, which had evolved from the Holy Roman Empire. In 1860 some limited political independence was allowed to Bohemia and other countries within the Austrian Empire. This helped to boost a focus on local cultures, including music. Bedřich Smetana was to the Bohemians what Glinka was to the Russians. He was appointed music director of a new Czech theatre in Prague, where in 1866 he staged his most famous work, *The Bartered Bride*. This is an opera in the Czech language, set among ordinary village folk. Like all educated Bohemians, Smetana had been brought up speaking German: the native language, Czech, was only spoken by the poorest and least educated layers of society, and Smetana had to learn Czech in order to set it to music.

In Smetana's orchestra at the opera house in Prague was a young viola player, Antonin Dvořák, who, inspired by Smetana, rose to be his successor as the leading Bohemian composer. Dvořák was the son of a village innkeeper and butcher, so unlike Smetana he was brought up speaking Czech. Dvořák wanted to reconcile national Czech elements with both the 'New German' freedoms of Liszt and Wagner and the older 'classical' styles of Beethoven and Mendelssohn. Brahms, a highly influential figure in Viennese circles, helped him to gain an Austrian State Stipend, which gave him an income to compose. Dvořák wanted to stay true to his roots, but Viennese critics were sometimes hostile to the Bohemian folk ingredients of his music. The skill with which Dvořák found his way through this minefield is remarkable. His mature works – Symphonies Nos 6–9, his opera *Rusalka* – feel pastoral and Bohemian (with an ingredient of African American spirituals in the Ninth Symphony), but at the same time they are as rigorously structured as the music of Brahms.

In the next generation after Dvořák came Leoš Janáček. These days we think of both Dvořák and Janáček as 'Czechs', but Janáček was from Moravia, to the east of Dvořák's Bohemia. Janáček developed a deep interest in Moravian folk music, with its distinct dialect and speech rhythms, and its characteristics became fundamental to Janáček's own style. His music has a distinctly 'spoken' sound even when there are no voices. The full extent of Janáček's radical approach is heard in his operas, *Jenůfa*, *Kátya Kabanová* and *The Cunning Little Vixen*. The voices sing with a fascinating new version of the almost-recitative developed by Wagner. They stick closely to the rhythms of the Czech language, over an orchestral palette that is continually surprising with its stark and vivid colours.

Back in the 1840s, the virtuoso pianist Franz Liszt wrote and performed the first of his series of Hungarian Rhapsodies. Liszt was Hungarian by birth, and used the style of Hungarian Romani gypsies, with its alternation between melancholy and exuberance, to create powerful concert pieces. Partly through Liszt's influence, this gypsy style became a popular ingredient in formal works of music, from the finales of violin concertos (Bruch and Brahms) to Viennese operettas (Johann Strauss II's *The Gypsy Baron*).

By the turn of the twentieth century, another Hungarian, Béla Bartók, was studying with a pupil of Liszt at the Budapest Academy and learned to play Liszt's Hungarian Rhapsodies. But then, one day in 1904, he overheard a servant girl from the Hungarian countryside singing to a baby a folk song about an apple fallen in the water. It was a revelation. Bartók was used to listening to the gypsy musicians in the streets and cafés of Budapest, but suddenly he felt that he was hearing the true music of the people.

Bartók and a fellow student, Zoltán Kodály, embarked on a project that was to occupy them for thirty years. They travelled round rural areas of Hungary and the neighbouring countries with a phonograph, recording on wax cylinders the songs and dances of the people. Bartók's own music was transformed. He took the complex rhythms, the insistent repetitions, the free melodies with their sometimes Arab-sounding scales, and treated them as raw ingredients for new works. He combined the 'primitive' and the sophisticated, the Western and the Oriental, the modern and the ancient, in fascinating ways. Some of his music is very tough in its acerbic harmonies, such as the string quartets, or the mysterious and violent ballet *The Miraculous Mandarin*. Others are more easily accessible, including the *Music for Strings, Percussion and Celesta* and the *Concerto for Orchestra*.

Similar influences were at work in England, Spain and Finland. The same year that Bartók encountered the song about the falling apple, 1904, the composer Ralph Vaughan Williams joined the English Folk-Song Society. He was already in his thirties and, like the younger Bartók, had not yet found his feet. He knew the German masters, but more importantly, he loved English church music and discovered the qualities of English folk song. Combining these elements helped him to develop his own style, beginning with his first great success, the *Fantasia on a Theme by Thomas Tallis*. It evokes the grandeur of a cathedral with Tallis's hymn, but also brings in folk elements that give it a pastoral character.

In Spain, the composers Isaac Albéniz and his successor Manuel de Falla brought a strong sense of 'Spanishness' to their music. They did so by drawing on the character of flamenco, with its intense singing style, poignant melodies and harmonies, and complex dance rhythms. Albéniz was a virtuoso pianist, and his most important work is *Iberia*, a substantial and highly challenging suite for piano. Falla is at his most characteristic in his ballet scores, particularly the brilliant *The Three-Cornered Hat*.

The Finnish composer, Jean Sibelius, was a great admirer of the spacious symphonies of Bruckner. But when he was a student, Sibelius came across the *Kalevala*, a collection of traditional Finnish epic poetry. He then travelled in the countryside, listening to traditional singers of Finnish epics. These two sources had a profound effect on his music, and he developed a unique style of writing that seems both epic and down to earth, brusque but full of aspiration.

Vaughan Williams and Bartók, Albéniz and Sibelius, lived a thousand miles apart, in quite different countries. Yet they all, at roughly the same time, felt a pull towards the traditional music of the people. Why? It was partly to do with the politics of the time. Hungary, like Bohemia and Moravia, was a reluctant member of the Austrian Empire. To Bartók and others, searching for a 'true' Hungarian style was partly a political act. And this came to seem like an act of defiance after the First World War, when Hungary suffered under communist dictatorship and then military rule.

Finland was still ruled by Russia when Sibelius had his first triumph with his grand choral symphony, *Kullervo*. His assertion of Finnish character, through all his succeeding seven symphonies and other pieces inspired by the *Kalevala*, turned him into a national hero.

England was facing a different situation. For a hundred years the British Empire had been the leading power in the world, but now there were signs that its supremacy was beginning to crumble. The English, brought up to see their empire as a benign force, felt a strong sense of nostalgia for the qualities of 'Englishness', which seemed under threat. Vaughan Williams, with his love of old English music, was swept up in this wave of sentiment. Somewhat similar forces were at work in Spain. By the twentieth century, Spain had lost its mighty overseas empire, and, as in Britain, composers such as Albéniz and de Falla were looking for a sense of 'Spanishness'.

The effects of all this have been extremely varied. This is partly because folk music of different countries is itself extremely varied. And when you stir into the mix other influences, notably church music, the picture becomes even more complex.

Liszt was criticised for his naive view that gypsy music was pure Hungarian folk music, when it turned out that much of it had been recently composed and published. But notions of 'purity' are shifting sands. Bartók himself was sometimes naive in his assumption that peasant cultures were untouched by modern, urban civilisation. And if a peasant tune made up by an unknown musician a hundred or a thousand years ago is pure, why does that make gypsy music composed recently of lesser value, and, by implication, 'impure'? Twentieth-century history teaches us that these are dangerous waters, particularly when politics become involved.

If I ask you to imagine Spanish music, you might think first of flamenco. But flamenco has its roots in the music of gypsies who migrated to Spain from India centuries ago, and it was long influenced by Spain's exposure to Arab music and to the dances of African slaves. Interestingly, the composers who were internationally most successful in evoking traditional Spain in music were French rather than Spanish. Georges Bizet set the trend in 1875 with his opera *Carmen*. Later, Claude Debussy and Maurice Ravel wrote Spanish-inspired music which even the Spanish composer Manuel de Falla admired for its convincingly Spanish character.

When a composer brings in elements of other people's culture, this is most often seen as homage, particularly when the result is as satisfying as the music of Bizet, Debussy, Ravel or Bartók. But the relationship between the original musicians and the composers who drew on their music is not entirely straightforward. Today, we have become much more aware of the issues surrounding the 'appropriation' of the work of other cultures. This most often raises its head with physical objects that have ended up in the museums of Europe and North America. Of course, music is not an 'object', so if a composer takes it and makes use of it in a different context, the original still exists. But it is increasingly acknowledged that musicians from traditional cultures have rights. Bartók's peasants were certainly never consulted about any 'rights' to their music, and until recently it would have been considered ridiculous even to think along such lines. But these are issues that increasingly crop up in the modern world. Composers are now obliged to tread carefully in order to avoid accusations of appropriation, or even legal challenges, from cultural groups whose music they have used or referenced.

CHAPTER 31

Westernising and Modernising

Claude Debussy had a gift for evoking a Spanish atmosphere. But a more profound influence on his style was from much further afield. In 1889 the Paris World Exhibition was held, in which there were groups of musicians from around the world, including Africa, India and Java. Of these, the one that most struck French musicians was Javanese *gamelan*, the orchestra of gongs and metallophones that I described in Chapter 6. Debussy spent hours listening to them, and wrote, 'Their conservatoire is the eternal rhythm of the sea, the wind among the leaves and the thousand sounds of nature which they understand without consulting an arbitrary treatise.'

Debussy was attracted to the mysterious and the atmospheric. And he certainly found the *gamelan* players mysterious, with their complex patterns and the tuning of their instruments that seemed to have little connection with familiar Western harmonies. There are distinct hints of the 'noble savage' and 'orientalism' in Debussy's descriptions of the Javanese musicians. But his fascination with them had a remarkable effect on his own music. He developed ways of evoking this sort of mystery through the use of floating, multi-layered counterpoint, and unconventional scales. He made particularly striking use of the whole-tone scale, which avoids any suggestion of a key. This was the nearest approach that Debussy could find to the effect of *gamelan* scales within the confines of the Western tuning system.

This brings us back again to the question of the relationship between the West and the rest of the world, which reached a new climax in the late nineteenth and early twentieth centuries. There is no indication that Debussy took any interest in the Indian or African musicians at the exhibition. India and Africa were, for most Europeans at this time, countries to be exploited rather than admired. India had by now been subsumed into the British Empire. As for Africa, the scramble for domination of the south of the continent was boosted by the discovery of diamonds and gold. By 1914, 90 per cent of the continent was under European rule. After centuries of the trans-Atlantic slave trade, Africans now had to endure the wholesale occupation of their countries and plundering of their resources.

As early as the seventeenth century, Dutch owners of estates in South Africa had orchestras of African slave musicians who were trained to play European music on European instruments, and by the nineteenth century this tradition extended across Africa. There were brass bands played by Africans from Ghana in the west to Kenya in the east. The singing of Christian hymns was encouraged by missionaries. These imports gradually affected traditional African musicians, encouraging them to simplify complex native rhythms, and to adopt the harmonies of European hymns and use European instruments.

Conversely, African rhythmic elements crept into performance of European music. South Africa developed a particularly rich blended culture of working-class music in the late nineteenth century, when the mining of diamonds and gold brought workers from Europe and the United States together with Africans, leading to the evolution of new styles of dance music. Similar things were going on in the plantations across the Atlantic in the Americas, with profound consequences for the future of music.

North Africa had been connected to Europe and Asia through trade and religion since ancient times, so the ground was laid for interaction between European and North African music. After the Europeans defeated the Ottoman army at Vienna in 1683, Europe was increasingly seen as 'advanced' by the Islamic world, and this tendency increased as the Industrial Revolution got going in the nineteenth century. Europeans invested in railways in Asia and North Africa, and as European technology was promoted, so was European music.

In Egypt, the Suez Canal was opened by the French in 1869, creating a direct route for European shipping through to India and the Far East. Its grand opening was celebrated by the staging of operas by Verdi at the newly built Cairo Opera House, including the specially composed *Aida*, with a spectacular setting in ancient Egypt. This was the climax of a century of European domination of Egypt and its culture that had begun with Napoleon's invasion in 1798.

The French went on to conquer Algeria in 1830, with similar importing of European culture. Concerts of European music, sponsored by the government, became a regular part of Algerian life. There were some examples of interest in North African musical culture. In the 1850s a French composer, Francisco Salvador Daniel, spent four years travelling from Algeria across North Africa, collecting folk song. He published volumes of Arab and Kabyle (Berber) music. But he thoroughly Europeanised the melodies by adding elaborate piano accompaniments in order to make them suitable for French audiences.

Much more widespread was the adoption of Western musical influence across the Islamic world. In Turkey, the Sultan established an opera house in Istanbul in 1797. Giuseppe Donizetti (brother of the composer Gaetano Donizetti) was appointed director of court music in 1828. Turkish music was increasingly influenced by Western styles, with the use of Western instruments, and the adoption of new scales and notation. The wholesale Westernisation of Turkey was introduced in 1923, when the president of the new republic, Kemal Atatürk, banned traditional Turkish music from state radio, and encouraged the teaching of Western musical styles and their incorporation into Turkish music. Chopin's Funeral March was adopted as the official state funeral march, played by European-style brass bands.

In Iran too, Western-style military bands were introduced by the emperor in the 1860s. A French musician was brought in to train them and to teach the principles of Western music. By the 1920s there were two parallel music conservatories, one devoted to Western music, the other to traditional music, and a symphony orchestra was founded.

A landmark moment in this drive towards Westernisation was a conference on Arab music, held in Cairo in 1932. Its purpose was to discuss how to 'civilise' Arab music, and to 'rebuild it on acknowledged scientific principles', in order to compete in the modern world. The guests at the conference included not only Arab musicians but also European composers Paul Hindemith and Béla Bartók, as well as leading European musicologists. The conference discussed the merits of traditional Arab scales with their subtle tunings, and the increasing use of pianos whose Western-style tuning conflicted with them. Some, including Bartók, argued that it was important to preserve the great Arab tradition. Others, including Hindemith, argued for the adoption of Western tuning, so that Arab music could develop European-style polyphony.

The modernisers won the argument, and the use of Western tunings and instruments, and Western notation, were encouraged across the Arab world. This in turn encouraged the general 'Westernising' of Arab music. Traditions such as *maqam* were in danger of losing many of their most vital characteristics: tunings, improvisation (which was eroded by the drive to use notation), and traditional instruments and vocal styles. Small groups became bigger, in imitation of Western orchestras, and performances increasingly took place in large concert halls rather than more intimate performing spaces. This in turn encouraged a more emphatically virtuoso style of performance, in line with European taste.

Amid all the discussion of losses and gains, there were musicians ready to grasp the new possibilities. In Turkey, Tanburi Cemil Bey, a great virtuoso player of lutes and bowed instruments, composed pieces in a semi-European style, but with elements of traditional *maqam* and its non-Western tuning. Singers across the Arab world found different ways of compromising. Two of the most successful were Egyptian. Mohammad Abdel Wahab became a star of recordings and musical films, with songs accompanied by an orchestra. He wrote several songs for another prominent Egyptian star, Umm Kulthum. Her rise to fame was truly remarkable, partly because she was a woman in a society in which women's roles were traditionally restricted. Like many traditional singers, she had been trained in recitation of the Qur'an and in the improvisation of *maqam*. From the 1930s onwards her regular radio broadcasts attracted an audience of millions across the Arab world. She too sang with an orchestra, with tunings that compromised between Western and Arab. But her skill in negotiating between the traditional, florid improvisation and more 'modern' approaches earned her immense respect and a devoted following over several decades.

In 1914 an English schoolmaster, A. H. Fox Strangways, published the first serious study in English of Indian music, *The Music of Hindustan*. Gustav Holst, most famous as the composer of *The Planets*, had a deep interest in Indian literature and mysticism. But these examples of engagement were unusual, and in general Indians and Europeans continued to view each other's music with mutual indifference. Local Indian patrons continued to support Indian musicians playing and singing in the traditional ways. Unlike the leaders of the Arab world, they had not come to think of European music as superior to Indian, or modernisation of their music as necessary, and they had not established opera houses or conservatoires teaching Western music. So the traditions of Indian music, north and south, continued.

It was with the rise of musical films from the 1930s onwards that new genres of Indian music began to emerge. At first the songs in films were abbreviated versions of traditional popular styles, such as the *ghazal*, a favourite kind of love song. But increasingly Western instruments were introduced and the music became more influenced by American popular styles. This led eventually to the 'Bollywood' genre. One of the most distinguished singers of

Bollywood died in her nineties as I was writing this chapter: Lata Mangeshkar. Taught by her father, a classical Indian musician, she was the most celebrated 'playback singer', who recorded thousands of songs in several different languages, to which Bollywood actors danced and mimed. She retained her elegant and emotionally charged Indian vocal style while singing a wide range of genres. Some were more traditional, some more modern, in many different Indian languages, and Mangeshkar was adored by millions across all classes.

Chinese culture had been admired by the thinkers of the eighteenth-century European Enlightenment, such as Goethe. But Chinese rulers tried to maintain their isolation from the West, until they suffered a series of military disasters in the nineteenth century. Europeans had little taste for Chinese music, despite their interest in other aspects of Chinese culture. But the Chinese began to bring European music and musicians into China in the later nineteenth century. In Shanghai a symphony orchestra was founded in 1907, a Conservatoire in 1927. During the following decades Russian musicians came to China, and a mixed style was developed in which Chinese traditional melodies were set to European harmonies.

During the brutal twenty-seven-year rule of Mao Zedong's Communist Party, which began in 1949, all music had to be an expression of the glorious new future, and all elements from the decadent past had to be eliminated. In practice, this meant the development of this hybrid of Chinese and European music, to create uplifting songs and marches. Orchestras replaced traditional ensembles, and Western tuning was adopted. The resulting 'music as propaganda' had much in common with the music promoted by the Soviet authorities in Russia during the same period. However, the performing of European classical music during Mao's regime was strictly prohibited. After his death in 1976, Chinese symphony orchestras were again allowed to perform European symphonies, and at the same time those who had secretly preserved the traditions of historic Chinese music set about reviving it.

The extent of Westernisation varied across East Asia. In Java and Bali the *gamelan* with its dance and puppet theatre remained important. But at the same time new hybrids with Western jazz and popular music evolved. Thailand was unusual in not being colonised by Europeans in the nineteenth century. Nevertheless it Westernised from the mid-nineteenth century while preserving its musical traditions. In Japan, 'modernisation' was official doctrine from the 1860s onwards, and traditional Japanese music was pushed into the background. By the beginning of the twentieth century, Japanese composers were blending Japanese and European styles, and the fusion has continued to this day. After Japan's catastrophic defeat in the Second World War, its rapid recovery was achieved by wholesale Westernisation, in music as in everything else. Japanese symphony orchestras, musicians and composers were soon respected world-wide. But, as part of the reconstruction, there was also a revival of interest in traditional Japanese music. This went hand in hand with the coexistence in Japan of new technology and ancient ritual.

In the Americas, North and South, interaction between indigenous peoples and colonisers had been going on for centuries, as I described in Chapter 16. Across Latin America from the seventeenth century onward, missionaries had brought European music and instruments, and the result was a fascinating genre known as 'Latin-American Baroque' music. Later, symphony orchestras and opera houses were established in the major centres of South America.

In North America, settlers and colonists generally confronted the Native Americans rather than engaging with them. The Czech composer Dvořák, resident in New York in the 1890s, took an interest in Native American music, and by around 1900, American composers were beginning to incorporate some Native American material into their music. But the most successful embracing of Native American references was not by an American, but by an English-born son of a white mother and a Black father from Sierra Leone, Samuel Coleridge-Taylor. His *Hiawatha's Wedding Feast* set the poetry of Longfellow in the grand English choral style. It premiered in London in 1898 and was an immediate triumph. Coleridge-Taylor toured the United States conducting his choral works, earning the nickname the 'African Mahler'. He was sometimes allowed to conduct a chorus of mixed races, a very unusual concession against the prevailing segregation.

But any influence of Native American music on European-style music in America was far outstripped by the influence of African-derived music brought to the Americas by slaves and their descendants. Coleridge-Taylor himself went on to compose music incorporating 'Negro melodies'. Florence Price, an African American based in Chicago, did the same in the next generation. She was the first Black woman to have major works performed by symphony orchestras in the United States. Much of her music was forgotten until a collection of manuscripts was discovered in 2009 in an abandoned house where she had lived. Her music is gradually being revived.

Dvořák had urged American composers to take the music of African Americans seriously, and to draw on it as Europeans were drawing on their own folk traditions. This was in the 1890s, a time when references to the music of African Americans by the white European-origin population were generally trivial, sentimental or insulting. 'Blackface minstrelsy' had been popular since the mid-nineteenth century, providing an increasingly crude carica-ture of the songs and dances of the plantations. Then there were the sentimental imitations of African American songs designed for the genteel drawing rooms of respectable white America. I have already mentioned Stephen Foster, the most successful composer of these, with songs that have remained famous to this day, such as 'Swanee River', and 'My Old Kentucky Home'.

The African American spirituals and other songs on which Foster's imitations were based were already mixed African and European in style. But the great fusion of African and European was only just beginning. African American music was to have enormous consequences for the future of music, not only in the United States but worldwide. That is a large topic which I'll return to in Chapter 34.

CHAPTER 32

Into the Darkness

Tracing the Western impact on different countries in the previous chapter has meant straying well into the twentieth century. But now we need to return to the early twentieth century to consider one of the major events of history and its aftermath.

The First World War was an international catastrophe that still dominates our historical memory. But it didn't come out of the blue. It was the climax of decades of tension and wars between the powers of Europe, with confrontations across the world that they struggled to control. This almost continuous pattern of tension and warfare had a deep effect on society, with a widespread sense that all the usual certainties of life were in danger of collapse. This feeling was deepened by a flu pandemic that followed the First World War and killed more people than the war did.

Reactions to this sort of crisis vary enormously. We were reminded of this in the Covid-19 pandemic that began in 2020. Some people are constantly fearful, some try to be sensible but not to worry too much, and some throw caution to the winds, saying that there is no point in our lives unless we enjoy them to the full. No doubt a similar range of reactions has applied across human history.

As for the expression of human emotions in art and music, the years leading up to the First World War were a time of unprecedented variety. Writers, painters and musicians ranged from those who seemed to be throwing all the old rules and conventions up into the air to those who desperately sought to preserve tradition. Some seemed to be looking forward recklessly, others looking to the past for reassurance. Some aimed to disrupt, others to comfort. For some, this was clearly a reaction to war and instability, but for others the picture is more complicated and subtle.

Perhaps it is possible to sum this up by saying that, at times of tension and anxiety, the expression of the public mood in art tends to go in two opposite directions, to the dark or to the light. Exploration of the dark side of mental lives was in the air, with studies of the powerful forces of sexual feelings and the working of the unconscious mind. Sigmund Freud, a doctor and neurologist in Vienna, developed the technique of psychoanalysis and published his *Interpretation of Dreams* in 1899. The composer Gustav Mahler consulted Freud at a time of crisis in his marriage to his wife Alma. Freud reported that Mahler showed an impressive capacity for psychological understanding, and immediately understood the point of psychoanalysis. You could say that there is a lot of 'psychoanalysis' in Mahler's music, with its huge range of mood and emotion, sense of yearning, evocation of memories, and tortured striving for release and resolution. And towards the end of his career, in the years before the First World War, Mahler's music conveys a powerful sense of struggling to hang on to the important things in life, while preparing for the last farewell. This feeling is strong in his ninth and incomplete tenth symphonies, but it is most explicit in *Das Lied von der Erde* (The Song of the Earth, 1909). This is a setting of Chinese poems for solo voices and orchestra, contrasting the beauty of the earth with the pain of human sorrow. The mood ranges from drunken desperation through charmingly pastoral scenes to poignant resignation. The last movement is a long and haunting 'Farewell' to the earth, ending with words that Mahler added to the Chinese poem: 'Everywhere the dear earth blossoms and is green in spring, forever, forever, forever.' It is Mahler's most powerful expression of the darkness and the light, and the human experience of living with both of them.

Arnold Schoenberg went much further into the Freudian darkness, throwing out the possibility of light altogether. His early, massive cantata, *Gurre-Lieder* (composed 1900–11), is Wagnerian in its extravagant richness. But by 1909 he had already turned thoroughly to darkness with *Erwartung* (Expectation). This is a nightmarish monologue with orchestra, in which a distraught woman searches through a wood at night for her lover, only to find him dead. It is like an extreme extension of Mahler's darkest music, with its dissonance rarely relieved by any sense of conventional harmonies. On a smaller scale, in 1912 Schoenberg wrote *Pierrot Lunaire*, a sort of cabaret-setting of poems by Albert Giraud full of strange and violent images, for which Schoenberg composed strange and violent music. The singer has to half-sing, half-speak (*Sprechgesang* = 'speech-song') to give a weirdly theatrical effect. This too was 'atonal', without obvious reference to traditional harmonies.

Schoenberg found it impossible to go on composing extended pieces of music like this. He needed something to create new order out of the nightmare. In 1922 he came up with his 'twelve-note' (or 'twelve-tone') method. All themes were to be derived from a row, or 'series', of all twelve notes of the chromatic scale (all the black and white notes within an octave of the keyboard). These were to be put in a chosen order for each composition to create a theme that could then be manipulated in various ways: played backwards, upside down, simultaneously in chords, leaping across different octaves. This method came to be known as 'serialism', and the result is music that has its own fearsome logic, but has struggled to attract a wide audience over the hundred years since Schoenberg devised his method.

Schoenberg treated all notes as equals, referring to this as the 'emancipation of the dissonance'. There was already plenty of dissonance in the music of other composers, but dissonance was now a constant feature of the new 'serial' music. Traditional harmonies would be a distracting reminder of the past and were therefore to be avoided. You could see this as a divorce from the fundamental root of harmony, the harmonic series. But Schoenberg saw it as an inevitable way out of chaos, and the means to secure the great line of German music for the future.

Schoenberg's two most famous pupils, Anton Webern and Alban Berg, began studying with him long before his development of the twelve-note method, and travelled with him on the journey into this strange new landscape. Webern began by writing lush, late-Romantic music in a style similar to early Schoenberg. Later, he pursued the logic of his teacher's new method zealously, creating brittle, meticulously crafted soundscapes. It is easy to hear these as cold and intellectual, but Webern said that, after the death of his mother in 1906, almost all of his music was inspired by memories of her.

When Berg began studying with Schoenberg in 1904, Schoenberg reported that he could only write songs. Indeed, it is Berg's lyrical gift, applied to instrumental as well as vocal music, that makes his music so accessible, despite its complexity. His greatest achievement is the opera *Wozzeck*, on which he worked from 1914 to 1922. It plots the descent into madness of a soldier, Wozzeck, who murders his wife and drowns himself. It shares the nightmarish qualities of Schoenberg's *Erwartung*, and is similarly atonal, with singers half-speaking in Schoenberg's *Sprechgesang*. But Berg incorporates references to traditional harmony which help the listener to find the way through the dissonances. He continued to do this even after he had adopted the twelve-note method. His Violin Concerto (1935) is a work of great intellectual complexity, but also deeply affecting even if one cannot follow all its intricacies. It is dedicated to the memory of Manon Gropius, teenage daughter of the architect Walter Gropius and Alma Mahler.

There were others exploring the possibilities of new harmonies and new approaches without throwing out the basis on which listeners had always orientated themselves. Richard Strauss, a leading

German conductor as well as composer, had refused to conduct Schoenberg's Five Orchestral Pieces (1909) in conservative Berlin, and wrote to Alma Mahler (Gustav Mahler's then wife), 'The only person who can help poor Schoenberg now is a psychiatrist.' Strauss himself did not shrink from the use of dissonance when he thought it appropriate. His orchestral style is already extravagantly complex in the series of orchestral 'tone poems' that he composed in the last years of the nineteenth century. In his operas *Salome* (1905) and *Elektra* (1909) he relishes the violence of their plots with savage dissonances and dense interweaving of orchestral textures, but in a way that is dramatic, and can easily be understood. His next opera was *Der Rosenkavalier* (1911), a period comedy set in aristocratic Vienna, for which Strauss uses much more traditional harmonies and incorporates Viennese waltzes.

Bartók, who used folk song as a basis for a new approach to composing, sometimes wrote in a straightforwardly 'folk-like' manner. But his acerbic harmonies sharpened the percussive edge to take it in a direction that had more to do with the modern trends of the twentieth century than with folk inspiration. And his percussive rhythms often became wilder and more complex than any folk dance.

Several composers opted for an extravagant lushness of chromatic harmonies. The Russian Alexander Scriabin used it to create a sort of fevered ecstasy, naming his best-known orchestral work *Poem of Ecstasy* (1905–8). Frederick Delius used it to evoke intense nostalgia for a lost Englishness. Another English composer, Arnold Bax, used it to evoke exotic richness.

If I had to name a single work that defined the early twentieth century, and truly set music on a new course, it would have to be Stravinsky's *The Rite of Spring* (1913). This is a ballet for orchestra which depicts an ancient ritual of annual dance and sacrifice to the gods of the earth. A young girl is chosen by the elders for sacrifice, and dances herself to death. The subject matter is drawn from research into ancient tribal cultures, and Stravinsky invented a musical style to match. He didn't collect folk songs, as Bartók did, but he quoted a few actual Lithuanian folk songs in the score, elaborating on their characteristic dissonant clashes. He created a network of little 'folk-like' cells of melody and rhythm, repeating them with variation of orchestration and harmony, in the manner pioneered by Glinka. But Stravinsky took this method to an extreme, with fragmentation and relentless repetition building paragraphs of enormous power.

The other pioneer on whom Stravinsky drew was Debussy, with his unusual ways of juxtaposing chords and rhythms, giving them quite new effects. Debussy himself wrote to Stravinsky about *The Rite of Spring*, 'it is a special satisfaction to tell you how much you have enlarged the boundaries of the permissible in the empire of sound'. The premiere of *The Rite* in Paris provoked outrage. But this was mostly because the audience of ballet fans objected to the deliberately jerky and violent style of the choreography by Vaslav Nijinsky. Later concert performances were a triumph. With its very direct power and energy, it struck audiences immediately, and has continued to do so to this day.

The nature of the revolution that Debussy and Stravinsky put in train was quite different from Schoenberg's revolution. Their musical language is at heart still founded on the harmonic series, and the traditional notions of scales and chords that are derived from it. These are distorted, have additional dissonances, are juxtaposed in surprising ways, and, in the case of Stravinsky, subjected to persistent and irregular rhythms. But the ordinary music-lover still has some echo of the familiar to cling on to. This approach – what you might call de-familiarising the familiar – has proved much more durable, and ultimately influential, than Schoenberg's attempt to create a new language from notes which have been removed from all traditional harmonic roots.

All of this was happening at a time when there were radical developments in the other arts, a trend which came to be labelled as 'modernism'. Schoenberg was also a painter, a member of *Der Blaue Reiter* (The Blue Rider), one of several groups in Berlin and Vienna before the First World War who challenged the orthodox thinking of the arts establishment. You can certainly see and hear parallels between Schoenberg's nightmarish atonal music and some of the nightmarish 'expressionist' paintings of the time by Gustav Klimt, Egon Schiele, Oskar Kokoschka, as well as Schoenberg himself.

At the same time, the Spanish painter Pablo Picasso was drawing on what he saw as the 'primitive' power of African masks. Together with Frenchman Georges Braque, Picasso experimented with fragmentation in various ways, breaking up forms and combining different perspectives to create 'Cubism'. Both primitivism and fragmentation are fundamental to *The Rite of Spring*. Stravinsky never quite returned to the direct confrontation with the 'primitive' in later works. But fragmentation, what you might call 'musical Cubism', remained a basis for his composing for the rest of his life. You can hear its influence on many composers over the following decades.

CHAPTER 33

Reaching for the Light

In the years before and after the First World War some composers and artists explored darkness and the 'primitive', while others satisfied a public need to turn away from everyday anxieties. Operetta was all the rage, both sides of the Atlantic. The popularity of the French Offenbach and the Viennese Johann Strauss II continued. The satirical operettas of Gilbert and Sullivan, written in the 1870s and 1880s, had become a national institution in Britain and were exported wherever English was spoken. In the United States, the operettas of Victor Herbert were popular, bringing together elements of Viennese operetta and Gilbert and Sullivan. There were many different versions of operetta and other popular musical genres around at the turn of the twentieth century, some aimed at the well-to-do, others at the working classes. But the smash hit of the early twentieth century was a Viennese operetta in the tradition of Johann Strauss II: Franz Lehár's *The Merry Widow*, staged in Vienna in 1905 and in London and New York soon after.

The Merry Widow's enormous popularity was one of the factors that encouraged the development of a new genre of music theatre that came to be known as the Broadway musical. One of the earliest teams to score a major success on Broadway in New York was the combination of composer Jerome Kern, librettist Guy Bolton and lyricist P. G. Wodehouse (who would go on to become even more famous for his books about Bertie Wooster and his manservant, Jeeves). Their most successful show, *Oh Boy!*, opened on Broadway in 1917 and ran for 463 performances.

The same year, in Paris, a strange cabaret-ballet, *Parade*, was staged, a collaboration between writer Jean Cocteau, choreographer Léonide Massine, painter Pablo Picasso and composer Erik Satie. With its jaunty score, deliberately clumsy 'Cubist' costumes and awkward dance steps, it had a droll narrative of a fairground in which performers try unsuccessfully to entice a bored audience into their show. *Parade* provoked almost as much uproar as Stravinsky's *The Rite of Spring*. It was anti-traditional and anti-establishment, doubly provocative because it poked fun during a terrible war.

Satie had started his career playing the piano at a cabaret in Paris, and *Parade* was a satirical reimagining of the genre. Cabaret had also taken off in Germany, at first relatively mildly compared with the French. But after the First World War, with the country and society destroyed and humiliated, German cabaret took a dark turn, with a bitter vein of satire. This was powerfully expressed by the team of playwright Bertolt Brecht and composer Kurt Weill in *The Threepenny Opera* (1928), a sour reworking of the eighteenth-century success *The Beggar's Opera*, with a cast drawn from criminal low life.

One element that the Broadway musical and French and German cabaret all had in common was an element of jazz. We'll be getting onto that huge topic in the next chapter. The rhythms of ragtime and jazz were not only an enlivening element, but were also regarded with alarm. From around 1910 there was a renewed fashion for nightclubs in London, with a combination that authorities thought dangerous to social order: dancing, alcohol, the mixing of the sexes (unlike in the old-established men's clubs) and the new 'syncopated' music from America. During the war, the concerns became so extreme that army officers were threatened with prosecution if they were found in a nightclub.

For some writers and musicians, the prime sentiment arising from the First World War was one of longing for peace, or for an imagined past. Two of Vaughan Williams's most peace-evoking works were specifically related to the war. *The Lark Ascending* is a pastoral meditation for solo violin and orchestra. Vaughan Williams sketched the first ideas for it in 1914 as he walked the chalk cliffs overlooking the English Channel, in which ships of the Royal Navy were exercising in preparation for war. During the war, Vaughan Williams worked as an ambulance officer in France, where, at the end of the day of transporting wounded soldiers in dangerous conditions, he would go up the hill to look at the landscape bathed in a glorious sunset. It was there that he developed ideas for his Pastoral Symphony (No. 3). Poised somewhere between bleakness and serenity, it is, as Vaughan Williams said, 'really wartime music'.

Across the Atlantic, the United States entered the First World War in 1917, the year that *Oh Boy!* opened on Broadway. Americans' relations with war were different from those of Europeans. Their principal memory was of the Civil War that tore America apart in the 1860s, and before that, the American Revolutionary War surrounding the declaration of independence from Britain in 1776. As in Europe, composers in the early twentieth century were inevitably influenced by present and past tensions, as well as by writers and thinkers and the inherited stories of the national history. One of the most fascinating American composers to have drawn on this material is Charles Ives. Largely ignored in his lifetime but esteemed since his death, he was an eccentric figure who earned his living running an insurance firm. Ives composed in his spare time, feeling bound by no rules. His father was a bandmaster, who encouraged him to experiment.

The influences that fed into Ives's music were contradictory. He loved the old hymns, and the writings of the 'Transcendentalists', led by Ralph Waldo Emerson. Emerson believed in the freedom of human thought, 'the infinitude of the private man', and the vital link between nature and the human soul. During the Civil War, Emerson was a fierce opponent of slavery, and argued that the destructive force of war was necessary to create a new society. Ives's music is full of similar contrasts: the evocation of nature, the force of destruction, and the struggle through chaos to achieve serenity. His orchestral set, *Three Places in New England* (1908–17), shows his range as well as any of his works. The first piece honours a regiment of Black soldiers and their white commander, with ghostly fragments of 'The Battle Cry of Freedom' and 'Marching through Georgia'. The second piece is a chaotic welter of marching songs evoking a boy's dream of revolutionary soldiers on the march. And the third piece plunges deep into nature, with the sound of singing from a distant church.

Of course, it is always the composers with new and challenging ideas that get the most prominent places in the history books. But even in the tumult of the early twentieth century there were composers who just tried to plough their own furrow, sticking to what seemed right, and trying to ignore the noise. Several prominent composers left Russia at the time of the revolution. I have already mentioned Sergei Rachmaninoff, who emigrated to the United States in 1918. He was an acclaimed pianist, whose recordings of his own music are still treasured. He clung to memories of life back in Russia, and wrote piano concertos and symphonies using tried and tested methods handed down by Tchaikovsky and other Russians. He brought to his music a personal quality of sonorous melancholy that often suggests echoes of Russian Orthodox chant. He felt himself left behind by modern developments, saying in an interview in 1939, 'I feel like a ghost wandering in a world grown alien. I cannot cast out the old way of writing, and I cannot acquire the new.'

Another Russian, Sergei Prokofiev, settled in Paris for some years, but returned to Russia in 1933, to face a difficult life under the Soviet regime. He too was a brilliant pianist, and began his career as an impish provocateur rather in the mould of Stravinsky, writing bold piano concertos and enjoying audiences' reactions to their brash dissonances. But later he developed a spiritual streak partly inspired by Christian Science, and declared in 1941, 'We must seek a new simplicity.' His combination of brilliance and lyricism is at its most intense in his ballet score, *Romeo and Juliet*.

The English composer Edward Elgar found himself in a similar quandary to that of Rachmaninoff. He achieved his first success with his *Enigma Variations* in 1899, just as composers elsewhere in Europe were exploring more neurotic pathways. Elgar knew the latest orchestral works, and you can hear in his music something of the flamboyance of Richard Strauss (then regarded as the leading German composer). But while Strauss was shocking his audiences with *Salome*, Elgar had no intention of shocking anyone, and remained, at least outwardly, a traditionalist. He wrote symphonies, concertos for violin and for cello, 'Pomp and Circumstance' marches, and oratorios. He had the appearance of an Edwardian country gentleman, with his moustache and tweeds. But scratch beneath the surface and you find someone a great deal less comfortable than he appears, in life and in music. His music reveals a great deal of nervous uncertainty, particularly when it is played with the dash that he brought to it in his own recordings. This combination of the traditional facade with an underlying nervous energy gives his music a character that often strikes listeners as peculiarly 'English'.

Rachmaninoff and Elgar demonstrate that, in the end, posterity values music for its sense of a sincere, personal voice, not for the degree to which it was 'new' in its time. The same applies to Sibelius. I have already mentioned the inspiration that Sibelius drew from the Finnish epic, the *Kalevala*. His highly individual way of writing symphonies and other works arose not just from his main influences – the music and poetry of Finland, Bruckner, Russian composers – but from a particular cast of mind. You have to find your way between his utterances to what he means. When a climax comes, it is after fighting its way round many stumbling blocks. Sibelius, in the fevered world of the early twentieth century, was an enigmatic but powerful figure, and that is how he remains.

Finally, where had Italian opera got to by the early twentieth century? Giuseppe Verdi had ended the nineteenth century with two contrasted masterpieces based on Shakespeare's plays: the tragedy *Otello* (*Othello*) and the comedy *Falstaff*. By the time Verdi had retired, a new trend in Italian opera had emerged, a style known as *verismo* (realism). This arose from writers of novels who set out to portray the lives of ordinary people truthfully, showing the bad as well as the good without flinching. The first well-known *verismo* opera was Pietro Mascagni's *Cavalleria Rusticana* (Rustic Chivalry), followed by Ruggero Leoncavallo's *Pagliacci* (Clowns). Both are stories of love and raw jealousy ending in death. *Pagliacci* is all the more remarkable because Leoncavallo himself wrote the brilliant libretto. Indeed, the Shakespearean libretti that Arrigo Boito wrote for Verdi's *Otello* and *Falstaff*, and Leoncavallo's libretto for *Pagliacci*, demonstrate how the libretto continued to be important for Italian composers right through from opera's beginnings around 1600 to the start of the twentieth century.

It was another *verismo* opera that opened the twentieth century: Giacomo Puccini's *Tosca* premiered in Rome in January 1900. Puccini had already composed *La Bohème*, and other operas followed, including *Madama Butterfly* and *Turandot*. These well-loved operas retain their appeal to audiences because they have extraordinary directness. The singers are real actors in the drama, and their music is dramatic and lyrical at the same time. There are aria-like moments but always for dramatic reasons, not for mere vocal display. Puccini's harmonies are carefully judged to be completely understandable, while being spiced with modern touches of dissonance; and he uses the full resources of the post-Wagnerian orchestra to colour and drive the drama, and weaves some Wagner-style *leitmotifs* through his music. Puccini insisted that, despite these Wagnerian ingredients, 'I have always remained, and still remain, Italian. My music is rooted in the peculiarity of my native country.'

One essential feature of opera in Italy in this period is that it retained something that was not generally the case in other countries: it had a genuinely popular appeal, appreciated by people of a wide social range. The tickets at the great opera houses in Italy were expensive, as they were elsewhere. But there were many smaller theatres and opera festivals where the tickets were cheaper and people from all classes came.

By the time Puccini died in 1924, leaving his final opera *Turandot* unfinished, Stravinsky's *The Rite of Spring* was a decade old and Schoenberg had already developed his twelve-note method of composition. It is difficult to imagine that there has ever been a period in Western history when the music being written or performed was so varied in style and approach, so full of contra-dictions and antagonistic points of view. But the most potent and lasting revolution in music in the early twentieth century came from outside the conservatoires, opera houses and concert halls, and from a level of society that had had little input into the official progress of music up to this point. I have touched on it from time to time, but now is the moment to turn our attention to it.

CHAPTER 34

From Blues and Ragtime to Jazz

In 1860, Abraham Lincoln was elected president of the United States. He was strongly opposed to slavery. The Southern states relied on mass slavery for their cotton and other plantations, and responded by declaring their separation from the Northern states. The anti-slavery North won the Civil War that followed, but this did not resolve the fundamental conflict. Although slavery had been abolished, a fragile peace was achieved only by allowing the Southern states to continue with policies of segregation and discrimination. For many former slaves, life was scarcely different from slavery. The four million slaves who worked the plantations of the Southern states by 1860 were only a small fraction of the total – many more were in Brazil and the Caribbean. In the history of music, the dispersal of African culture through all these slave populations was important. But it was from the Southern United States that a musical revolution was to emerge that would sweep the world, and whose effects are with us to this day.

On the slave plantations, singing, drumming and dancing with hand-clapping were an outlet for yearning, dreams and religious expression. Work songs matched the rhythm of work and helped to alleviate the back-breaking labour. The words were, on the surface, yearning or even joyful, but, as a freed slave Frederick Douglass wrote, 'Every tone was a testament against slavery, and a prayer to God for a deliverance from chains.' Over time, as more and more slaves converted to Christianity, their songs adopted Christian imagery, drawing on stories from the Bible.

Long before the Civil War, New Orleans was a centre for the music of African Americans. Sunday afternoons were the time when both enslaved and free Black people would gather in open spaces to sing and dance. Congo Square became famous for these gatherings, attracting visitors from far away. An architect, Benjamin Latrobe, left a detailed description in 1819. A drummer begins a 'throbbing pulsation', and is joined by others: 'One voice, then other voices join in . . . A dance of dark bodies forms into circular groups – perhaps five or six hundred individuals moving in time to the pulsations of the music, some swaying gently, others aggressively stomping their feet. A number of women in the group begin chanting.' This characteristically African mass dance in a circle was accompanied by shouted call and response. We can hear just this sort of 'ring shout' in a recording made by John and Alan Lomax in Jennings, Louisiana (near New Orleans) in 1934, 'Run Old Jeremiah'. With its religious words, its hypnotic, repetitive beat, and the fervent call and response between the singers, it transports us right back to the days of slavery.

People of mixed Black and white descent came to be known as Creoles, and they were an important element in the new musical developments. With famine in Ireland in the 1840s, many Irish immigrants joined them, looking for work. Various mixtures of music arose, bringing together, for example, African-style dance rhythms with Irish-style fiddle-playing. One of the popular developments from this mixture was the minstrel show, and from the 1840s groups of minstrels toured the United States. These included not only Black and white, but also 'blacked up' white musicians.

The church was another very important influence. As well as regular church services, in the South through the nineteenth century there were huge 'Revivalist' meetings, in which thousands of worshippers sang and danced. There were meetings for whites, others for Blacks, and sometimes Blacks were allowed into the white meetings. The African tradition of fervent call and response added a characteristic, ecstatic edge to the hymns, with solo singers calling with increasing passion and the congregation responding rhythmically. It has been suggested that this fervour carried echoes of the Islamic call to prayer – many slaves had been brought up as Muslims. In the voices of African singers, these hymns, like the work songs, carried messages of yearning for freedom from slavery and oppression, in their call for the 'promised land' and for 'rest'. It was from these hymns that the wider genre of the spiritual and gospel music developed. The harmonising of hymns, a hybrid between European and African customs, fed into other songs of the African Americans, the work songs and spirituals, which developed their own style of harmonisation.

One of the most characteristic ingredients in African American music is the contrasting of the regular beat with a melody that is rhythmically free, wandering from the beat or kicking against it. This 'syncopation' became a feature of their instrumental music, and they applied it to the military march. Marches had become immensely popular, largely through John Philip Sousa, the most successful bandmaster in American history. Sousa toured with his band from 1893, scoring enormous success with marches composed by himself. Many are still famous, including 'The Liberty Bell' and 'Stars and Stripes Forever'. Minstrel and other African American bands took to playing marches, introducing their characteristic syncopation of the melodies, and this created the genre that swept into popularity across the United States and Europe around 1900: the ragtime. And with ragtime the entire history of popular music through to our own time has begun.

The first successful composer of ragtime was Scott Joplin. He was the pianist of the band at the Maple Leaf Bar at Sedalia, Missouri, and began publishing ragtime including his most famous piece, 'Maple Leaf Rag'. As he became well known, Joplin moved to St Louis to further his career. He had been taught European classical music by a local German piano teacher when he was a boy, and he had ambitions to create something bigger than ragtime. He wrote two operas, only one of which survives: *Treemonisha*. It is set in a former slave plantation, and brings together scenes in operatic style with choruses that burst joyfully into ragtime. Joplin managed to have it sung to an audience, with himself at the piano, but it was not staged until the 1970s, long after Joplin's death. His ragtime style, however, was widely imitated, particularly by white composers in New York. One, Irving Berlin, had the good fortune to compose 'Alexander's Ragtime Band' in 1911, just as recordings were becoming widely available and affordable (Joplin made a few piano rolls, but no sound recordings). So Berlin's success eclipsed that of Joplin, who died in an asylum in 1917. By that time, ragtime and its offspring, jazz, were big business on both sides of the Atlantic.

Around the same time that ragtime was on the rise, the 'blues' developed into another popular genre. It, more than ragtime, expressed the deep yearning of the oppressed African Americans. It became popular in the bars and brothels of Storyville, New Orleans, where audiences also enjoyed sexually explicit lyrics expressing a different kind of yearning. The simple form of the blues encapsulated the sense of dogged persistence in the face of repeated disappointment: a twelve-bar tune, three chords in a repeating pattern, and characteristic 'blue' notes, pulling down the third and seventh notes of the scale.

W. C. Handy was an early exponent of the genre. He took inspiration from the music of poor Blacks of the Mississippi Delta, and formalised it into the first published blues, 'Memphis Blues', in 1909. Handy was a trumpeter and bandleader, not a singer. But blues had its origin in the emotionally intense yearning of church singing, and it was singers who gave it its most powerful expression into the era of radio and recordings. An early pioneer, Ma Rainey, said that in 1902 a girl had taught her a sad song about a man leaving a woman, just the sort of narrative that characterised what became 'the blues'. Rainey went on to work with legends including 'King' Oliver, Louis Armstrong and Sidney Bechet.

About ten years later, Ma Rainey encountered a gifted younger singer in her backing chorus, Bessie Smith. Smith was an orphan from Tennessee who had busked on the streets from the age of nine, and rose to become one of the highest-paid singers in the 1920s. Her voice had the penetrating emotional directness of the Black churches – her father had been a Baptist church minister. But Smith retained the character of a tough, working-class woman who was not to be kept down.

In 1925 she recorded W. C. Handy's 'St Louis Blues' with Louis Armstrong. Four years later a short film was built round her performance. Smith sings and plays the part of a woman, 'Bessie', whose lover leaves her for another, fancier woman (as in 'St Louis Blues'), and then returns to steal money from her. This is the only film of Bessie Smith, and it is a precious document. But it also presents us with a recurrent problem. We naturally hear the music of these African American singers as steeped in their centuries of struggle to survive, and that is part of the source of the film's power. But nobody becomes a great musician simply through oppression. As well as talent, a musician needs advice, practice, determination.

Blues and early jazz performers did not often talk about their training, wishing to give as spontaneous an impression as possible. Not much is known about how Smith acquired her phenomenal qualities as a performer, beyond instinctive talent, singing in the church, and possibly some help from Ma Rainey. But there were many early Black jazz performers from poor backgrounds whose talents were nurtured by dedicated music teachers at schools for Black children. Trumpeter Louis Armstrong was first taught by a bandleader at his school, the Colored Waifs' Boys Home in New Orleans. W. C. Handy attended the Florence School for Negroes in Alabama. The school had no piano or organ, but the music teacher, with nothing but a pitch pipe to give the notes, taught the pupils the notes of the scales, the different keys, how to sing in parts, and they learned to sing classical works in chorus. Many musicians had stories of how they were helped by dedicated teachers in deprived circumstances, illustrating a recurring human phenomenon that it is often those who have least who most support each other.

Blues and ragtime represent opposite sides of what rapidly became jazz. The factor that transformed instrumental jazz into a popular genre was its appeal as dance music across the social classes. Previously, dancing for the white majority had centred on European dances. These included quadrilles and other group dances, and, for couples, polkas, mazurkas, gallops, and above all waltzes. Upper-class households employed dancing masters and mistresses to teach young people the correct steps and deportment, and dancing to appropriate music was part of formalised social life.

Ragtime and jazz, together with associated American dances, loosened all this up. Already in the 1880s, the American Barn Dance, with its country music, had started to push aside the quadrilles of Europe. Now around 1900 ragtime came in, with dances that were irresistibly energetic and simple to learn: the One Step, the Two Step, the Turkey Trot, the Charleston, as well as the Argentine Tango and Brazilian Maxixe. Despite the alarm of the older generation, the new trend was unstoppable, and by the end of the First World War everyone, both sides of the Atlantic, was dancing to jazz. Recordings and radio accelerated the take-over. The dance bars and clubs were the place to be, but you didn't need musicians to start dancing in your own living room: you could put on a record or listen to the radio.

Early jazz bands played for dances, weddings and funeral parades in the Southern states of the United States, improvising a synco-pated polyphony with trumpet or cornet, trombone, tuba, clarinet, maybe with banjo and other instruments. It was not 'show-off' virtuoso performance, but music that expressed community by its close ensemble of near equals. This is the style of early jazz bands, such as the 'Original Dixieland Jazz Band'. They made the first recordings of jazz in 1917, including 'Tiger Rag', and toured abroad to London and Paris. Kid Ory and King Oliver, who both began their careers in the bars and brothels of Storyville, New Orleans, were among those who rose to fame through early recordings.

Individual display was less important than the sense of togetherness. But a change in style was given impetus by trumpeter Louis Armstrong. He too was from New Orleans, worked with various bands and then, in 1925 in Chicago, formed 'Louis Armstrong and His Hot Five'. Armstrong became known for his brilliant solos, introducing a competitive element into jazz improvisation that was to be a persistent feature over the years. This was one of the elements that conspired to ensure that, apart from singers and the occasional pianist, jazz was overwhelmingly a man's world as it entered the era of the big band.

CHAPTER 35

From Big Band to Bebop

Larger dance venues encouraged larger jazz bands, and by the 1920s the 'big band' sound was driving all before it. The brilliance of the trumpets, the solidity of the trombones and the warm richness of the saxophones created a uniquely varied and satisfying combination of sonorities. They could play everything from straightforwardly swinging dance music to highly sophisticated pieces almost as substantial as classical concertos or symphonies. Unlike earlier small groups, which relied on largely improvised polyphony played by ear, big bands required extensive preparation and rehearsal. In the most famous bands, the level of musicianship and discipline was extremely high. They rehearsed with a mixture of notated parts and 'head arrangements', in which the players learned their parts by ear during rehearsal, without notation. The development of the head arrangement is attributed to two white musicians, Paul Whiteman and Bix Beiderbecke, both with experience of the classical music world. White and Black musicians adopted the method, among them the Black bandleader Fletcher Henderson.

His recordings with his own band pioneered what was to become the classic big band sound. In the 1930s, with the rise of famous bands promoted by recordings and radio, Henderson supplied arrangements to them. But there was a problem: he had never written them down. When Benny Goodman's band was offered a regular radio series, he bought many of Henderson's pieces. But first, Henderson had to go back to his own recordings, and transcribe the arrangements from them.

The combination of spontaneous-sounding swing with impressive discipline made the big bands of the 1930s and 1940s a phenomenal success. But the big band provided the opportunity not just for popular success but also for sophistication and seriousness to rival the classical orchestra. And the outstanding figure in this was Duke Ellington, who himself composed much of his band's repertoire. He encapsulates several of the contradictions of the era. His band played at the Cotton Club in Harlem in New York from 1927. The audience was all-white, and among the club's entertainment were 'jungle-themed' nights: Ellington himself had made records in what was known as 'jungle style'. This could be seen as skirting dangerously near racial stereotypes. But Ellington's originality, with a distinctly ironic, 'modernist' edge, suggested not so much stereotype as a parody of the stereotype. By the 1930s, Ellington's reputation was so high that he was able to get the Cotton Club to relax its segregation policies. He and his band toured Europe to great acclaim, earning the admiration of music critics, who compared him to classical composers Ravel and Stravinsky.

Ellington had ambitions to produce something more than the three-minute pieces demanded by recordings. He had already written some more substantial items, and when the band played a landmark concert at New York's Carnegie Hall in 1943, Ellington composed a three-movement suite for the occasion, *Black, Brown and Beige*. The concert was a great occasion celebrating Ellington's twenty years in New York, and he was presented with a commemorative plaque signed by many of the leading musicians of both the jazz and the classical worlds. *Black, Brown and Beige* was based on the history of Black struggle and aspiration, and was a work of serious intent. But it was not well received at the time. Classical critics saw it as a failed attempt to be 'symphonic', jazz fans saw it as having lost jazz's essential dance origins. Much later, in 1958, Ellington set words to a saxophone solo from the first movement and called it 'Come Sunday'. This turned it into a powerful hymn, in which the singer Mahalia Jackson implored God to look after her people.

Meanwhile, Harlem's rival to the Cotton Club, the Savoy Ballroom, had a policy of non-segregation, admitting white and Black together. It became renowned as a centre for the latest dance craze, the Lindy Hop (also known as the Jitterbug). Among the bands who played there were those led by Benny Goodman (clarinettist), Chick Webb (drummer) and Count Basie (pianist), and the rivalry between them was formalised into Battles of the Bands, with the winners chosen by the public. This rivalry would continue in jazz bars with 'cutting contests', to see who could dominate by playing faster and higher. This was an indication of the macho, overwhelmingly male world of the famous jazz bands. Women performed as singers with the bands, referred to as 'song birds' – the teenage Ella Fitzgerald was engaged by Chick Webb after winning a talent contest in 1934. And there were some notable women jazz pianists, among them the remarkable Hazel Scott. Taught by her classically trained mother, she became so well-known in the jazz venues that she went on in 1950 to become the first musician of African heritage to be given her own television show.

Benny Goodman also aspired to bridge the gap with the classical world, not, like Ellington, by composing, but by being accepted as a classical clarinettist. He commissioned Béla Bartók to write a trio for clarinet, violin and piano, Contrasts, in 1938. This turned out to be a thoroughly Hungarian-inspired, rather than jazzy, work. Then in 1947 Goodman asked American composer Aaron Copland to write a Clarinet Concerto for him, which has a jazzy finale. The bandleader Woody Herman commissioned Igor Stravinsky to compose Ebony Concerto for his band in 1945. But although Stravinsky had flirted with jazz rhythms, he had no feeling for jazz's dance-based freedoms. The band found the music extremely awkward, and it remains one of Stravinsky's less admired pieces.

It was in 1924, three years before Duke Ellington had begun his residency at the Cotton Club, that bandleader Paul Whiteman put on a concert billed as 'an experiment in modern music'. It was one of many attempts to make jazz more 'respectable' to white audiences by bringing it into the concert hall. The highlight was the first performance of *Rhapsody in Blue*, a piece for piano and orchestra by a young songwriter and pianist, George Gershwin. For the concert, Whiteman engaged his usual band which included many of the finest white jazz players, together with classical string players. Following the concert, Gershwin was asked by Walter Damrosch, the conductor of the New York Symphony Orchestra, to compose a piano concerto.

Gershwin had scored his first major success as a song composer in 1919 with 'Swanee', which was taken up by the rising star Al Jolson, who sang it in blackface. But Gershwin had studied classical music, and his aspiration to write big works reached a climax in 1935 with his 'American folk opera' *Porgy and Bess*. It was performed by an all-Black cast, and achieved the success that had eluded Scott Joplin with his *Treemonisha* twenty years earlier – though critics were quick to point out the irony of a successful white composer evoking the life of a poor Black community in an opera. Gershwin's career was already dazzling, and he would undoubtedly have achieved much more. But a brain tumour killed him at the age of thirty-eight.

Paul Whiteman's combination of classical strings with the woodwind and brass of the jazz band created a synthesis that was to prove potent in the Broadway musical. The composer Jerome Kern had already made his mark with *Oh Boy!* in 1917. It was Kern and lyricist Oscar Hammerstein II who, in 1927, took the musical to a whole new level with *Show Boat*. Musicals had previously been lightweight comedies. But this one was serious, tackling head on issues of race and discrimination, with a love story across the racial divide. It was *Show Boat* that set in train the history of the musical as drama, not just entertainment. There were still highly popular comedies, but it was the successors to *Show Boat* that tried to explore the serious possibilities of the musical. In *Oklahoma!* (1943), Richard Rodgers with Hammerstein tried to ensure that each song formed part of the drama, helping to push the story on. This endeavour reached its climax with *West Side Story* (1957), with music by Leonard Bernstein and lyrics by Stephen Sondheim. It is the heir of *Show Boat*, reworking Shakespeare's *Romeo and Juliet* with doomed lovers from rival gangs across the racial divide. And its score, by a brilliant classical composer, is the most complex and subtle of all Broadway musicals.

I have given the names of the lyricists (who wrote the words of the songs) for all these Broadway musicals. It is one of the most important features of this genre that it is the words as much as the music that make the songs work. The best lyricists had a knack of combining the simple and the emotionally telling in a way that sounds natural rather than banal or contrived. You can hear this even in the titles of the songs: 'They can't take that away from me' (Irving Berlin), or 'People will say we're in love' (Oscar Hammerstein). Simple touches, like ordinary speech, elevate melodies to create songs of great subtlety. Stephen Sondheim, the lyricist for *West Side Story*, went on to compose his own musicals. He took the genre in the direction of sophisticated wit, with intricate plots and ensemble numbers that demand concentration from the audience and great skill and co-ordination from the actor-singers. Other musicals since *West Side Story* have tended to move away from subtlety, satisfying a public craving for bold, singable tunes and big effects, often carried by spectacular stage productions.

Jazz itself has gone in many different directions since the heyday of the big bands. While the bands and Broadway musicals were attracting the crowds into the 1940s, not only in the theatres but through radio and film, smaller-scale jazz tended to aim more for an audience of connoisseurs, exploring the emotional and intellectual possibilities of the music. They retained more improvisation than was possible in the context of a big band, but at the same time experimented with a more daring vocabulary of harmonies and key changes. The leading African American musicians in this movement wanted to distance themselves from the mainstream entertainment industry dominated by white money-makers, which they saw as having swallowed up their musical culture. And unlike big band music, this was essentially music to listen to, not to dance to.

The saxophonist Charlie Parker was an influential figure, inspiring many others to experiment. He described a moment in 1939 when, in the middle of improvising on a tune with a guitarist, he started using the upper notes of chords as the bass notes of new chords, in effect playing in two keys at once (a favourite effect of classical composers from Debussy onwards). Parker, with others including trumpeter Dizzy Gillespie and pianist Thelonious Monk, developed these new ideas at jazz clubs in Harlem in the 1940s to create the quirky, challenging genre known as 'bebop'.

One musician who idolised Charlie Parker was trumpeter Miles Davis, who had trained at a classical music school but found the teaching 'too white'. He learned the new, complex chord changes from Parker and Gillespie, and then experimented with ways of simplifying the language without losing its newness. The result was a more contemplative style of jazz. The landmark recording that attracted a wider audience to this new 'cool' jazz was Davis's *Kind of Blue* (1959), in which he was joined by saxophonist John Coltrane, pianist Bill Evans and others. In the studio, Davis presented the musicians with certain scales or modes, some fragments of melody, but not the traditional chord sequences or songs. The result is almost static, hypnotic, oscillating between very few chords, with floating improvisations that have none of the assertive raucousness of much bebop. It seems to take jazz almost in the direction of Indian or Arab improvisation.

'Cool' jazz was highly influential. Among its most successful exponents was the Modern Jazz Quartet, in which Milt Jackson's vibraphone gave a particularly haunting quality to slow numbers. Echoes of cool jazz are still with us to this day. Keith Jarrett's long, meditative solo piano improvisations are a recent manifestation. And he and other pianists have explored new harmonic devices, often deploying chords built on intervals of fourths to create a sense of timeless floating.

If there is often a vaguely spiritual feel to this floating, that too is an echo of African American musicians of an earlier generation. Miles Davis said that *Kind of Blue* was partly inspired by memories of his childhood, evoking sounds of gospel singing as he returned from church: 'that feeling I had when I was six years old, walking with my cousin along that dark Arkansas road . . . when the owls came out hooting'. African Americans' continued link with a religious basis is one of the things that distinguishes them from the experience of most white musicians. Saxophonist John Coltrane described music as 'the spiritual expression of what I am: my faith, my knowledge, my being'.

The relationship between Black and white musicians and audiences through the twentieth century is complicated, musically and socially. In the cool jazz scene, Black and white musicians (such as Bill Evans) worked together, and though most of the big bands were either all-Black or all-white, some were mixed. But quite soon, most of the big money was being made by white managers and organisations, a situation that is only changing slowly in modern times. Given the foundation laid by African American musicians at the dawn of the twentieth century, there are some unavoidable questions.

George Gershwin declared in 1927 that jazz was 'the voice of the American soul . . . It is black and white. It is all colours and all souls unified in the great melting-pot of the world'. You could see this as an act of generous acknowledgement from a white composer of his Black fellow musicians, but some have seen it as Gershwin offering his fellow European Americans something that was not his to give. Not many people went as far as bass player and composer Charles Mingus, who declared, 'Jazz – it's the American Negro's tradition, it's his music. White people don't have the right to play it.' That is an extreme position, but Mingus follows it with something that is more difficult to argue with: 'You had your Shakespeare and Marx and Einstein . . . but we came up with *Jazz*, don't forget it, and all the pop music in the world today is from that primary cause.' As I said about folk music, music is not an object that one can steal, like a bronze statue or the sculptures on an ancient temple. The original is still there, whatever use other people make of it, and white musicians have certainly contributed wonderful things to jazz. But it is as well to have our eyes and ears open to where those riches came from in the first place.

CHAPTER 36

Reacting to Repression

Music has always had a use in war, to scare the enemy, to strengthen the resolve of fighters, to keep up the spirits of those at home. In wars throughout history, people have made music themselves or have had it supplied by musicians in person. During the Second World War musicians toured the army camps on both sides. But this was the heyday of radio, and the musicians who toured could also be heard across the world by soldiers and civilians. German pilots had a particular love of American jazz, much to Hitler's annoyance.

Music on the radio was a comfort but could also be used for propaganda. A powerful example was 'Lili Marleen', a soldier's love song. The German singer Lale Andersen made a cheerful, march-tempo recording in 1939 that was immensely popular among German soldiers. Then, in 1944, the USA's 'Morale Operations' got German-born singer Marlene Dietrich to record a melancholy version of the song, which was broadcast from secret radio stations across Germany. It was reported to be very effective at making German soldiers feel homesick.

Music was played and composed in prisoner-of-war camps, and even in the appalling conditions of the Nazi concentration camps. A rich repertoire of works by Jewish prisoners has gradually emerged. In London, the pianist Myra Hess was the figurehead for a series of lunchtime concerts at the National Gallery that continued daily for the six years of the war. Bud Flanagan and Chesney Allen, singing comedians from the British music hall, became famous during the war for their gentle songs mocking Hitler and celebrating the friendship of ordinary people.

After the war, there were some striking changes. One arose from Hitler's repression of certain kinds of music. The Nazis condemned jazz because of its association with an 'inferior' race. At the same time, the regime condemned all music that was dissonant or intellectually challenging. This was partly a veiled attack on Jewish musical intellectuals, particularly Schoenberg, but it extended to others who were seen as tainted with dissonance. This went hand in hand with the condemnation of modern art. An exhibition was organised of 'Degenerate Art' in Munich in 1937, followed the next year by an exhibition of 'Degenerate Music'. The music ranged from jazz to modern classical composers. Both exhibitions were extremely successful, not because people wished to be educated about degeneracy, but because they wanted to see the art and hear the music.

Stalin in Russia also repressed dissonant music. And as the Cold War with Russia developed, Hitler and Stalin's repression of challenging music provoked a reaction in the West. The music that they condemned came to be seen as somehow representing freedom, and therefore deserving of promotion. Governments and arts organisations across Europe and the United States adopted a policy of financing the most 'advanced' music, with the implication that it was more important than music that was easy to understand. In Britain, the BBC had broadcast regular concerts of new music ever since its establishment as a corporation in 1927. In 1946, a year after the war ended, the BBC launched its 'Third Programme', devoted to serious arts and discussion. Its promotion of modern music became particularly intense during the 1960s when it commissioned and performed works by many of the most challenging composers.

A focus for new musical thinking after the war was the Vacation Courses for New Music, held annually at Darmstadt, Germany, from 1946. Their purpose was to repair the damage done by the Nazis and reconnect Germany to the latest thinking in music. The twelve-note 'serialism' of Schoenberg and his pupils was revered at Darmstadt, particularly the work of Webern. A group of young composers, including Karlheinz Stockhausen and Pierre Boulez, set about developing new ways of building on Schoenberg's and Webern's principles. Like Schoenberg, they developed an almost religious belief that these principles were an inevitable consequence of history, not merely a subjective choice. Boulez emerged as the most determined member of this group, applying the organising principle of serialism to every aspect of music, not just the pitch of a note, but its length, tone-quality, volume and attack. This led on to methods of extraordinary complexity and subtlety, in which these different components of music were treated as independent from each other, and organised according to various determining principles. Stockhausen developed huge structures whereby everything in a composition, from the tiniest detail to the overall structure, derives from a 'super-formula'. This reached a climax in his massive cycle of seven operas, *Licht*, which he began in the 1970s, and, at twenty-eight hours of music, is truly Wagnerian in its ambitions.

Obsession with musical structures was only one aspect of the new thinking. There was also an urge to expand the range of sounds and tone-colours available to musicians, rather than just accept the available instruments and voices. This quest had begun much earlier in the century, with the French composer Edgard Varèse. He had emigrated to the United States in 1915 and explored ways of creating music that made Stravinsky's *The Rite of Spring* seem almost traditional. Varèse's *Amériques*, composed between 1918 and 1921, is for an enormous orchestra, including many percussion players, and stretches the possibilities of the orchestra to breaking point, with climaxes of utter destruction. Already in 1916, Varèse had said, 'We also need new instruments very badly', in order to open up entirely new ways of composing. By the 1950s, the instruments that would make Varèse's visions a reality were coming into being: computers and tape recorders. And as part of the post-war thrust towards modernity, which seemed so 'anti-fascist', organisations in Germany, the United States and France were pouring money into electronic studios.

Of all the early experiments with electronic music, one of the most complex is Stockhausen's *Gesang der Jünglinge* (Song of the Youths), which took over a year to create (1955–6). Stockhausen recorded a choirboy singing fragments of melody and text from the Bible. Everything was layered and organised with mind-boggling complexity, creating what Stockhausen called 'swarms'. All of this was recorded on magnetic tape – this was before computer memory became available. Despite the incomprehensible complexity of its design, the work is fascinating for its multi-layered mixture of human and electronic sounds.

The official promotion of electronic music in France reached a climax in 1970 when the president of France, Georges Pompidou, authorised the establishment of an electronic research institute, IRCAM, headed by Pierre Boulez. It was to be housed next door to the prestigious new Pompidou Centre in the heart of Paris. Even in Soviet Russia, after the death of Stalin in 1953, the government encouraged the development of electronic instruments as part of the drive towards 'Socialist modernity'.

Meanwhile, electronic research was adding a new dimension to broadcasting and popular music. In Britain in 1958, the BBC established its Radiophonic Workshop, with Delia Derbyshire and Daphne Oram as lead innovators. It was Derbyshire who created the arrangement of Ron Grainer's theme for *Doctor Who*. In the 1960s, the Moog Synthesizer, developed from earlier Russian prototypes, made electronic music widely available, and it entered the field of experimental pop. It was famously used by Kraftwerk from the 1970s, and Laurie Anderson in 'O Superman' (1981). Over the following decades, the possibilities of electronic music were explored by many musicians in the pop world, creating genres that overlapped with the experiments of Stockhausen and others in the classical field.

The idea of using any kind of sound, rather than just musical notes, was taken further by American John Cage. In 1952 he devised *Water Music*, which involves pouring water from one vessel into another, shuffling a pack of cards, and finding different stations on a radio, all according to detailed instructions. He went on to experiment with the use of chance, or random events, creating what we would now call 'performance art'. Notoriously, also in 1952, Cage came up with *4′33″*, in which a pianist sits playing absolutely nothing. The only sounds heard are those in the room. This could be seen as a mere joke, a provocation. But Cage was interested in removing the 'performance' from music, of opening minds to what was all around them.

Cage's *Variations IV* (1963) is described as being 'for any number of players, any sounds or combinations of sounds produced by any means, with or without other activities'. A sheet with points and a circle is cut up and thrown onto a map of the performance area, to choose places where actions might be performed. A recording of the premiere, performed by Cage with David Tudor, consists of a jumble of sounds including voices and music from radio channels, street sounds, people clinking glasses at a bar, and so on. The event lasted from 7 p.m. to 1 a.m. But this is just one of an infinite number of possibilities: there is no 'work' to be performed, merely the establishment of circumstances in which events may take place.

Cage's ideas were strongly influenced by Eastern religions, particularly Zen Buddhism, with its aim to remove oneself from all desire or expectation. But, of course, Cage still retains expectation: he demands to be heard, to be reacted to. There is no question of his disappearance.

Boulez was a close friend of Cage for a time in the 1950s. But he stayed committed to order and precision, and this remained his guiding principle throughout his long career, both as a composer and as a conductor. He first leapt to public fame with the premiere in 1955 of *Le Marteau sans maître* (The Hammer without a Master), a song cycle for alto voice, flute, viola, guitar, vibraphone and percussion. Analysts have established that Boulez used complex and subtle ways of manipulating his note-row. But this is not discernible by ear. What the listeners hear is a web of leaping fragments, with no obvious suggestion of themes or melodies, not even in the voice. The kaleidoscopic effect, using a deliberately un-blending combination of instruments, carries suggestions of South-East Asian percussion ensembles. Stravinsky called *Le Marteau sans maître* 'one of the few significant works of the post-war period of exploration'.

As the Cold War developed between the United States and the Soviet Union, music that was seen as sympathetic to the opposite side came under suspicion. The Russian composer Dmitri Shostakovich had survived the years of the Stalin regime, and was seen in the West as a heroic figure during the war. His Symphony No. 7 was composed in 1941, as the German army besieged Leningrad (St Petersburg), resulting in the death of 600,000 people. Shostakovich vividly, and brutally, evokes the struggle against oppression. Microfilm of the score of the symphony was flown to London, where it was performed at a Promenade Concert.

In 1949, with the Cold War between the United States and the Soviet Union under way, Shostakovich, at the request of Stalin, attended a Conference for World Peace in New York. He gave a speech in which he attacked Stravinsky (then living in the USA) as a corrupter of Western art, and acknowledged that he himself had sometimes been led astray. It was clear to the listeners that Shostakovich had been obliged to say these things as an expression of Soviet policy.

As the fear of communism grew in the United States, musicians with any hint of socialist views found themselves under suspicion. Prominent composers were called to appear before Senator Joseph McCarthy's Un-American Activities Committee, which aimed to root out communist sympathisers. Aaron Copland, who sought to write music accessible to anyone, was called in 1953 to defend himself against accusations of affiliation with communist organisations. The persecution of musicians in America extended to all genres. Hazel Scott, whom I've already mentioned as a brilliant jazz pianist and singer, was a fierce supporter of civil rights. She was summoned to appear before McCarthy's committee in 1950, following which her TV show was cancelled. She suffered a nervous breakdown, and never fully rebuilt her career.

Meanwhile, composers in communist countries continued to face persecution. In Hungary, György Ligeti lived through first Nazi and then Stalinist repression, escaping in 1956 to Austria when the Russians crushed the Hungarian Revolution. He was inspired, like his predecessor, Bartók, by Hungarian and Romanian folk music, and also fascinated by maths and physics as well as all the latest musical developments. But Ligeti was not free to explore these possibilities in public. While still in Hungary, he was obliged to write easy-going settings of folk songs for public performance, but in secret he was experimenting, particularly exploring new ways of writing for the piano. His *Musica Ricercata* (1951–3) is a sort of demonstration of how to compose, starting with one note only, adding another note for each piece, and ending with all twelve notes of the octave. It is a fascinating exploration of possibilities of counterpoint, rhythm, and the sonorities of the piano. It wasn't performed in public until 1969. Exiled in Austria and Germany, Ligeti was free to experiment openly. Late in his career, he composed three books of piano Études (studies), which are fascinating in their complexity. They draw on inspiration from many sources, including *gamelan* and African drumming patterns.

As before the war, there were plenty of composers who ploughed on without being either at the forefront of modernity or stuck in traditional ways. One of the most difficult to pigeonhole is the French composer Olivier Messiaen. He had a reputation as a teacher of everything from Monteverdi to Stravinsky and Schoenberg. Messiaen was a generation older than Boulez and Stockhausen, and both of them attended his classes. He was a deeply religious man. Messiaen wrote a large quantity of organ music, and was celebrated as a great improviser on the organ. He considered his music a meditation on the world as a manifestation of God's love, and Messiaen drew very widely on that world. He was fascinated by the complex rhythms of Indian music and Balinese *gamelan* (in an echo of Debussy). In the

1940s he brought these different influences together in his massive *Turangalîla Symphony*, an exploration of love through the myth of Tristan and Isolde. Another of God's gifts that Messiaen celebrated was birdsong. He studied it seriously, and brought transcriptions into his compositions, culminating in the 1950s in a collection of piano pieces based almost entirely on birdsong, *Catalogue d'Oiseaux*.

Messiaen's music is highly unconventional without being attached to any fashion or school. More traditional in their approach were the two leading composers in Britain after the Second World War, Benjamin Britten and Michael Tippett. The two had much in common. They were both pacifists and conscientious objectors during the war. They both aimed to write music that was accessible without being old-fashioned. And they were both concerned to reach out to ordinary music-lovers. Tippett taught at an adult education college, and conducted an orchestra of out-of-work musicians. He made his name with *A Child of Our Time* (1944), a cantata that hopes for a reconciliation of the 'dark side' of human nature, and incorporates spirituals rather as J. S. Bach used Lutheran chorales in his cantatas. Among Tippett's operas are the exuberant *The Midsummer Marriage* (1955) and the powerful tragedy *King Priam* (1962).

Britten's reputation was established with the opera *Peter Grimes* (1945), based on a poem by the Suffolk poet, George Crabbe, in which he vividly evokes the fishing community of a Suffolk town, and their attitude to a cruel, isolated fisherman. Britten himself lived near Aldeburgh in Suffolk, and established an annual festival there in 1948. If there is one event that demonstrates how alienated Britten and many other composers felt from the avant-garde of Darmstadt, it is the opening of this festival. Britten composed for the occasion *Saint Nicolas*, a cantata that brought together professional instrumentalists, school choirs, and audience participation. This is a very long way from the remote intellectual complexity of Boulez or Stockhausen.

CHAPTER 37

Just Rattle Your Jewellery

I remember vividly the moment in 1963 when my family first acquired a record of the Beatles. It was 'She Loves You', I was eighteen, and it was a blast of fresh air.

Paul McCartney, John Lennon and George Harrison had got together as a skiffle group when they were teenagers in Liverpool (drummer Ringo Starr joined them a few years later). Skiffle was essentially a rough-and-ready, amateur genre, something that any working-class boy could quickly get involved in. It echoed the many groups that had sprung up in the United States, often with home-made instruments and maybe a cheap guitar or banjo. With the development of the electric guitar, this grassroots activity on both sides of the Atlantic formed the basis of the rock 'n' roll band.

Early rock 'n' roll had reached the UK from the United States with Bill Haley and His Comets and 'Rock around the Clock' (1955). The song was so successful that it was used as the basis of a film of the same name the following year. Here, Haley and the Comets perform for young girls in party frocks, and for adults dancing formal dance steps. I remember myself being taught the 'official' steps of rock 'n' roll at teenage dance classes. This was fun, but tame stuff compared to what was to follow.

Elvis Presley, white like Bill Haley, sang in a much more intense, emotional manner, modelled on Black rhythm and blues singers whom he acknowledged as his inspirations. Elvis scored a huge success with his early records, such as 'Hound Dog' and 'Don't Be Cruel' (1956). Later white rock 'n' roll singers followed Elvis in adopting a 'semi-Black' style of singing, rendering it acceptable to the majority white audience. Elvis had a particularly seductive quality of voice, which he coupled with overtly sexual hip-movements. In his early days he was regarded as a threat to public order by the authorities, despite having been brought up singing in church. He certainly attracted young crowds, and they certainly screamed.

Rock 'n' roll quickly knocked the existing popular musicians off their positions as the most successful entertainers. Crooner Frank Sinatra, who had inspired the adoration of the crowds, rightly saw himself threatened by the new craze. In 1957 he published an article in a London newspaper, in which he praised jazz as America's great ambassador, loved by people all over the world. But he deplored rock 'n' roll, 'the most brutal, ugly, degenerate, vicious form of expression . . . sung, played and written, for the most part, by cretinous goons . . . This rancid-smelling aphrodisiac I deplore.' Sinatra was fighting a losing battle. Three years later he felt obliged to invite Elvis Presley onto his TV show, in which they both looked awkward. But the tide had turned, and rock 'n' roll was the future.

The Beatles knew all the Black, blues-derived influences of rock 'n' roll, but their approach had a more home-grown appeal. Their songs, mostly written by Lennon and McCartney, seemed simple, but had an elegant, almost folk-song style of melody. With their Liverpool accents, this gave them an instantly recognisable personality. And, compared with other rock 'n' roll groups, they sang with unusually sophisticated two- and three-part harmonies and surprising chord changes. This even attracted the approval of classical commentators who had previously ignored the rock 'n' roll scene. Lennon and McCartney's musical relationship was intense, as footage of their rehearsals shows, and the public quickly recognised this as something special. 'She Loves You' sold three-quarters of a million copies in less than a month, the fastest-selling record in the UK to that date, and over six years the Beatles had a string of seventeen No. 1 hits.

Meanwhile, in the United States, the Beach Boys had their first hit 'Surfin' USA' in 1963, the same year as 'She Loves You'. The Beach Boys had, rather like the Beatles, started as a garage band, with teenager Brian Wilson and his younger brothers. They developed an approach as sophisticated as that of the Beatles, with not only three-part vocal harmony but also the use of tape resources to create double-tracking and overlaying of voices. This gave a rich, super-realistic dimension to their sound. Rather than working-class Liverpool directness, the Beach Boys projected California sophistication and aspiration, a world full of bronzed girls and sunshine.

The Beach Boys were one of the few American groups that continued to prosper through the 'English invasion', led by the Beatles. When the Beatles toured the United States in 1964 and performed on *The Ed Sullivan Show*, they attracted the largest audience ever recorded for a US television show (73 million). Wherever they went, either side of the Atlantic, they were, like Elvis, mobbed. Their concerts were accompanied by such loud screaming that, despite amplification, the music was sometimes barely audible (the Beatles came to hate these events). This was despite the fact that their stage performances had none of the overt eroticism of Elvis.

The Beatles arrived at just the right moment. It was less than twenty years since the end of the Second World War. After the post-war Labour government, admired for its establishment of the National Health Service, Britain had reverted to the Conservatives. Harold Macmillan, the very image of the prosperous establishment, had been prime minister for six years. Despite the promise that Britain would be transformed into a fairer society after the war, the dream was fading fast. The teenagers taking to skiffle and the like had no role in how they were governed: the voting age in the UK and in the United States was still twenty-one. There was frustration at the persistence of the old guard and their stuffy values. And despite the coming of skiffle and the beginnings of rock 'n' roll, for most families their diet of popular music consisted largely of songs and dances in the style of the previous generation.

Rock 'n' roll challenged all this, demanding that tradition should give way, and that everyone should be pulled onto a less inhibited dance floor. And, crucially, the principal target of popular music shifted from whole families to the young. 'Teenager' was a word scarcely used before the 1940s; it now became the defining term of youth culture and its music. The idea took root that the young were more important than the old and that youthful vigour was more important than aged wisdom, and it has not left us yet.

What was particularly clever about the Beatles was that they managed to appeal to the young without threatening the older generation, while retaining the appearance of authenticity by adhering to their working-class, Liverpool roots. My whole family enjoyed them. The same year we acquired 'She Loves You', 1963, we watched the Beatles appearing in front of the Queen at the Royal Variety Performance on TV. They were immaculately presented, joyful, witty and cheeky. Before their last number, John Lennon invited the audience in the cheaper seats to clap their hands, 'and the rest of you, if you'll just rattle your jewellery'. Lennon smiled and ducked his head at this point, like a small boy cheeking his dad and avoiding a smack. That gesture said it all. The Beatles cheeked the establishment without seriously worrying them.

As for their musical sophistication, this was skilfully managed over the years, particularly by their producer George Martin. It was Martin who added a string quartet to 'Eleanor Rigby' and a high trumpet solo to 'Penny Lane', as if musicians from a classical session in the next studio had popped their head round the door. This sort of mock-classical touch was to feature in several other successful groups over the years: Led Zeppelin's 'Stairway to Heaven' with its opening using recorders, Queen's 'Bohemian Rhapsody' with its exuberant operatic fantasy.

All of this represents rock 'n' roll at its most respectable, you might say. Other rock groups adopted more of the intense style associated with African American singers. The Rolling Stones, formed in 1962, were pioneers of what came to be known as 'hard rock', with a more aggressive vocal style and heavy, driven guitar rhythms. They were followed by other groups such as the Who and The Kinks (both formed in 1964). In contrast with the benign air of the Beatles, an undertone of menace and potential violence was part of their appeal, which, in the case of both the Rolling Stones and the Kinks, sometimes spilled over into actual violence at concerts. A decade later, this dark side was to be exploited by 'punk rock', with its overtly anti-establishment message. But for now, the violent edge didn't stop hard rock contributing to the 'Swinging 60s' in Britain, with its emphasis on confident, fashionable young people who were not going to be told how to behave.

One element in these developments was the electric guitar, which, in standard and bass forms, created the gritty, energetic sound of the rock band. This was the latest product of a technology that had started back in the 1920s: amplification and the use of microphones. At first, microphones were used to make people audible in large spaces – singers with a big band, politicians addressing rallies. The musical world soon divided into genres for which amplification was appropriate, and others for which it was not. The classical world generally coped without it, except in the recording studio. To this day, singers in opera are expected to project their voices without help, unless they are in unusually large venues or outdoors. Popular music embraced amplification. This didn't just make people audible: in the world of singers, it made possible whole new styles. A singer could sing in an intimate, unforced style alongside a big band, and be audible across the hall and on the radio. This had made possible the careers of the crooners, such as Bing Crosby and Frank Sinatra, who were now yielding their place to the new rock stars.

The electric guitar played a crucial role in this development. As with amplification, there were divisions between different genres. Singer-songwriter Billy Bragg recalled that when he was starting out in the English rock clubs around 1980, 'I played electric guitar because if I had played acoustic the rock clubs would have sent me to the folk clubs.' In the United States, country musicians stuck to the traditional acoustic guitar. This was in line with the aura of clean-living, simple, rural life that surrounded country music, as distinct from the more dangerous edge of urban music.

The first country singers to become recording stars were the Carter Family of south-west Virginia, who began recording in 1927. Their lead singer, Sara Carter, played acoustic rhythm guitar or autoharp, while harmony-singer Maybelle played guitar in a style that came to be known as 'Carter Scratch', picking out the tune in the bass and interspersing alternating chords above it. The next generation of the family were joined in 1949 by Chet Atkins on electric guitar. This led on to 'country and western', a beefed-up version of country music more able to compete in the era of rock 'n' roll.

The country field was predominantly white. But in 1965 a Black singer, Charley Pride, made his first recordings of country songs, and went on to become RCA's biggest-selling artist since Elvis Presley. This was not straightforward. The publicity material for his first record did not include the usual photograph of the artist. As it became known that he was Black, it became more difficult for him to get bookings. Despite his enormous recording success, he was a 'guest' in a white genre.

Meanwhile, the electric guitar was becoming the dominant instrument in popular music. African American musicians took advantage of it to add power to the blues. Singers such as Muddy Waters and B. B. King developed a style of guitar-playing involving note-bending, vibrato, and other effects to mimic the human voice. Male performers used the power of the electric guitar to create a macho style of playing, so it came to be predominantly a man's instrument. But one of the most prominent singers and guitar players was a woman, Sister Rosetta Tharpe, who combined the tradition of powerful female gospel-singing with electric guitar.

In the church gospel community from which she had come she was a controversial figure. Although religious concerts were accepted, not everyone thought it appropriate to take such music into settings such as the Cotton Club, where she first appeared in 1938. But her blending of the spiritual with the new highly rhythmic styles made Tharpe a powerful figure. She gave the men as good as she got, and often took part in 'guitar battles', similar to the 'cutting contests' of the jazz world. Her electric-guitar-based spiritual blues was a major influence on 'rhythm and blues', as the record labels now called the new style, and this came to dominate over jazz in the dance halls of major American cities.

Tharpe was one of the major influences on early rock 'n' roll musicians, both Black and white: Little Richard and Chuck Berry (Black), Johnny Cash, Elvis Presley, Jerry Lee Lewis (white). And the influence carried over to the more blues-oriented British groups and guitarists, notably Eric Clapton, Jeff Beck and Keith Richard (of the Rolling Stones). Again, the assertive style was predominantly a man's sport, and women found it difficult to break in. It was not until the 1970s that the rock scene acquired a major female guitar-playing star in the bass-guitarist Suzi Quatro, who in 'Can the Can' provided a joyfully raucous answer to all the macho male rockers.

CHAPTER 38

From Protest to Pop

Sister Rosetta Tharpe was an early example of a singer who made the transition from Black gospel to rhythm and blues. This popularising of music that originated in the Black church communities was taken up in the 1950s and 1960s to create 'soul' music. Its singers were Black men and women, but its appeal crossed racial boundaries. Ray Charles had an early hit in 1954 with 'I Got a Woman'. In the 1960s this combination of intense singing, dance beat, and simple lyrics of everyday life and love proved irresistible, whether the singer was male or female. Otis Redding's 'Respect' was an even greater hit when Aretha Franklin recorded it.

Despite the influence of the African American musical tradition on the popular music scene, by the late 1950s the white-dominated record corporations with their predominantly white recording artists were making most of the money. In the American city of Detroit, there was an attempt both to correct the balance and to break through racial barriers.

In 1960 two African American songwriters, Berry Gordy and Smokey Robinson, established the Motown record label in Detroit, publishing and promoting recordings of predominantly Black artists. Smokey Robinson's own group, the Miracles, gave them their first hit, 'Shop Around', and others soon followed from artists including Mary Wells, the Marvelettes, the Supremes, Marvin Gaye and Stevie Wonder, who made his first recordings at the age of eleven. The predominant Motown style was upbeat and joyful, taking soul to another level in its popular appeal, and helping to break down barriers. Alice Cooper, a white male singer in a Detroit-based hard rock group, remembered how Black Motown and white rock musicians would go to hear each other: 'It's a rock dungeon, and it's sweaty, and it's hot. And you look down and there's Smokey Robinson. And you look over the other side and there's one of the Temptations, or one of the Supremes. All of the Motown acts loved hard rock because of the energy behind it. And when they played, we would all go down there. Even after the riots, if you had long hair, and you were in a band, you could walk into any Black bar downtown, and you were fine.'

Cooper's mention of riots is a reminder that the United States in the 1960s was very far from resolving its tensions. A series of laws against racial discrimination was introduced in this decade, but prejudice against Black people was not so easily broken down. Civil rights movements grew, urging people to achieve in practice what the law said in theory.

The Black Power movement confronted discrimination head on, led by Malcolm X until his assassination in 1965. Meanwhile, the preacher Martin Luther King Jr led a peaceful civil rights movement, culminating in a great march on Washington in 1963. King addressed the huge crowd in his most famous speech: 'I have a dream that one day this nation will rise up and live out the true meaning of its creed: "We hold these truths to be self-evident, that all men are created equal."' That was a quotation from the American Declaration of Independence of 1776, and it summed up the belief that had been fought over for the intervening two centuries.

Music played an important role in these struggles. Nina Simone and James Brown were prominent voices in tune with the Black Power movement. In 1964, Simone dared to sing 'Mississippi Goddam', a song of protest against the murders of Black adults and children, to a predominantly white audience at Carnegie Hall, New York. Its recording rapidly became famous but was banned in Southern states. Four years later, Brown recorded 'Say it Loud – I'm Black and I'm Proud', which also became a popular anthem. With its insistent rhythms and repeating phrases, creating a hypnotic 'groove', it was a powerful example of what came to be known as 'funk', a style that was to influence a wide range of musicians.

It was not only Black musicians who supported King's civil rights movement. The singers who performed on the march on Washington included Black singers Mahalia Jackson, Odetta, and opera-singer Marian Anderson, together with white singers Joan Baez, Bob Dylan, and Peter, Paul and Mary.

I mentioned that in the USA and the UK the voting age was still twenty-one. This had much more serious consequences in America than in Britain. For a decade the United States had been fighting a war against the communists in Vietnam. The brutal fact was that an eighteen-year-old American was too young to vote, but not too young to be drafted into the army and sent to Vietnam to die. Protest against this appalling and unwinnable war took different forms. At its most gentle it involved young people dropping out of the competitive culture in favour of peaceful sharing, love and hallucinogenic drugs. These were the hippies, the 'flower children'. Some 100,000 gathered in San Francisco in 1967 for a 'Summer of Love'. Scott McKenzie recorded an easy-going folk ballad, 'San Francisco (Be sure to wear flowers in your hair)', which became a best-selling anthem for the peace movement. San Francisco-based groups who performed at the Summer of Love included the Grateful Dead, a funky rhythm and blues band, and Jefferson Airplane, who set the tone with their 'psychedelic rock', including lyrics that referred to drug use. These groups, and most of the audience, were white. But there were also appearances from Black artists, including Otis Redding and guitarist Jimi Hendrix.

Peaceful sharing proved to be no match for the growing anger among young Americans, Black and white. The following year, 1968, marked the climax of that anger, with echoes across the Atlantic in Europe. The civil rights movement took a shocking turn when Martin Luther King was assassinated. As word got around, crowds gathered in Washington where the Democrats were holding their Convention. Rioting led to window-smashing and looting, and buildings were set on fire. After four days thirteen people were dead. Two years later, protests against the Vietnam draft at Kent University led to the death of four students, killed by members of the Ohio State Guard. These were just the most high-profile protests of many across the country.

Again, music was an important way of giving voice to the emotions behind these protests – anger, mourning, helplessness at human folly and destructiveness, dreams of a better future. The most spectacular response to destruction was the performance at Woodstock in 1969 by Jimi Hendrix of the national anthem of the United States, 'The Star-Spangled Banner'. He used his electric guitar to distort the anthem into a cry of rage. This was a shocking gesture, and also a powerful expression of the sense that the younger generation had been betrayed by their elders. But Woodstock was more than a protest: it was a great music festival, seen as an important moment in the modern history of music, expressing the hopes as well as the frustrations of the new generation. The music ranged from hard rock all the way to gentle folk music, from the Who to Joan Baez. It was the folk-like songs that most expressed both the feeling of loss and the sense of possibilities. Afterwards, Joni Mitchell wrote a song, 'Woodstock', to express the spirit of the festival. The lyrics imagine the bombers of Vietnam turning into butterflies, and the chorus evokes a return to the Garden of Eden, from which God banished Adam and Eve.

Joni Mitchell and Bob Dylan were the new stars of this 'folk-ballad' style. It's a style that goes back centuries and continues to have a life parallel to that of the heavy rhythms of pop music. Both Mitchell and Dylan are masters of poetic lyrics that suggest a meaning rather than stating it directly. One of Dylan's most famous songs is 'Blowin' in the Wind', which he wrote in 1962. It has images that, like many of Mitchell's, could have come from the Bible, and its melody is based on an old African American spiritual. The meaning is in the end left deliberately vague, but the call for a new spirit of compassion is clear. The song was taken up as another of the anthems of the protest movements, both civil rights and anti-Vietnam.

The comparison between Dylan and Mitchell is fascinating. Dylan's great inspiration was the folk singer Woody Guthrie, who had pioneered lyrics with grand, socialist themes in his songs, most famously 'This Land Is Your Land'. Dylan accompanied his own early songs with an acoustic guitar, interspersing the singing with bursts of simple riffs on a mouth-organ. But by 1966 he was already alternating between acoustic and electric backing, a move which some of his fans considered a betrayal, but which gave birth to 'folk-rock'. He has been unpredictable over his long career, with sudden bursts of inspiration and periods where he seemed to have run out of steam. And his public image, and his way of singing, gives the impression of a man who doesn't really care whether people like what he does, he's going to do it anyway.

Joni Mitchell's music and lyrics are a match for Dylan's, but her character and her attitude are quite different. Many of her songs are more deeply personal, and she seems intimately engaged with her audience. And although she too has engaged with different genres to vary her style, her output through her equally long career has been much more even.

In 2016, Bob Dylan was awarded the Nobel Prize for Literature, an award that prompted predictably divided responses. Is it possible to imagine Joni Mitchell being awarded a Nobel Prize? History teaches us that troublesome and unpredictable men have a habit of getting attention that steady and equally talented women do not. The fact is that both Dylan and Mitchell have been immensely influential over the years, encouraging talented singers to carry on writing serious songs, despite the increasing barrage of commercialisation.

Following on from the protests of the 1960s, in the following decade Jamaican reggae rose to become a leading musical genre of

Black power. Reggae was one of several Caribbean genres which blended the influence of rhythm and blues with other African elements. Bob Marley's 'Get Up, Stand Up' (1973) urged people to stand up for their rights. 'No Woman, No Cry' (1974) was his first international hit, a message of hope that everything would be all right in the end. Reggae, with its speech-style lyrics and repetitive rhythms was one of the genres that gave rise to hip-hop and rap. These emerged in the 1970s in the poor Black areas of American cities, starting in the Bronx, New York. In its hardened, urban form rap was direct, confrontational, often angry. It began as an expression of the lives of Black men who were forced to lead downtrodden lives in crime-ridden communities. It could be playful, but its words were sometimes violent, directed against white power and the police, and sometimes aggressively misogynistic in their attitudes to women. By the 1980s, women were challenging this masculine dominance, using hip-hop and rap to present a very different view of society and of men and women's places in it.

Over the years the rap style has taken many forms, from highly assertive to mild and entertaining. And where once it was a predominantly Black genre, it has been taken up by white men and, increasingly in recent years, women. It can still have a political edge. At the 2018 Brit Awards, Black British rapper Stormzy used a rap to attack the then prime minister, Theresa May, for her failure to respond to the terrible fire in a London block of flats, Grenfell Tower, in which seventy-two people died. Four years later the Black female rapper Little Simz won the Mercury Prize for best British album of the year. In Pakistan, there is a female rapper, Eva B, who attracts millions of viewers to her videos. She said, 'I come from a place where only a few girls get to work and my society doesn't consider a girl who raps to be respectable – I wanted to challenge that.'

The growth of the popular music industry over the last fifty years has been overwhelming, with the big corporations worth many billions of pounds, and the top recording artists extremely rich. On the other hand, the Internet has meant that it is now possible for a musician to make recordings at home and upload them to streaming channels. A number of musicians have become famous by this route, bypassing the official gatekeepers in the big corporations.

The balance of fame and income between white people and people of colour, male and female, has shifted. Several of the top-earning musicians are now women of colour, such as Beyoncé and Rihanna, with millions of fans across all races and genders. In 2016, Beyoncé released *Lemonade*, an album and video exploring her emotional journey after the infidelity of her husband, the rapper Jay-Z. Beyoncé wrote that she comes from 'a lineage of broken male-female relationships' going all the way back to a slave-owner who married a slave. And she added, 'Connecting to the past and knowing our history makes us both bruised and beautiful.' The album brings together issues of feminism and Black history in a powerful way and has been widely praised.

The range of styles in modern pop music is very varied, from a single singer with guitar or piano, through all-male and all-female groups, to bands with enormous power, elaborate studio produc-tion, huge stage displays with explosive sonic effects, and the videos to match. All of the different genres of music that I have discussed in the last two chapters have been echoed and developed. The audience is huge, relishing the intimate, and loving the sensa-tion of being overwhelmed by power. There is a downside: in 2015 it was estimated that over a billion young people were at risk of significant hearing loss because of exposure to loud pop music, either through headphones or at concerts.

All of this could fill another chapter. But when future historians look back at this period, I suspect the thing that will most strike them is the extent to which music that originated in the United States and Britain has spread round the world, leading to new engagement with other cultures. In Chapter 31, I talked about Westernisation. Now we have 'globalisation', in which the influence is not just from the West to other cultures but is a freer-flowing influence both ways.

CHAPTER 39

Music in the 'Global Village'

It was in the 1960s that Marshall McLuhan coined the term 'global village' to describe the interconnections of the modern world. In the twenty-first century those connections are ever more complex and unavoidable. After a period when modernisation seemed to mean embracing Western technology and values in order to compete, now many countries have reasserted the importance of their own cultures, including music. And for the first time since European music started its idiosyncratic development, the West has started a process of genuine engagement with the other musical cultures of the world. Of course, this is not the first time that there has been interest in other cultures. But now we have the beginnings of an exchange of ideas in which the respect and the influence work both ways. Here are just a few examples of this process across the world.

Interaction with the music of the West has taken very varied forms, as I said in Chapter 31. Japan had been undergoing Western-based 'modernisation' since the 1860s. Following the Second World

War, revival was driven once again by the need to rebuild. One result was that Japanese musicians came to excel in Western classical, jazz and pop. Curiously, Japan was becoming interested in Western modernism just at the point where Westerners were beginning to turn elsewhere. In 1961 the 'East-West Music Encounter Conference' was held in Tokyo, partly funded by an American anti-communist organisation. Several of the leading modernist composers from the United States and Europe attended and exchanged ideas with Japanese composers. The following year, John Cage visited Japan, and collaborated with Japanese groups who were already exploring new ways of improvising.

At the same time, there was a realisation that Japan's ancient traditions needed to be preserved. And in recent years interactions between Japanese and Western musical traditions have led to many new works and ideas, both inside and outside Japan. The Japanese flute, the *shakuhachi*, has become popular in the West, not just for its unique range of sounds, but because of its association with meditation and Zen Buddhism. The American musician John Kaizan Neptune has become well-known for his use of the *shaku-hachi* in a wide range of music, from traditional Japanese through jazz to Indian-inspired music.

The major international figure to emerge from Japan since the Second World War was the composer Tōru Takemitsu. He first got to know Western music through radio broadcasts during the American post-war occupation of Japan, and was particularly attracted to contemporary music. At this stage he felt alienated from Japanese culture and did not know traditional Japanese music. Then he discovered the music of the Japanese puppet theatre, *Bunraku*, and this led him to combine elements of Japanese and Western in his own music.

In China, as the terrible Cultural Revolution of Mao Zedong came to an end in the 1970s, Chinese musicians were able to rekindle their love of Western classical music. Students flocked to join the conservatories, interest in the piano revived, and Chinese pianists began to win international competitions. The success of international superstar Lang Lang led to a boom in pianos and piano-playing. By 2012 it was estimated that China was manufacturing 80 per cent of the world's pianos. As I write, Lang Lang is using his own money to set up 'Piano Labs' in junior schools, first in the United States and China, and later in Britain. It is an ironic sign of the times that a Chinese pianist who has earned a fortune from performing European classical music is using it to fill the gap in music education left by Western governments.

Meanwhile, those who had preserved the traditions of historic Chinese music set about re-establishing it. The *qin* (zither), traditionally an instrument for meditation, has been revived with new pieces being composed, and collaborations with jazz and rock musicians. A recording of the piece *gaoshan liushui* ('High Mountains') played by Guan Pinghu, a modern *qin* master, was sent on the Voyager space probe in 1977 as one of the samples of Earth's music.

In the early twentieth century, Korea was part of the Japanese Empire, and therefore modernised early. It was partitioned into communist North Korea and Western-oriented South Korea in 1945. Since the 1970s, South Korean musicians have been prominent in Western music, with many Korean musicians achieving international reputations, particularly violinists. There are Korean jazz genres, and blends of traditional and Western popular music. In the 1990s 'K-Pop', a blend of influences ranging from pop to reggae, emerged from music clubs in Korea to become a major commercial genre, with elaborately produced videos performed by Korean pop stars and marketed worldwide in several different languages. The 2012 video 'Gangnam Style', by the South Korean pop star Psy, became the most watched video internationally, and provoked many parodies. But 'Gangnam Style' is itself already a conscious parody of K-Pop, cleverly playing on the interaction between Eastern and Western stereotypes.

Of all the musical traditions of South-East Asia, the one that has long fascinated Westerners has been the *gamelan* of Java and Bali. I have already written about its influence on Debussy and Messiaen. Steve Reich is one of several American composers who studied *gamelan* in the 1970s. Its layered and shifting patterns fed into what came to be known as 'minimalism', in which music is built from patterns that repeat again and again, gradually shifting and evolving. In 1976 a *gamelan* ensemble, *Gamelan Son of Lion*, was founded in New York by three composers, Barbara Benary, Philip Corner and Daniel Goode. They and others have composed many new works for *gamelan*. In 2009, Javanese *gamelan* players took part in a recording project, *In Nem*, in collaboration with British musician Daniel Patrick Quinn, in which they improvised together on short themes that they had composed. The Javanese musicians who took part in these experiments had little difficulty learning their parts, but admitted to being unsure what the point was. More obviously meaningful is the use of the *gamelan* as a popular activity for children and students in the West, giving them experience of a kind of communal enterprise that is very different from Western ways of organisation. While these new ideas were developing, traditional *gamelan* continued as an important part of village life in Java and Bali.

Further west in Asia, the most high-profile coming together of cultures in the twentieth century occurred in India. The flamboyant style of 'Bollywood', combining Indian melody with Western beat, became a mass market with the coming of audiocassettes in the 1970s. Meanwhile, classical Indian musicians were becoming known in the West and collaborating with Western musicians. Sitar player Ravi Shankar and American classical violinist Yehudi Menuhin played concerts together, improvising on *raga*. Famously, Shankar also collaborated with the Beatles. In 1966, George Harrison visited India and spent six weeks being taught to play the sitar by Shankar. Harrison played the sitar on several Beatles songs, notably 'Norwegian Wood', and he and Shankar worked on collaborative concerts after the Beatles broke up. Shankar performed at Woodstock in 1969, but he became uncomfortable with his identification in the West as part of the hippie scene. Shankar also influenced American minimalists. Philip Glass was among the composers who studied with him, and Shankar and Glass collaborated in recording an album together.

The area in which collaboration between Indian and Western styles has been most fruitful is in new genres of jazz. With their training in improvisation, jazz musicians have a natural link with Indian traditions, and many jazz drummers now play the *tabla*. British-Indian guitarist and pianist Nitin Sawhney in the 1990s began to speak of a potential 'renaissance' in music through such cross-fertilisation. His early influences range from Indian classical music through flamenco and Cuban music to jazz and rock, and there are echoes of all of them in his music.

Meanwhile, the traditional performance of Indian *raga* by singers and instrumentalists remains strong, with increasing appreciation in countries that spent centuries disdaining Indian music. Until recently, all the lead singers and instrumentalists were traditionally men. But now more and more women are adopting these high-profile roles. There are still barriers that sometimes limit women's participation, but they are gradually breaking down.

Similar change has been happening across the Arab world. There have been prominent women singers in the past, notably the Egyptian Umm Kulthum, but now some have become more widely known in the West. One is Palestinian Kamilya Jubran, who took up her father's instrument, the *oud*, and moved to Europe in 2002, settling in Paris. Her performances range from song firmly rooted in Arab tradition, accompanying herself on the *oud*, to haunting Arab-jazz fusion with the Swiss composer-trumpeter Werner Hasler.

Africa has given rise to an enormous amount of cross-cultural fusion. As we have seen, African slaves created the foundation of what became Western popular music, so you might say that we have already covered the most important African contribution to the music of today. But here are a few examples of musical currents emerging directly from Africa itself.

I mentioned in Chapter 31 the new working-class musical fusions that emerged in South Africa in the late nineteenth century. By the mid-twentieth century these had evolved into vigorous street music, whose insistent, dancing rhythms came to symbolise the dynamism of Black South African culture. In 1986 the white American singer-songwriter Paul Simon brought this music to the attention of the wider world through his album *Graceland*, in which he worked with Black African musicians and wrote songs inspired by them. This was at a time when South Africans were subject to the brutal segregation of Apartheid, which did not come to an end until the 1990s. The album was widely praised for its breaching of racial boundaries. But some argued that Simon, the star of the album, had exploited African musicians. These are arguments that return again and again in different contexts.

In Zimbabwe, there was a movement from the 1970s to promote the local culture after its suppression under colonial rule. One result was the revival of the *mbira* (thumb-piano). Traditional African religion requires the spirits of ancestors to be consulted about where and when the *mbira* may be played. As the *mbira* became popular beyond Zimbabwe, this presented a problem: the instrument had not traditionally been played for the mere pleasure of an audience. But this does not mean that the spirits have been forgotten. Forward Kwenda, a leading *mbira* player, tours internationally, but retains a strong belief in the role of the spirits when he plays: 'The music is so much greater than a human being can understand . . . I just have to get out of the way so spirits can make my *mbira* play – it isn't me – I'm just amazed.'

There have been many other adaptations of traditional music. The hereditary praise-singers of Mali have increasingly taken to the public stage. And the *kora*, traditionally used to accompany the praise-singer, has become popular as a solo instrument. The most celebrated of these *kora* soloists is Toumani Diabaté, from a long line of praise-singers, who takes part in multi-cultural events and ensembles. You can hear how the 'ragged' relationship between melody and bass in *kora*-playing easily appeals to listeners brought up with the freedoms of ragtime and jazz – which, of course, have their roots in African rhythms.

Finally, there is the question of 'Pan-Africanism', and the idea of music as an expression of the whole continent. Can such an idea have any meaning across such a huge area? One figure who promoted the notion is the Nigerian, Fela Kuti. He studied the trumpet in London, and returned to Nigeria in 1963 when the country was newly independent. He had formed a band which mixed several influences – jazz, calypso, funk and African traditions – and already referred to his music as 'Afrobeat'. Then in 1969 he spent almost a year with his band in the United States, where he encountered the Black Power movement and James Brown's 'Say it Loud – I'm Black and I'm Proud'. By the time Kuti returned home, Nigeria was under military rule, and he and his music became political. He formed a controversial commune which he declared independent of the state, performed traditional Yoruba ceremonies, and married (and later divorced) twenty-seven wives. In 1977 his song 'Zombie', aimed at the Nigerian military, provoked an attack on his commune in which Kuti was beaten and his mother was killed. He remained a controversial figure throughout the rest of his career.

Kuti's domineering character and appeal to universal 'Africanism' had supporters but also detractors. Many came to resent his macho attitude to women. And one of the most striking features of African music in recent decades has been the prominence of powerful women singers, echoing those on the other side of the Atlantic. One of the best-known was Miriam Makeba, who took part in the tour of Paul Simon's *Graceland*. Born in South Africa, she rose to become a prominent campaigner against Apartheid, moved to the United States in 1960, and became involved in the civil rights and Black Power movements. She was one of the most important ambassadors for the broad notion of African music, influencing the succeeding generations of African and African American singers, notably Nina Simone, Aretha Franklin and Angélique Kidjo.

The term 'melting pot' is often used to describe today's music scene, and you can easily see why. Cultures around the world are interacting with Western classical, jazz and popular music in all sorts of ways. Cities across the world continue to build opera houses and concert halls, young people from China to Venezuela are being trained to play Western classical music. 'World Music' festivals were pioneered in the 1980s by English rock musician Peter Gabriel with WOMAD (World of Music, Arts and Dance). Now festivals in the West routinely host musicians from all the continents of the world, and musicians from many different cultures play together with Western musicians.

Where is this all going? I'll have to leave it to historians of the future to give the answer to that question. But I can at least try to sum up where I think we are now, and how we have got here.

CHAPTER 40

Yesterday, Today and Tomorrow

When I was at music college in London back in the 1960s, a brilliant piano student performed from memory Boulez's Second Piano Sonata, a work then only fifteen years old, which Boulez himself described as having 'an explosive, disintegrating and dispersive character'. It was an extraordinary achievement, and we applauded him enthusiastically. But during the performance of this violent, dissonant piece, most of the audience was silently heaving with the attempt not to laugh. We were all trained musicians, but we couldn't make any sense of the torrent of sounds that were coming out of the piano, and we had no idea whether the pianist was playing the right notes or not.

This illustrates a more general problem. Until the twentieth century it had been routine for concerts to feature a high proportion of new works, which were composed in a language that audiences could understand. But by the late twentieth century many young composers, encouraged by their teachers to write in 'uncompromising' styles, would find themselves commissioned to compose a new work for a concert, and then have difficulty getting it repeated. The music-loving public struggled to make friends with perpetual dissonance, as it had always done. The result in concert programmes and sales of classical records and sheet music was the predominance of a 'museum culture' of the great composers of the past.

There were several consequences of this situation. One was that the classics were endlessly repeated, and, with the availability of recordings, became very familiar at home. This diet began to seem stale, and because musicians and audiences had little interest in new works, they sought other ways of refreshing their palates. This was one of the factors that drove the Early Music movement.

Already in the late nineteenth century, specialists had been exploring forgotten repertoire from the seventeenth and earlier centuries. It was in the 1960s that the Early Music movement really got into its stride. Across Europe and North America, musicians recreated the sounds of old music. Harpsichords, long out of fashion, were made again. For Renaissance music, there were shawms, crumhorns, cornetts, and styles of singing to go with them. In time the principle of using original instruments was also applied to more familiar repertoire: first the symphonies of Haydn, then on to Beethoven, Brahms, Wagner, even Debussy. Audiences discovered that the old instruments had a different character compared with the more powerful modern ones, generally lighter, brighter, clearer. This was highly refreshing, and 'period' performance of the well-known classics became commonplace.

All of this was made possible through recordings and radio, which spread the word far beyond the concert hall. People got used to these refreshed sounds, and came to think of the performances they had been accustomed to as rather heavy and staid. This influenced the way the classics were played by conventional orchestras and groups. By now, in the twenty-first century, the sound of period instruments playing Bach or Beethoven is normal and unsurprising. Even the 'refreshed' is in danger of sounding predictable.

Meanwhile, another great division was opening up. When the pop explosion got under way in the 1960s, the hallowed establishment of classical music, even more than the older popular genres such as jazz, found itself elbowed aside, at least in terms of commercial success. The contrast between popular and classical became much starker than it had been. To play in a big band or a Broadway musical required as much expertise and discipline as playing in a symphony orchestra. Now, with the new pop groups, the informal, technically simpler styles meant that pop musicians were not trained in the same way. Half the point was that it should sound as if you could do it yourself: it was democratic, anti-elitist.

The situation has evolved since the 1960s. Pop music has become ever more diverse and sophisticated in the way it is produced, presented and marketed. Jazz still commands a loyal audience, though not on the mass scale of the 1940s. And classical music has gradually been fighting back in various ways.

One way is with clever marketing and presentation. The 1990 FIFA World Cup final in Rome was preceded by a gala concert by 'the Three Tenors', Luciano Pavarotti, José Carreras and Plácido Domingo. It was viewed by an audience estimated at 800 million, and the CD of the concert became the best-selling classical album in history. Dutch violinist André Rieu and his Johann Strauss Orchestra are one of the highest-earning touring groups, classical or pop, whose success relies not just on the programmes of waltzes and light classics, but on spectacular sets and effects.

Outside such deliberate attempts to reach a popular audience, everyone gets to experience classical music without necessarily realising what it is. TV wildlife documentaries are drenched in what is, in effect, classical music: grand, processional music to accompany the sweeping plains of Africa or the great whales; skittering woodwind for lizards and insects; snarling brass and drums for crocodiles attacking their prey. On a larger scale, and often more subtle, are film scores. American composer John Williams is widely regarded as a master of creating the right music for the narrative and images of films. His scores for the *Star Wars* series, *E.T. the Extra-Terrestrial*, *Schindler's List* and many others have not only won him many awards but have earned the respect of classical musicians for their traditional craftsmanship.

Composers of such traditional classical-style music tend today to work in specialist areas. As well as TV and films, another area is choral music. Choral societies are mostly amateur, and they are naturally reluctant to devote their evenings to struggling with highly dissonant music. The leading composers of choral music are those who are comfortable within a traditional classical style, largely sidestepping the modernism of the last hundred years. John Rutter is one such, whose carols and other choral works are popular. Scotsman James MacMillan is admired for his religious choral music, its challenges often tailored for a particular choir. Welsh composer Karl Jenkins has successfully combined his classical training with his experience in a jazz-rock group to create large-scale 'crossover' choral works: *The Armed Man: A Mass for Peace* (2000) has been widely performed by professional and amateur choirs.

There are other composers who have turned away from daunting complexity to find a way of doing something that sounds new. I have already mentioned the 'minimalists'. Minimalism is a catch-all word to describe music that is based on simple phrases, but creates complexity by repetition, overlapping and gradual variation. Terry Riley is credited with setting the movement going in 1964 with his piece *In C*. Steve Reich enriched minimalism by bringing various influences to bear on it, from the jazz improvisations of John Coltrane to Ghanaian drumming and *gamelan*, which he studied in the 1970s. John Adams and Philip Glass are particularly known for their minimalist operas. In both composers, the repetitive, slowly changing patterns in the orchestra become almost hypnotic. Over this flow of music, the voices generally sing in a rather stately, chant-like manner. The effect is more like a ritual than a conventional operatic drama.

Reich, Adams and Glass are all Americans. Two European composers brought a strong religious impulse to minimalism. With Estonian composer Arvo Pärt this went hand in hand with the study of European Renaissance music. There is a strong evocation of the antique in his music, creating an atmosphere of deep meditation. Polish composer Henryk Górecki began his career writing complex, dissonant works. But in the 1970s his music underwent a fundamental change, and, like Pärt, he took to composing much simpler, contemplative works. When his Symphony No. 3, the *Symphony of Sorrowful Songs*, was first performed in 1977, the critics were dismayed by Górecki's switch from intellectual complexity to simplicity. One wrote, 'This non-composition has irrevocably paved the way down the wrong path to a childish "new simplicity"'. But twelve years later when it received its London premiere, the critics were more sympathetic to its 'piercingly simple melodic lines', and a recording of the symphony suddenly brought the work to a vast audience, topping the classical charts.

'New simplicity' might well describe the music of Ludovico Einaudi, but, as with Górecki, opinions are sharply divided. Sitting priest-like at the piano, he fills major concert halls with mesmerised fans, but the critics are deeply unimpressed. One wrote that it's as if Einaudi 'has cannily pureed his musical language down to an inventory of generic, soulless chord sequences'. It seems that 'new simplicity', childish or not, is what many people crave in a world of conflict and challenge.

The great divide between critics and the ordinary music-lover was starkly shown by reactions to the death in 2022 of Harrison Birtwistle, regarded as the leading British composer of complex, dissonant music. Critic Richard Morrison wrote an appreciation of his 'magnificently uncompromising' epics. Among the hostile respondents, one described Birtwistle's opera *Gawain* as 'an aural tsunami of screeching nonsense'. Morrison went on to argue that Birtwistle had become 'a lightning rod for the contempt that a large proportion of the British public feel (and have always felt) for all creative artists . . . who don't produce immediately accessible and ingratiating work'.

Morrison was echoing the words of Schoenberg who, ninety years earlier, had declared that 'the hostility of the majority always turns against those who forge ahead into the unknown regions of the intellectual realm'. But the public does not always reject challenge in the arts. Bookshops are full of substantial books by living authors. An eager public flocks to the theatre to attend the latest plays, and to art galleries to see exhibitions of contemporary artists. There is no lack of challenge in these new works. But the challenges are not like the challenges of musical modernism, and there remains a core understanding that writers and artists have to connect with the public.

Of course, there have been plenty of works that the public has found baffling in the visual arts, from Cubism to entries for the Turner Prize. But in an art gallery, if you find something baffling, you don't have to spend half an hour staring at it, you can move on to the next work. And the successful marketing of avant-garde works of art has added the excitement of financial value, so that people are intrigued even if they don't understand. Nobody pays $3 million for a modern classical music score.

In the popular music fields, on the other hand, huge fortunes are made. Bob Dylan in 2020 sold his back catalogue for an estimated $300 million, Bruce Springsteen in 2021 sold his for around $500 million. Against this background it is not surprising that disputes about ownership increasingly end up in court. In 2022 one of the most successful singer-songwriters, Ed Sheeran, won a court case about his song 'Shape of You', one of the highest-selling tracks in the history of pop. Sheeran had been accused of taking a repeating phrase, 'Oh I', from the song 'Oh Why' by Sami Switch. The judge threw out the claim, ruling that, though there were similarities, the phrase was 'so short, simple and commonplace' that Sheeran could well have come up with the idea himself. Welcoming the judgement, Sheeran said, 'There's only so many notes and very few chords used in pop music. Coincidence is bound to happen if 60,000 songs are being released every day on Spotify.'

Reactions to this statement were revealing. They ranged from loving support from Sheeran's many fans to criticism of a music industry that makes so much money out of such simple and repetitive ideas. It is true that modern, commercial pop music tends to rely on formulas that are guaranteed to be successful. This has been encouraged by the rise of TV competitions such as *Pop Idol* and *The X Factor*, which have been duplicated across the world. You might put this positively and say that pop shares a common language that everyone understands. Everything is calculated – by musicians, producers, video designers and promoters – to have the maximum appeal, and that has more to do with familiarity and image than with traditional notions of originality or talent.

The world of classical music has had the opposite problem. Classical music has, ever since it fragmented in the early twentieth century, struggled to retain any sort of common language – common not just among musicians, but shared with the audience. Highly complex, intellectual music has tended to be taken seriously by critics but largely disliked by audiences and even musicians (such as my fellow students). Undemanding music has tended to be disdained by critics but accepted by audiences. The divide has been difficult to bridge, but it is at last beginning to heal.

In a 2019 survey, 174 composers were asked to name their top 50 composers of all time. The living composer who came highest in the poll (at no. 17) was the Finn, Kaija Saariaho. She studied under teachers of tough, post-Schoenberg serialism, but found music without connection to traditional harmonies and melodies empty, saying 'I don't want to write music through negations.' At Boulez's IRCAM in Paris she used electronic analysis to explore the 'sound-spectrum' of different instruments, that is, the harmonics that make up their characteristic tone-colours. From this she developed ways of creating dense and fascinating 'clouds' of sound that gradually transform themselves – often dissonant, but not brutally so. In 2016 she became only the second female composer ever to have an opera staged at New York's Metropolitan Opera.

Another composer who is regularly cited as one of the most important of our time is the Tatar-Russian, Sofia Gubaidulina. Brought up in Stalin's repressive Soviet Union, she had to hide her deep religious faith even from her parents. There is a strong spiritual quality to her music: she says, 'Music ... allows us to approach the highest of our being. The art of music is capable of touching and approaching mysteries and laws existing in the cosmos and in the world.' She too is unafraid of dissonance, but most often uses it like a destructive force against which harmony and melody have to battle for survival. One of her most extraordinary works, *De Profundis*, is for Russian accordion (*bayan*), which uses everything from exhausted breath through low moans and snarling dissonance to an ecstatic chorale.

It is a sign of the times that both of these leading composers are women. There have been many women composers over the centuries, but until recently they always had to battle against the overwhelming dominance of men in the musical establishment, including the writers of music histories. In no earlier period would it have been possible for a woman to be listed as the greatest living composer: the world was against such a possibility, and women rarely had the opportunity for public exposure. Now, with a high proportion of women composers emerging from conservatoires around the world, the situation is very different.

So many of the old divisions are breaking down – between genders, races, genres of music, and between the West and the rest of the world. In popular fields, there have been many individuals and groups that have transcended boundaries – from Kraftwerk and Brian Eno to Kate Bush, Annie Lennox, David Bowie and Björk. There have been popular musicians with one foot in jazz or classical music. Folk singers play ancient instruments and bring together the folk music of different cultures. At the same time classical composers find themselves negotiating the minefield of opposing styles to find their own voice. Free jazz, experimental pop, the possibilities of electronic music, crossovers between different genres, all mean that the conventional labels become increasingly unhelpful. The catch-all term 'contemporary' is increasingly used for music that is difficult to categorise. I wrote in the previous chapter about the engagement between different cultures, and if you add to that all the crumbling borderlines between different genres, once again the term 'melting pot' seems right.

Humans have been making music for millions of years, and throughout that long period we have explored ways of creating the right music for our circumstances. Music has always been a fundamental form of human expression, essential to our health and well-being. And whatever the future holds, we can be sure that music will continue to evolve with us.

Index